ENDORS

"Drs. Mashihi and Nowack are anything but clueless. .... *reatise on coaching! Aimed at practitioners and designed to help coaches guide their clients, Clueless offers practical information in an easy-to-follow, easy-to-implement format. Seldom have I seen such a clear road map for coaches to follow as they improve their business practices and provide more enhanced services to their clients. Clueless points out the pitfalls and potholes into which even the most seasoned coaches sometimes fall."*

Marshall Goldsmith - million-selling author of the New York Times bestsellers, *MOJO* and *What Got You Here Won't Get You There*

"If you are a coach, you've probably seen umpteen books on the how to's of coaching. What you may not have seen is the research, the data, the thinking of those who have studied this particular niche and are willing to put all that they have learned....out there....for you to use as the situation demands...this book is a must read."

Beverly L. Kaye - Founder/CEO of CareerSystems International and Best Selling Author of *LOVE 'EM or LOSE 'EM: Getting Good People to Stay*

"Changing behavior is one of the hardest things in the world, as anyone who has tried to lose weight, quit worrying, or stop some other problem behavior will tell you. It seems like we ought to be able to decide to change something about ourselves and then just do it – it's simple, isn't it? Ken Nowack and Sandra Mashihi tell us,

"Yes, it's simple – but not easy." As psychologists and behavioral consultants, they work with individuals and organizations, helping to bring about behavior change to enhance productivity, boost profitability, and promote happiness. They understand human behavior in a way that few people do. I love their formula: *"Enlighten, Encourage, Enable." It really works!"*

BJ Gallagher - coauthor of *YES Lives in the Land of NO*

"Clueless, a practical guide for coaching, does a masterful job of providing a clear framework for behavior change, relevant research and conceptual models as well as useful strategies and skill building exercises. Not only does it help coaches learn what to do, it shows them why and how. While aimed at coaches, this book is also a critical how-to resource for practitioners such as trainers, managers and those involved in professional development."

Anita Rowe, Ph.D. - Partner, Gardenswartz & Rowe, Co-author, *Emotional Intelligence for Managing Results in a Diverse World*

"Clueless fills the science-practitioner gap with just the right balance of empirical data and practical exercises to address individual behavior change. The model of change is straightforward and easy for clients to understand. As a practitioner in an academic environment, I really appreciate tools that have an empirical foundation!"

Sue Anderson MS, SPHR - Staff Employment and Development Manager, University of California, Riverside

"Clueless is a remarkably accessible and very practically-focused collection of resources for coaches. Using simple but powerful models for each of the key phases of the coaching cycle that the authors term "Enlighten, encourage and enable" an excellent balance of theory and practice is provided. Their guide includes over 100 clearly explained and easy to use applications for use as self-reflection and for client interventions. The book, complete with extensive literature references is a valuable resource that can be used by the novice and more experienced coach alike. I highly recommend it."

Barry Bar-El - Director, Organization Development and Learning, Cedars-Sinai Medical Center

CLUELESS

COACHING PEOPLE WHO JUST DON'T GET IT

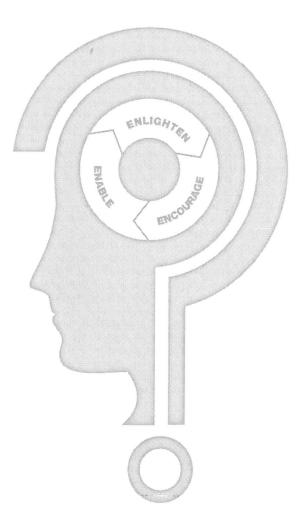

SANDRA MASHIHI, PH.D.
KENNETH NOWACK, PH.D.

Envisia Learning Inc.
3435 Ocean Park Blvd.
Suite 203
Santa Monica, CA 90405
www.envisialearning.com

ISBN: 978-0-615-54562-2

Printed in the United States of America
First Printing: 2011

PREFACE

We have written this book to help coaches (executive, career, lifestyle modification, and personal) initiate and sustain successful behavioral change in the clients they work with. We hope that it will provide some useful models, research, and practical tools that you can use to enable your clients to move ahead with their developmental journeys that will include some degree of enhanced self-awareness, skill acquisition and deliberate practice until these new skills become a natural part of your clients' behavioral repertoire.

We will be introducing a very powerful model of behavioral change, based on strong theoretical models coming from the leadership, health psychology, and behavioral medicine literatures. Our individual behavioral change model contains three stages, which we call *Enlighten, Encourage, and Enable*. Each stage represents a milestone for your clients to move through, and if successful, they will be able to transition from *successful adopters* to *successful maintainers* of new behaviors. We think you will find this individual behavioral change model useful, intuitive, and valuable as you work with your clients along each critical stage from an initial readiness to change to the unconscious competence of the most effective performers in any field.

We will begin the book with an introduction to the various evidence-based factors that influence behavioral change and then describe each of the *Enlighten, Encourage, and Enable* stages in separate chapters along with *practical exercises and coaching tools* you can use with your clients on their developmental journey. Our hope is to give coaches and others a comprehensive and practical model and toolkit to guide each of your clients to successful behavioral change.

The Three Necessary Conditions for Initiating and Sustaining Successful Behavioral Change

1 - ENLIGHTEN	2 - ENCOURAGE	3 - ENABLE
We must first be aware of what we want to change, in order to initiate new behaviors.	You have to be motivated and feel confident in order for your change efforts to be successful.	It's hard to start new behaviors but even more difficult to sustain them over time! During this phase, you will understand how to develop an appropriate development action plan and review methods for sustaining change interventions.
During this phase, you become more enlightened and aware of ways to identify your signature strengths to leverage further or become more aware of development areas to focus more time and attention on.	During this phase, you will identify ways to assess your motivation to implement behavioral change action plans.	

Contacting the Authors

This book represents an ongoing exploration of how to facilitate successful behavioral change in individuals. We welcome reactions from our readers and although we are not always able to respond to every e-mail, we enjoy hearing from (and learning from) our readers. To reach us via e-mail, please use the following address:

Sandra Mashihi: sandra@envisialearning.com
Kenneth Nowack: ken@envisialearning.com

TABLE OF CONTENTS

ACKNOWLEDGEMENTS

It is often said that if when we are through changing, we are through. We have written this book to help coaches and practitioners who help facilitate successful behavior change in their clients -- particularly those who are "clueless" and also resistant to change. Whether through observing Ken's "running club" members, raising guide dog puppies for the blind, reflecting on our own coaching experiences, and trying to make personal changes in our lifestyles we are reminded just how challenging it is to initiate new behaviors and successfully maintain them over time. We hope our evidence based approach and practical exercises in the book will be useful for those involved in roles of helping others change.

There are a number of people in writing a book that contribute directly and indirectly and few of these people we would like to acknowledge. Several dear colleagues we have had the pleasure to work with over the years have been invaluable for many of the ideas and exercises included in the book including William "Bo" Bradley, B.J. Gallagher, Bruce Heller, Soren Eilertsen, Joy Hawkins, Anita Rowe, Lee Gardenswartz, Scott Wimer, Jeanne Hartley, Beverly Kaye, and Professor Charles Healy.

Sandra would like to acknowledge her colleague and friend, John DiFrancesca for his constant support and guidance. She would also like to thank her coaching clients for being an inspiration of growth and development for this book.

Ken would like to acknowledge his wife Denise who has been a constant supporter and a wonderful sounding board for many decisions about the book from the very beginning--her guidance and love have been invaluable to me. Our most recent guide dog puppies we have raised as volunteers for Guide Dogs of America, Ajax and

Rocco, have been inspirations for me to observe and learn about learning new habits and the power of feedback and support.

We would both like to thank Andy Parkinson, for his insights, input, support, and leadership in all aspects of writing and publishing this book. A special thanks to Aaron Mahnke, our designer, for all his creativity and hard work throughout the process.

PART I:

Factors that Influence Behavioral Change

"People don't resist change. They resist being changed!

PETER SENGE

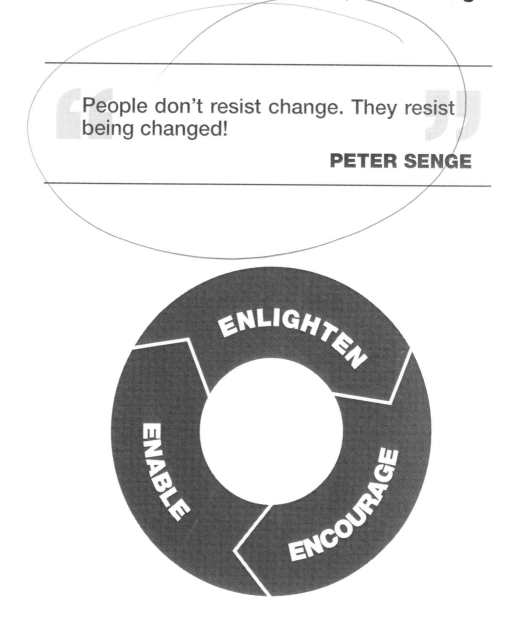

Introduction to the Enlighten, Encourage, and Enable Behavioral Change Model

> **I** put a dollar in one of those change machines. Nothing changed.
>
> **GEORGE CARLIN**

Behavioral change efforts are often not linear. They tend to be progressive, regressive, or even static. However, to successfully change behavior we all move through *three* specific stages. This chapter will introduce a powerful model for translating the behavioral intentions of your clients into actual implementation goals that can be sustained over time. We call the steps of this individual-based behavioral change model *Enlighten, Encourage, and Enable*. Each will be described briefly below.

ENLIGHTEN

Most people don't wake up in the morning and spontaneously want to change or try new behaviors at work (for example, attempting to listen more effectively, becoming less autocratic, or trying to be more participative and involvement-oriented). Coaches must try to get clients to adopt new behaviors and styles that are, at best, awkward and uncomfortable. People only change for a good reason, and becoming enlightened or more self-aware is a *necessary but not sufficient condition* required to leverage any behavioral change effort. This individual behavioral change stage is characterized as helping clients to perceive, understand, and accept information and data about their thoughts, feelings, and behaviors, either through internal reflection and/or feedback from others.

Insight and awareness are key to helping your clients understand more about how they are perceived by others, as well as providing the impetus to make behavioral changes that are important to their own health and well-being. For example, learning one has high blood pressure might be the information that prompts a person to learn more about how to control it or that increases one's motivation to change a specific lifestyle habit. To maintain homeostasis in our bodies, internal and external feedback is the key to correcting and modifying both conscious and unconscious behavioral change. *Feedforward* (Goldsmith, 2002) from others is a great way to help clients learn about the consequences of their behavior and style of leading, communicating, or interacting with others and learn some things they might consider doing more, less, or differently in the future to become more effective. Most coaches have a large "toolkit" to enhance insight and awareness of their clients. In fact, this is one of the key roles that coaches play in helping clients to grow and become more successful. Some useful approaches and techniques for increasing *insight and self-awareness* in your clients include:

- **Utilizing a 360-Degree Feedback Process**. Comparing self-perceptions to those of others is a critical first step to increasing awareness and understanding. Your clients might find value in soliciting feedback from their manager, direct reports, or team members and peers, by using popular, multi-rater feedback assessments that can be done online and will result in detailed summary reports highlighting potential blind spots, as well as strengths.

- **Providing Specific Behavioral Feedback**. Motivation to change can be enhanced when clients are given specific, behavioral feedback in a manner that minimizes defensiveness and denial. Individuals are most likely to change when they believe feedback is constructive and accurate, and when they are helped to identify specific steps they can take to grow and develop.

- **Matching Feedback to an Individual's Self-Insight**. Some individuals have an accurate appraisal of their strengths and development areas. Others lack true insight about how they are perceived by others. Tailor your feedback to increase motivation by matching your client's self-insight to your approach in delivering strengths and development opportunities. For example, when clients possess a cognitive distortion of "underestimating" their strengths, you might need to help them focus on what they are perceived to be seen as doing frequently and effectively, rather than the tendency to highlight data and information that appears to be negative or critical.

- **Using Journals and Self-Monitoring Techniques**. We tune into things we try to tune into. Encouraging some clients to keep a daily journal of behaviors, feelings, and thoughts can help build mindfulness and insight about their pattern of response to situations and other people.

ENCOURAGE

There is an old joke that asks how many coaches does it takes to change a light bulb. The answer is: Only one, but the light bulb has to really want to change! Similarly, in coaching assignments, our clients have to be motivated to change, or any interventions will not result in lasting performance improvements. This behavioral change stage is characterized as moving clients along a readiness to change continuum and building their confidence so they can actually practice new ways to think, feel, and behave. To maximize "readiness" and encouragement, coaches might consider using one or more of the following strategies:

- **Using Motivational Interviewing**. Motivational interviewing (MI) is a useful approach for coaches who work with behavioral change engagements that assist clients in reflecting on and targeting specific performance goals to work on. It is a style that emphasizes the client's values, interests, and motives and utilizes reflective listening and probing to help the client make lasting behavioral changes.

- **Assessing Readiness Level**. Identify and determine how "ready" your client is to initiate new behavioral change.

- **Providing a Change Model**. Introduce clients to one or more of the popular individual, team, or organizational change models in the human resources or mental health professions. This can better help clients understand the typical stages, emotional reactions, and feelings that accompany change.

- **Using Analogies and Telling Stories**. Effective coaches are able to "connect" with others in a manner that motivates and inspires behavioral change. One simple tool and approach that works well to establish rapport and teach others is to tell relevant stories.

- **Find "What's in it for the Client" To Maximize Motivation to Change**. Integrate the behavioral change efforts with the client's own career and professional goals and aspirations.

ENABLE

Not all enlightened and truly encouraged clients are successful at changing their styles or specific behaviors. In order for behavioral change to be sustained, clients must know what to change *and* be committed to sustaining it over time. The key to successful long-term behavioral change is the consistent application of a complex set of skills over an extended period of time. This stage is characterized by helping clients track and monitor progress on the implementation of their goals. This includes building a support network at work and home to help prepare for inevitable lapses that are a part of behavioral change efforts, as well as defining rewards for success in actually accomplishing change goals. Some strategies and techniques to facilitate the enablement required for successful behavioral change include:

- **Maximizing Individual Choice**. People are much more likely to grow and develop in areas when they decide which competencies or skills to focus on and when they are capable of setting their own goals. To stretch clients, it is particularly important to maximize choice, whether they focus on behavioral goals or on the type of learning to engage in (e.g., experiential).

- **Breaking Down Learning into Manageable Steps**. When a client achieves success on specific developmental goals, it paves the way for setting new and more challenging goals. It is important to "stretch" individuals by structuring goals into small, attainable, and manageable steps. Learning and developing competence is maximized when goals are challenging but still realistic and attainable.

- **Using Experiential Techniques**. Reading books, listening to tapes, and attending seminars may be useful, but current research suggests that successful behavioral change can be facilitated much more rapidly and successfully by using more active group and experiential approaches, such as work sample simulations, case studies, and on-the-job activities (e.g., special projects, stretch assignments, etc.).

- **Building Social Support.** It is well known that we develop best in a social environment where mentors, friends, coworkers, and even family members going through the same change process can help facilitate a person's confidence, hope, and motivation.

- **Providing Relapse Prevention Training.** "Lapses" and "slips" are part of the inevitable journey of personal behavioral change. Understanding what leads to these "lapses" and how to effectively cope with periods of personal stress will enable individuals to continue to grow and learn over time, without totally relapsing back to old, entrenched behaviors and styles.

- **Becoming a Professional "Nag" by Using Reminders.** People will often need someone to "remind" them about what is important and not just urgent. Many people have rows of workshop materials and assessments from previous training programs but still have not altered their behavior.

To maximize coaching success, coaches must use and understand the three key drivers of sustained behavioral change: *enlightenment, encouragement, and enablement.* Coaches who attempt to maximize all *three conditions* will have a much higher probability of seeing a payoff in their clients, than if only one condition exists alone.

Successful behavioral change is not without challenges. Sometimes, the best we can do as coaches is try to help our clients become more self-aware and motivated to try new behaviors. After that, a number of social, organizational, and environmental factors play a big role in how well our clients maintain the new behavior until it becomes automatic and part of their natural style and repertoire in dealing with work and non-work situations and challenges. Of course, all of our clients come with unique personalities, styles, experiences, and genetic set points that also can limit their ability to perceive information, to remain diligent with maintaining goals, and to overcome adversity.

Coaching is never done in a vacuum, and great coaches always consider their work as part of a broader "client system" that involves the client's work or home environment, as well as the skills and experiences that the coach will bring to the intervention. In fact, the best coaches are aware of their own limitations, biases, and experiences that can help or hinder the coaching engagement. They also look to engineer the external environment with their client's permission to ensure that new behaviors are recognized, reinforced, and rewarded (e.g., encouraging the client's manager to meet periodically with the client to provide ongoing feedback about his or her progress and provide words of encouragement along the way).

We do know some of the necessary conditions and factors required to ensure learning and lasting behavioral change. In fact, the focus of this book will be on how to leverage each of the three individual change conditions *Enlighten, Encourage, and Enable* to ensure a successful coaching intervention with any client.

Does Coaching Really Work?

Coaching models, assessments and practitioners seem to be increasing exponentially these days (Nowack, 2003). There are even organizations and training institutes devoted specifically to this particular intervention, each with different models, approaches, and even ethical or professional guidelines. It seems "everyone" is now doing "coaching" for a variety of clients and presenting problems. Many of the larger human resources consulting and outplacement companies now provide and specialize in coaching services. Overall, the question still remains: Do people *really* change as a result of coaching?

Recent published research on evidence-based outcomes on coaching is expanding rapidly. In fact, the total number of coaching publications from 1937-2009 was 518, with at least six recent studies, including randomization and between-subject designs (Grant, 2008). No doubt more evidence-based coaching evaluation studies will be available to guide practitioners on "best practices" in the next few years. It is important to define the most typical categories of

9

"outcomes" commonly described in evidence-based coaching studies. Not all "outcomes" are the same or easy to compare when evaluating the coaching literature. These coaching "outcomes" might be conceptualized as:

- Behaviors/Habits: establishing new behaviors or modifying existing habits (e.g., health/wellness, interpersonal relations)

- Skills: developing new skills or abilities (e.g., managing stress, leadership)

- Development: increasing self-insight, self-esteem, meaning, values, or mindfulness (e.g., hope, optimism, self-awareness)

Support for positive coaching outcomes (behaviors, skills, and development) has been found in several recent, randomized, controlled longitudinal studies (Grant, Cavanagh, & Parker, 2010). In three recent studies, executives received 360-degree feedback, a half-day leadership workshop, and four individual coaching sessions over 10 weeks, using a cognitive-behavioral, solution-focused approach. Compared to controls, coaching resulted in *significant increases* in goal attainment, increased resilience, reduced depression, and enhanced workplace well-being (Grant, Curtane, & Burton, 2009; Spence & Grant, 2005; Green, Oades, & Grant, 2006). Furthermore, Green, et al., (2006) found that gains from participation in the 10-week solution-focused, cognitive-behavioral coaching were maintained at a 30-week follow-up. These well-designed coaching studies and positive results have been replicated with diverse presenting issues and audiences such as teachers (Grant, Green & Rynsaardt, 2010), students (Green, Grant & Rynsaardt, 2007), coaches in training (Grant, 2008), and those with chronic illness (Giesser, Coleman, Fisher, Guttry, Herlihy, Nonoguch, Nowack, Roberts, & Nowack, 2007).

A recent study highlighted the impact of mindfulness training used *in conjunction* with coaching on goal attainment (Spence, Cavanagh, & Grant, 2008). In this study, mindfulness training included a training manual and exercises recorded on MP3 that aimed to develop clients' selective attention and sustained attention abilities, as well as behaviors focused on controlled breathing and reducing negative thoughts and emotions. It was hypothesized that the efficacy of health coaching could be enhanced through the inclusion of Mindfulness Training (MT). To test this, 45 adults were randomly assigned to three health programs for eight weeks. Using a crossover design, two groups received an alternative delivery of MT and cognitive-behavioral, solution-focused (CB-SF) coaching, while the third group served as a control and participated in a series of only health education seminars. Results showed that goal attainment was *significantly greater* in the facilitative and coaching groups than the health education groups. No significant differences were found for goal attainment between the two MT/CB-SF conditions, suggesting that the delivery sequence had little to no bearing on outcomes.

Taken together, these evidence-based coaching studies begin to build a case that successful behavioral change is indeed possible and improve on the earlier and weaker non-experimental or quasi-experimental designs for evaluating coaching interventions. Initiating and sustaining behavioral change for anyone is challenging in the most ideal of situations. The growing base of evidence-based research on coaching supports the idea that *successful* behavioral change depends on a complex interplay of intrapsychic, interpersonal, and organizational factors ("who" may benefit most, for "which" kinds of coaching efforts, and under "what" circumstances). In the next section, we will summarize the main three factors that appear to influence the success or failure of behavioral change interventions.

Factors Influencing Successful Behavioral Change

There are a number of factors that contribute to an effective coaching process. Figure 1-1 shows four circles that represent factors that effect successful behavioral change. In the center, the three E's of *Enlighten, Encourage,* and *Enable* represent the process coaches can use to foster change for their clients. The three outer circles represent three factors that simultaneously influence a client's success, which include:

1. Coach factors
2. Client factors
3. Environmental factors

Each of these can increase or decrease the likelihood for successful behavioral change. Let's explore each of these factors and how they can influence behavioral change within a coaching engagement.

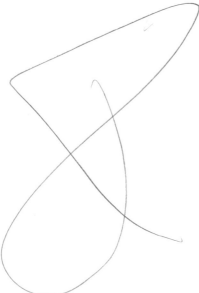

Figure 1-1

Factors Influencing Successful Behavioral Change

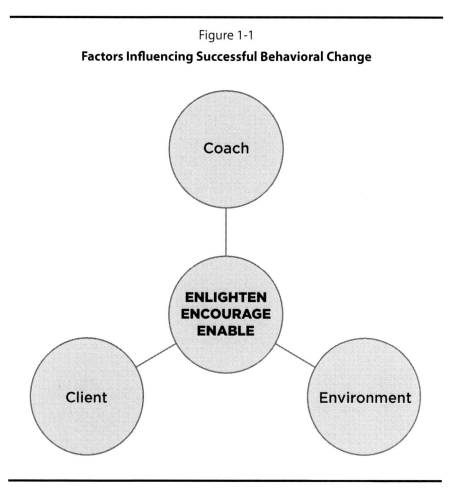

Chapter 1:

Coach Factors that Influence Behavioral Change

> Consider how hard it is to change yourself and you'll understand what little chance you have in trying to change others.
>
> **JACOB BRAUDE**

The background, training, skills, and experiences that executive, lifestyle, personal, and life coaches bring to coaching interventions play a critical role in both the initiation and sustaining of successful behavioral change in their clients (Nowack, 2003). In this chapter, we will explore how all these factors can increase or decrease a client's rapport with a coach, the perception of their coach's credibility, and the level of coachability.

Credibility of the Coach

Education/Training Level of the Coach

Coaches work in a variety of specializations. Personal/life coaches, career coaches, lifestyle modification coaches, and executive coaches are just a few. Education and training will vary with each coach's area of practice and can include professional certificates, business degrees, and advanced academic degrees. Each of these backgrounds may be well suited for different types of client needs. For instance, an executive coach working with a CEO will typically use skills relevant to assessment, adult learning, organizational systems and development, change management, and leadership development. On the other hand, a coach working with a sales manager to improve productivity may need skills such as business knowledge, performance management, sales, marketing, interpersonal relations, and sales industry knowledge. The field of coaching is relatively young, growing, and somewhat of a "wild west" for clients to accurately discern relevant training, background and credentials to ensure both competence and adherence to professional and ethical practices. Unfortunately, there is little agreement upon a common set of competencies required for the different types of coaching, few published professional practice guidelines, and multiple professional associations with diverse training requirements to become a "certified" coach.

A recent study by Dr. Joyce Bono from the University of Minnesota has helped to answer some important questions about the ongoing debate about the practice of coaching and similarities and differences between psychologists and non-psychologists in the field (Bono, et al., 2009). Bono's survey was completed by 428 coaches (172 psychologists and 256 non-psychologists), focusing on coaching practices (46 questions), coaching outcomes (23 questions), and information about the coach (education, preferred title, income, ethnicity, formal training, etc.).

Coaches were asked to share three competencies they believed were critical to successful coaching. Results indicated that, compared to non-psychologists, *psychologists* who provide executive coaching services were significantly more likely to:

- Meet face-to-face
- Contract for fewer coaching sessions (38 percent of non-psychologists reported "often" holding 21-30 sessions, compared to only 19 percent of psychologists)
- Avoid using behavior modification, neuro-linguistic programming, or psychoanalytic techniques
- Assist clients with applying new skills back at the job
- Focus more on building rapport with their clients

- Incorporate and utilize more assessments into the coaching interventions (360-degree feedback assessments, personality inventories, interviews)

There was enough data in the survey even to compare differences between psychologists (industrial/organizational, counseling, clinical, and personality/social). The findings suggest that few differences occurred in the use of coaching methods or assessments/tools, but some statistically significant differences were found mostly for clinical psychologists (e.g., clinical psychologists tended to use personality inventories more frequently, as well as have more CEO/President levels). Indeed, like other helping professions, "helpers" can be effective, with diverse experiences, training, and backgrounds with particular clients and problems.

Theoretical Orientation of the Coach

Coaches have adopted their own theoretical orientations, models, processes, and preferred assessments when working with clients. Some coaches utilize insight-oriented theoretical approaches, while others use cognitive-behavior-oriented approaches. The effectiveness of these theoretical orientations often depends on the client's unique goals and needs. Turner & Goodrich (2010) suggest that some situations need multiple approaches and interventions over time. Using a single particular model of coaching might not be enough to be effective with diverse clients and situations that often emerge in coaching interventions.

Integrity/Ethics of the Coach

One of the crucial elements needed for effective interventions is a clear understanding between the coach and client about the nature of their agreement and the goals of the coaching assignment. The coach should identify barriers and roadblocks that are important to the client's long-term improvement (Kilburg, 2001). For instance, many professional coaches establish a written contract or coaching agreement at the onset of their coaching intervention, which specifies services with limits of confidentiality, stresses the importance of avoiding dual relationships (such as treating an executive for depression while coaching him/her), and evaluates the impact of the coach's services, based on agreed upon performance measures (Nowack, 2003).

Ethical standards foster accountability and can also guide coaches toward selecting the most appropriate care for their clients. Practitioners can base their practice on the ethical codes of their respective fields. For instance, licensed psychologists follow the Ethical Principles of Psychologists and the Code of Conduct published by the American Psychological Association (http://www.apa.org/ethics/code/index.aspx) which includes standards regarding psychologists' competence, human relations, privacy and confidentiality, public statements, record keeping and fees, education and training, research and publication, and therapy practices. Other coaches trained by the International Federation of Coaches (ICF) might adhere to that group's stated ethical principles and practices (http://www.coachfederation.org/ethics).

Coaching Experience

Having raw coaching talent is great, but it's what you do with it that matters most. "Only dead fish go with the flow," goes the old saying. If you don't work to get better, it won't just happen naturally. Nobody finds success in his or her career without hard work and deliberate practice. In contrast to the proposition that it is relatively easy to be a good coach, it appears to be much more difficult to become an "expert" coach. In a general sense, it is difficult to become a true expert in any profession requiring complicated cognitive and behavior skills (Ericsson, 2006).

Typically, the development of expertise in a complex activity such as chess, competitive sports, musical performance, or medicine requires at least 10 years of experience and/or 10,000 hours of regular practice (Ericsson, 2006). There is, in fact, a big difference between experts and those "who are expert" in what they do. Doing a lot of coaching might mean you have an expertise at this profession, but practicing *coaching skills* and applying them with difficult clients and situations are the ingredients for truly making you one of the *best of the best*.

Personal Attributes Clients Are Looking for in a Coach

If you were selecting a coach, what types of attributes would attract you? According to the *Executive Coaching Handbook*, "an individual who demonstrates the following nine categories of attributes may be more likely to be effective as an executive coach" (p. 87):

- Mature self-confidence
- Positive energy
- Assertiveness
- Interpersonal sensitivity
- Openness and flexibility
- Goal orientation
- Partnering and influence
- Continuous learning and development
- Integrity

In fact, research has suggested that coaches' attributes are more likely to increase a client's positive perception of a coaching experience than techniques that are used (Lambert & Barley, 2001). The techniques you apply on your clients might actually be *less important* than the trust, rapport, and confidence you establish with them.

The Client/Coach Match or Compatibility

The match, or client/coach compatibility, appears to be critical to facilitate trust, openness, and respect. Research suggests that a strong match provides the context in which specific techniques can exert their influence (Lambert & Barley, 2001). Empathy, positive regard, authenticity, genuineness, playful challenge, tactful exchanges, tolerance for interventions made, and the dimensions of diversity for both clients and coach can make or break a coaching assignment (Kilburg, 2001). Adult learning seems to work best when the client and the coach, along with other members of the organization, treat each other as equals, focus on mutual strengths, and believe in each other's integrity and commitment to both coaching and the organization. It also leads to a more positive perception about the progress of the client (Dolinsky, Vaughan, Luber, Mellman, & Roose, 1998). In an analysis of over 100 studies about the factors that influence the client's improvement, client-coach *relationship factors* accounted for approximately 30 percent of the success in therapeutic outcomes across diverse clients and presenting problems (Lambert & Barley, 2001).

Gender of the Coach

Clients may be *more likely* to identify with a coach of the same gender. Landes & Sullivan (2004) conducted a study on a group of women to examine differences in women's anticipated comfort with self-disclosure in therapy. Their study found that women actually prefer same-sex therapists and are more likely to self-disclose information to female therapists. It is important for coaches to be aware of how the role of gender might influence the coaching engagement and subsequent behavioral change efforts (e.g. helping women who "off-ramp" in their career clearly define and understand the issues involved and ways to transition back to work if that is a desired goal). Indeed, the "personal chemistry" within coaching relationships may be influenced by gender for some clients and should be explored and discussed further, if it appears to be a potential barrier for a successful coaching intervention.

Ethnicity/Cultural Background of the Coach

Many clients prefer to work with coaches that come from similar ethnic, cultural and socioeconomic backgrounds to them. Coaches need to be aware of their client's communication style, values, life experience and family dynamics that might influence their self-esteem and coping skills. For example, clients that have endured challenges associated with underprivileged backgrounds may be skeptical that a coach can understand them. Some therapists have observed that minority patients who are treated by non-minority therapists expect and fear being misunderstood and rejected (Sapountzis, 2007). Research further contends that professionals working with culturally diverse individuals at any level are often at a loss as to how to establish relationships that are both effective and respectful of cultural values (Gardano, 1996).

Within most multi-national organizations today, you may be working with clients of different ethnicities, nationalities, and cultures. You can set the tone for a stronger coaching relationship by understanding how employees from different countries and cultures may have different communication patterns, relationships to hierarchy, and norms regarding formality. This is especially vital at a time when organizations are facing constant changes and globalization is becoming increasingly common.

Coaches must also be aware of their own prejudices and biases. They can consult with their colleagues for insight about how these biases might influence their coaching engagement, or be willing to refer to other coaches if those beliefs might have a potentially negative impact on the client. To facilitate effective coaching outcomes, coaches should:

1. Recognize and learn as much as they can about cultural diversity.

2. Understand the role that culture and ethnicity or race play in the socio-psychological and economic development of ethnic and culturally diverse populations.

3. Understand that socioeconomic and political factors significantly impact the psychosocial development of ethnically and culturally diverse groups.

4. Help clients to understand, maintain, and resolve their own socio-cultural identification and understand the interaction between culture, gender, and sexual orientation on behavior and needs.

Age and Generation of the Coach

With times constantly changing, different generations have dealt with different challenges, advantages, and mindsets. By understanding generational barriers and needs, coaches can use appropriate methods (Fleschner, 2008). A Baby Boomer client who is working with a Generation Y coach is likely to want to feel valued and respected for his or her hard work. A Generation Y coach may have obtained success more easily, given the additional resources and opportunities that come with modern times (such as technological advances). Given this difference, can this coach effectively mirror and identify the Baby Boomer for his struggles and contributions? A Generation Y coach may need to be particularly cognizant of those needs. The reverse could also be true, in that the client may feel that the coach couldn't understand him or her through the lens of modern and changed times.

Being able to adapt to your client's learning style, values, and drives will enable you to be more effective as a coach working with today's diverse workforce. Figure 1-2 summarizes some of the characteristics and drivers across the different generations, as well as some possible implications for coaching and developing these individuals.

Figure 1-2

Coaching Talent Today Can Be Challenging

Generation	Characteristics and Drivers	Development Approach
iPod "Millenial" Generation **<25** YEARS OLD	Technologically Dependant No Organizational Commitment Self-Absorbed / Entitled Multi-Tasking/Productive Family/Friend-Centric Value Work/Life Balance	**"Connect Me"** Blended Learning Multi-Tasking Technology Enabled Entitled and Demanding Feedback
Generation X and Y 25-39 years old **25-39** YEARS OLD	Technologically Friendly Network Friendly Self-Reliant Community Centered	**"Network Me"** Coaching and e-Learning Risk Takers Interest in Work/Life Balance Bored with Routine Short Attention Span
Baby Boomers **40-59** YEARS OLD	Technologically Curious Competitive / Achievement-Focused Idealistic	**"Show Me"** e-Learning and Classroom Workaholics Encore Careers
Baby Boomers **60+** YEARS OLD	Technology-Phobic Organizational Commitment Rule-Bounded/Hierarchical Security Oriented	**"Teach Me"** Classroom Technology-Phobic

Religiosity/Spirituality of the Coach

Religion and spirituality are issues that might emerge in coaching interventions, particularly when the coach and client have strongly divergent beliefs. Suppose a client is an Orthodox Jew seeking spiritual enlightenment and the coach is a non-affiliated atheist. How can the coach guide this client without allowing his or her differing beliefs and values to interfere with the helping relationship?

In a recent study, Lijtmaer (2009) reviewed the effects of religious beliefs in a therapeutic setting, and suggested that it is important for the therapist to be aware of his or her own particular religiosity and spirituality and how it can impact the relationship with the client. Not surprisingly, other studies have found that clients with high religiosity would express stronger preferences for a counselor's use of religious interventions than those with low religiosity would (Schaffner & Dixon, 2003).

Chapter 2:

Client Factors that Influence Behavioral Change

A zebra does not change its spots.

AL GORE

Some individuals are unlikely to change, regardless of the intervention prescribed for them. Lambert & Barley (2001) summarized over 100 studies concerning the therapeutic relationship and therapy outcome. They found that 40 percent of clients' outcomes are attributable to factors that are *outside of therapy*. Surprisingly, only 15 percent of clients' outcomes were due to expectancy effects, 15 percent were due to specific therapy techniques, and 30 percent were predicted by the *therapeutic relationship*.

Coaches can assess their client's motivation, but sometimes, what clients say they will do and what they *actually do* are inconsistent. For example, a client may be eager to follow a coach's feedback but may or may not actually follow through. Is this due to the coach? Or, perhaps it's something that shows up as result of the client's personality? Specifically, what kinds of clients are most suitable for coaching, which are most prone to derailment, and which are most likely to sustain change?

Personality Factors of the Client

Personality refers to patterns of relatively enduring characteristics of behavior and the psychological classification of different types of individuals, ranging from normal to abnormal. Current research suggests that:

1. Personality measurements of the same factor or construct, by self-reports, other reports, or behavior simulation, tend to be *highly correlated* (Nave, Sherman & Funder, 2008).

2. Personality traits have proven genetic *heritability* (Stubbe, Poshuman, Boomsma & De Geus, 2005).

3. Personality measures appear to be related systematically to biological parameters, such as those assessed by fMRI (DeYoung, Hirsh, Shane, Papademeteris, Rajeevan & Gray, 2010).

4. Personality traits are resistant to a *large* magnitude of change and relatively consistent over long periods of time (Ferguson, 2010).

5. Personality measures correlated significantly with meaningful *life and health outcomes* (Ozer & Benet-Martinez, 2006; Deary, Weiss & Batty, 2011).

Normal ("Bright Side") vs. Abnormal ("Dark Side") Personality Traits

Two predominant normal or "bright side" personality models (Hogan & Hogan, 2001) have emerged that coaches should have knowledge about. The first is sometimes considered a "meta-personality" model called Core Self Evaluations (CSE; Bono & Judge, 2003) because it is composed of four broad personality traits that are thought to directly influence our thoughts, feelings, and behaviors that impact work/life success, satisfaction, and other personal and organizational outcomes. The second is referred to as the five factor personality model (FFM) which focuses on five broad dimensions of explaining complex human behavior.

Core Self-Evaluation (CSE)

Individuals who score highly on measures of core self-evaluations have been shown to demonstrate high performance, career success, and satisfaction in their job (Judge, 2009). Core Self-Evaluation (CSE) is described as a person's fundamental, bottom line self-perception of his or her abilities. It includes four traits:

1. *Self-Efficacy*: one's estimate of his/her capabilities to perform across many contexts.

2. *Locus of Control*: an individual's belief in his/her ability to control his/her environment.

3. *Emotional Stability*: the lacking of neuroticism (e.g., anxiety, anger, and other negative affects).

4. *Self-Esteem*: the approval of oneself and the degree to which one sees him/herself as capable, significant, successful, and worthy.

Presumably, these traits impact clients' orientation of behavioral change. Clients who feel like they can control the events of their lives, rather than, be the effect of the events are more likely to accept coaching and sustain change. On the other hand, clients who have a low core self-evaluation are likely to resist or fail intervention attempts.

While only a decade old, research on CSE explains much of the overlap among these trait measures while also predicting many work and other applied outcomes better than each of its individual traits. CSE has been found to be correlated with a variety of job, career, and health outcomes. Individuals with high levels of CSE perform better on their jobs (the average correlation coefficient of the four core traits in predicting diverse job performance outcomes ranges from .23-.30), are more successful in their careers, are more satisfied with their jobs and lives, report lower levels of stress and conflict, cope more effectively with setbacks, earn significantly higher levels of income, and report higher physical health and psychological well-being (Judge, 2009).

Five Factor Model of Personality (FFM)

In contemporary psychology, the "Big Five" factors of personality are broad domains or dimensions of personality that are used to describe normal human personality (McRae & Costa, 1997). The Five Factor Model (FFM) is now perhaps the most widely used trait theory of personality and has achieved the closest thing to a consensus in personality research. Evidence also indicates that the "Big Five" traits are highly heritable and reliable across cultures and countries (McRae & Costa, 1997). Despite some controversy about the model, most practitioners and researchers tend to have common descriptions for each factor. These five "bright side" personality factors are often characterized as *Emotional Stability, Extraversion, Agreeableness, Openness to Experience, and Conscientiousness.*

1. ***Emotional Stability*** is characterized by a tendency to be calm, relaxed, emotionally stable, and free from persistent negative feelings such as stress, anger, anxiety, jealousy, and depression. Individuals who score low on this trait have a tendency to experience negative emotions, low self-esteem, rumination, and a hypersensitivity to threat of punishment (Costa & McCrae, 1992). A low score on emotional stability has been suggested as

influencing goal striving processes and disrupting concentration on work tasks.

Emotional stability is strongly associated with subjective well-being, lack of turnover intentions, leadership effectiveness, and job satisfaction/engagement. Leaders who are high on emotional stability tend to remain calm in moments of crisis and change, be patient with employee development, and seem resilient in the face of group and organizational failures.

2. *Extraversion* is characterized by a tendency to experience positive emotions and to seek out stimulation and the company of others. This is defined by an individual's engagement with the external world. Linked to the tendency to experience happiness (Fleeson, Malanos, & Achille, 2002), extraversion would also be associated with the part of the brain system responsible for sensitivity to reward (DeYoung, Hirsh, Shane, Papademetris, Rajeevan, & Gray, 2010). Extraverts tend to be optimistic about the future and successful in mentoring and networking situations (Klockner & Hicks, 2008).

Extraverts are most commonly described as active, assertive, upbeat, talkative, and optimistic individuals. Importantly, extraverts experience and express more positive than negative emotions, as seen in the association among extraverts, job satisfaction ratings, and high subjective well-being. Extraverts' proclivity toward optimistic views of the future helps facilitate them to emerge as group and team leaders, be perceived as "leader-like" by others, and also to express behaviors consistent with transformational models of leadership.

3. *Agreeableness* is characterized by a tendency to be compassionate and cooperative, rather than suspicious and antagonistic towards others. This trait reflects individual

differences in general concern for social harmony. Agreeable individuals value getting along with others. This trait has been linked to psychological mechanisms that allow the understanding of others' emotions, intentions, and mental states, including empathy and other forms of social information processing (DeYoung et al., 2010). These individuals focus on teamwork and good relationships and often have personal-oriented careers (Klockner & Hicks, 2008).

As a personality trait, agreeableness tends to be positively associated with helping behaviors and interpersonal competence in positions and jobs requiring high emotional labor (i.e., those involving significant interpersonal relations). Although some evidence suggests only a modest or even weak correlation between high agreeableness and leadership effectiveness, there may be good explanations for why the associations in the research literature might be higher.

Agreeable leaders tend to be gentle, kind, fair, participative, inclusive, and cooperative while trying to avoid or smooth over conflict. As a result, agreeable leaders will try to promote collaboration, cooperation, and helping behaviors among team members; be very caring and sensitive when delivering critical feedback to others; and foster a fair and supportive work climate. In general, agreeable leaders take an interest in the concerns and challenges of others and will be interested in the satisfaction and professional development of those they directly supervise.

4. *Openness to Experience* is characterized by a tendency for having an appreciation for art, emotion, adventure, unusual ideas, imagination, curiosity, and variety of experience. Individuals who score highly in this trait are more likely to hold

unconventional beliefs. The brain functioning of those high in Openness to experience is associated with working memory, abstract reasoning, and the control of attention (DeYoung et al., 2010).

Those high in Openness to experience are intellectually curious and have a tendency to be creative, resourceful, insightful, and introspective. These individuals might be very willing to take risks and are often attracted to entrepreneurial opportunities. In their comprehensive, meta-analytic review, Bono & Judge (2004) found that open individuals score highly on inspirational motivation and intellectual stimulation, which are core components of transformational leadership. Such leaders tend to visualize and communicate a compelling vision and future for the organization and are willing to challenge existing ways of doing business.

5. *Conscientiousness* is characterized by a tendency to be disciplined in pursuit of goal attainment, have a strong sense of direction, and work efficiently. Conscientious individuals are detailed-oriented, polite in most interpersonal situations, and deliberate in their decision-making. As such, conscientiousness as a trait is typically positively associated with favorable work behaviors, such as job performance, and negatively associated with turnover and intention to commit deviant behaviors. Conscientious individuals tend to exhibit integrity and more tenacity and persistence in the pursuit of personal and organizational objectives, and they tend to foster work climates regarded to be just and fair.

Individuals who score highly on this trait tend to control, regulate, and direct their impulses. This personality factor is linked to both academic and occupational success, as well as behaviors that promote health and longevity (DeYoung et al., 2010). It is also considered to be related to commitment to change and professional growth (Klockner & Hicks, 2008).

Compared to individuals who are low in conscientiousness, these high flyers tend to be more motivated to perform well on the job and are more likely to achieve higher performance, due to their goal setting, drive, careful planning, and persistence to move through obstacles and challenges. But after a certain point, high achievers become rigid, unable to make decisions, inflexible, and almost compulsively perfectionist. Too much achievement orientation might result in paying too much attention to the small stuff and overlooking bigger goals, and having rigidity might actually interfere with ongoing professional development.

It appears that there is indeed a *threshold level* of conscientiousness (and emotional stability) that, once crossed, actually *interferes* with high performance (Le, Oh, Robbines, Illies, Holland, & Westrick, 2011). In a new study exploring the association among achievement striving, emotional stability, and performance, it appears that for high-complexity jobs (e.g., engineer, scientist), *more is, indeed, better,* compared to low-complexity jobs. Indeed, a curvilinear relationship was found among conscientiousness, neuroticism, and performance for low complexity jobs where the deliberate, cautious, diligent, and rigid attributes of high flyers could lead people to waste time, influencing both speed and accuracy.

These findings support a U-shaped relationship between personality and work/life outcomes. High conscientiousness will initially lead to better performance, but the relationship will become weaker and then eventually disappear after it reaches a certain point. This relationship depends on just how complex the job is. One implication of this finding is that for more routine roles where innovation and intellectual thinking isn't critical, it might be a mistake to hire applicants on "potential" and drive alone. In fact, they might fail in these roles but shine in more complex positions.

These normal, "bright side" personality factors (socially desirable assets) can also have some possible *negative effects* on leadership, job performance, and interpersonal relations. Extremely high or low levels of these five factor personality styles may also have socially *undesirable* outcomes. For example, conscientious people are typically experienced by others as driven, diligent, detail oriented, and goal oriented. Overuse or very high levels of conscientiousness might be associated with negative outcomes or experienced by others as overly cautious, risk-averse, over-controlling, and overly analytical behavior. The following figures illustrate both the *"bright side assets"* and *"dark side liabilities"* of each of the "Big Five" personality factors.

Figure 1-3

Conscientiousness

LOW EXPRESSION	HIGH EXPRESSION
Bright Side Assets	**Bright Side Assets**

LOW EXPRESSION — Bright Side Assets

- Multi-focused & less obsessed with pursuing goals
- Knows when to "cut losses" and move on with tasks and goals that can't be achieved
- Flexible and willing to give up, if prudent
- Big-picture oriented
- Greater openness to supporting other's agendas and goals
- Less concerned with perfection in decisions and actions
- Doesn't take on too many tasks/goals at one time
- More lackadaisical in working towards goals
- Flexible and open sense of direction in life
- Satisfied with a life with less ambition and relentless pursuit of goals
- Spontaneous and able to make more rapid decisions
- Greater work and life balance
- Accommodating and casual
- Willing to consult and seek advice
- Can keep work and family separate
- Free thinking
- Flexible in work practices
- Adapt quickly to new situations
- Casual/Liberal

HIGH EXPRESSION — Bright Side Assets

- Disciplined in pursuit of goal attainment
- Detail Oriented
- Deliberate in decision making
- Ethical in pursuing an agenda
- Determined/Strong-willed
- Conscientious
- Goal Oriented
- Polite in interpersonal interactions
- High tenacity/persistence
- Fosters a work climate regarded as fair
- Efficient
- Planned and Organized
- Good Time Management
- Strong sense of direction
- Organized and well planned/prepared
- Picks up new tasks quickly
- Strong sense of direction in life
- Decides carefully with all the data and researches information
- Can focus on immediate gains
- Measured and steady in their work

LOW EXPRESSION — Dark Side Liabilities

- Seen as lazy and unmotivated
- Undependable or unreliable
- Casual about deadlines
- Unprepared
- Eager to quit in the face of challenge & obstacles
- Procrastinates in beginning new tasks, chores, and assignments
- Easily discouraged when faced with adversity
- Hasty to speak out and not very deliberate
- Lack of commitment to achieve and excel
- Lacks confidence in abilities and may be seen as inept by others
- Tends to avoid making commitments
- Uncomfortable with personal responsibility
- Unwilling to accept direction
- "Drifter" and uncommitted to actions & decisions
- Irresponsible
- Rebellious
- Too independent
- Flighty
- Not very thorough and rushes to get things done
- Seen as lacking pride in what is accomplished
- Short-term oriented
- Unpredictable

HIGH EXPRESSION — Dark Side Liabilities

- Rigid/willful/stubborn
- Inflexible & too determined to stick with their views
- Compulsive perfectionists
- Prone to self-deception
- Wastes time correcting mistakes
- Slow in speed to get things done at the expense of accuracy
- Overly obsessive-compulsive and relentless
- Overly cautious and slow to adapt to change
- Unlikely to be seen as charismatic or inspirational
- Less willing to take risks and avoids innovation
- Workaholic and prone to burnout
- Delays critical decision making (overly analytical)
- Threatened by turbulent circumstances
- Stressed by organizational change and tries to achieve too much
- Overwhelmed by work overload
- Less adaptable to change
- Inflexible around procedures/policies
- Misses entrepreneurial opportunities
- Over-controlling and micro-managing
- Overly adheres to ethical principles and fulfills moral obligations as he or she understands them

Figure 1-4

Emotional Stability

LOW EXPRESSION	HIGH EXPRESSION
Bright Side Assets	**Bright Side Assets**
• Hypervigilant • Emotionally expressive • Realistically self-critical • Concerned and makes plans for future events • High standards and quick to feel impatience with sloppiness and inefficiency • Tunes into own feelings and anxieties • Moderate stress motivates one to action and decisions • Gets one ready for "fight or flight" in an emergency • Rarely overly optimistic in one's thinking about things • Not overly confident or optimistic to guard against impulsive actions and decisions • Increased alertness and readiness to act, think, and behave • Increases response time in a crisis situation	• Calm in the face of change, danger, and stress ("cool-headed") • Consistent in expressing emotions • Unlikely to express anxiety, stress, jealousy • Optimistic and hopeful about the future • Relaxed, unworried, & less likely to be tense or nervous • Seems to be more "in the moment" • Recovers from individual, team, and organizational failure • Views change as a challenge and not a threat • Possesses a sense of emotional control • Even-tempered & laid-back in interpersonal style • Slow to anger and patient with others • Rarely experiences or expresses extreme emotional "highs" and "lows" • Happy, content, and satisfied with work and life • Able to control their emotions and behavior in the face of stress • Serene, takes things as they come • Undemonstrative, doesn't panic • Optimistic • Focuses on events/situations as they get close • Capable of practicing mindfulness • Easy-going & slow to anger
Dark Side Liabilities	**Dark Side Liabilities**
• Prone to panic • Histrionic and overly emotive • Uncertain and moody • Pessimistic or negative about the future • Anxious, nervous, and overly cautious • Emotionally volatile and unpredictable • Unable to control emotions • Impatient and quick to express anger and hostility • Neurotic & excessive worrier who rubs off on others • Discontent and unhappy with work/life • Prefers to stick to what is comfortable and what they know • Pessimistic • Most likely to get hurt when let down by others • Easily discouraged and dejected when things go badly • Too sensitive/anxious to change • Overwhelmed and not able to concentrate under pressure • Prone to "choking" • Lets little things "get under one's skin" • Can be seen as too emotionally expressive and high strung • Inability to concentrate, think clearly, and make sound decisions	• Indifferent/Unresponsive • Overconfident to handle problems • Apathetic • Insular • Cold • Unconcerned and complacent • Impervious to criticism • Unemotional • Fails to see difficulties ahead • Emotionally unavailable • Overconfident in skills and abilities to handle crises and challenges • Can be perceived as aloof, apathetic, and lacking urgency • Can come across as uninterested and lacking empathy for others • Seldom injects emotions into relationships with others • Unexpressive leaders might conceal their true assessments of others • Less likely to use inspirational appeal as an influence tactic • Unwilling to face issues • Emotionally too controlled

Figure 1-5

Openness to Experience

LOW EXPRESSION	HIGH EXPRESSION
Bright Side Assets	**Bright Side Assets**
• Risk takers, so long as they agree to take the risks or there is a strong "upside" for them • Have to see a commercial point to doing something • Must have a clear "what's in it for me" (WIFM) • Less impulsive and more thoughtful about behavioral choices and decisions • Resists temptations and has high tolerance for frustration • Prudent risk takers • Practical and logical • Prosaic & prefers to keep mind on the task at hand • Controlled emotions & less emphasis on feeling states • Narrow, rather than broad, focus on activities, hobbies, and tasks • Conservative and more cautious • Analytical and logical • "Look before you leap" philosophy to ensure success • Stable, reliable, and predictable • Practical and more conservative ideas & thinking • Dependable and someone you can count on to do what they articulate they plan to do	• Intellectually curious and stimulated by learning or trying new things • Creative and innovative • Challenges the status quo • Seeks change and adventure & will try new things • High tolerance for ambiguity • Risk taker, flexible, adaptable • Aggressively pursues new opportunities • Introspective • Imaginative and resourceful • Utilizes divergent thinking to challenge the ways things are typically done • Sees change as adventure, rather than a challenge • Views failure as a learning experience • Possesses vivid imagination and can generate future visions that are often compelling to others • Open and tolerant of novel ways of thinking and behaving • Can detect an opportunity • Self-Development oriented & seeks to change self • Competitive • Radical ideas • Changes mind when excited about something • Passionate about initiating change • Sensation seeking
Dark Side Liabilities	**Dark Side Liabilities**
• Rigid, narrow, and lacking in imagination • Difficulty in coping with erratic or unpredictable behavior • Lack of spontaneity • Others might experience these individuals as boring and reticent to try new things • Finds change difficult and sticks with "tried & true" • Limited curiosity • Too dogmatic and not open to alternative views and ways of behaving • Misses out on entrepreneurial opportunities • Often expresses regrets about not taking more chances • Stays with what is known and rarely ventures out too far with new ventures, activities, or social interactions • Fails to see new opportunities and the "up side" to actions and decisions • Focuses more on what might go wrong or won't work than the opportunities for success	• Nonconformists • Prides oneself on being antiauthoritarian • Uncomfortable in hierarchical, conventional, and traditional organizational settings • Gets distracted by new and vogue ideas and proposals by others • Can be overly complex and philosophical • Too much emphasis on "possibility thinking" • Prone to bouts of deep analysis and reflection • Appears unable to develop a particular position on issues • Frustrating to others requiring simple and clear instructions • Big risk takers • Too committed to change for change's sake • Overly competitive • Radical but not people oriented solutions • Good getting things started but not finishing • Vivid fantasies and daydreaming that interfere with actions

Figure 1-6

Extraversion

LOW EXPRESSION   **HIGH EXPRESSION**

Bright Side Assets

- Respectful of others
- Introspective
- Intellectual
- Secure
- Non-Manipulative
- Gets energy from being alone
- Selective in whom they interact with
- Independent and less needy of others
- Unassuming
- Prefers to sort out problems alone
- Not dependent on others and self-reliant
- Maintains focus without others' input
- Takes time to establish relationships with others
- Seeks quality in friendships, rather than quantity
- Uses a private style and thinks deeply
- Prefers to be left alone and selects own company
- Prefers to work out problems alone after careful thought and consideration
- Lacks public need for recognition
- Operates out of respect and doesn't expect to be liked
- Emotional energy is charged in smaller and more intimate groups and friendships
- Better one to one in interpersonal interactions
- Data & thing oriented, rather than people oriented

Bright Side Assets

- Assertive and willing to speak "one's mind"
- Gregarious/Extraverted
- Charismatic
- Friendly/Outgoing
- Social
- Talkative
- Appears "leader-like" to others
- Gets energy from being around others
- Not inhibited socially
- Engaging interpersonally
- Outgoing and willing to meet new people easily
- Emotionally expressive and open with others
- Socially poised and confident
- Amenable to others and willing to fit in
- Interested in building long-term relationships
- Makes contacts and friends easily
- Compatible
- Responsive
- Agreeable
- Team oriented
- Interested in recognition
- High capacity to make friends
- Tolerant of diversity
- Less disturbed by awkward social interactions

Dark Side Liabilities

- Private, shy, and reserved
- Aloof and distant and keeps others away
- Domineering and opinionated
- Judgmental and evaluative of others
- Very selective in whom they support and court (political)
- Mysterious
- Closed and unwilling to share
- Troubled/Insecure
- May not seem obviously enthusiastic or involved with others
- Unwilling to share or divulge much to others
- Closed off emotionally
- Unwilling to mix and will ignore you unless you are needed
- Comes off as being better than others
- Doesn't care how others are doing things
- Too independent
- Submissive and lacking a "spine"
- Self-conscious and avoids groups and new relationships
- Slow to involve themselves in teams & new groups
- Easily misunderstood by others
- Inhibited and may have strong opinions and not share them

Dark Side Liabilities

- Too socially interactive and embarrassing to those who are quieter
- Bold and aggressive, both verbally and behaviorally
- Quickly bounces from one conversation to another (appears to lack focus)
- Can come across as disingenuous or friendly for self-gain
- Lacking in boundaries of what to share and disclose to others
- Attention seeking
- Overly talkative
- Draining
- Pushy
- Too dependent and in need of company
- Dependent on others
- Opinionated and inflexible
- Domineering
- Overly assertive
- Obstructive/Dogmatic
- Unwilling to take radical or independent views
- Needy for recognition from others

Figure 1-7

Agreeableness

LOW EXPRESSION	HIGH EXPRESSION
Bright Side Assets	**Bright Side Assets**
• Pragmatic and realistic • Quick to tell others what to do • Assertive • Determined to stick to their own views • Willing to take responsibility for actions • Outspoken • Direct • Blunt • Willing to give constructive feedback to others • Effective in confronting others • Holds own in face to face arguments • Can protect own interests • Healthy cynics • Capacity to see through flattery in others • High ability to see genuineness in others • Wary of others who take advantage • Can be tough when required • Strong negotiators • Can make decisions without feeling obligated to the feelings of others • Will challenge, defend, and argue to make important points • Understands and knows how to play "politics" • Less forgiving and more demanding • Argues using logic and structure	• Trusting and trustworthy • Responsive, open, and compassionate • Sympathetic and caring • Altruistic and kind toward others • Team oriented and willing to support & help others • Cooperative, accommodating , gentle, and kind • Inclusive and promoting affiliation • Facilitating and helping to minimize conflict • Pleasant • Fair and friendly—looks for the good in others • Empathetic in delivering negative feedback • Interested in the thoughts and feelings of others • Good, active listeners • Astute and "tuned" into other's feelings & behaviors • Psychologically minded and able to understand and mirror the feelings of others • Collaborative and seeks "win-win" outcomes • Amenable to others and tries to "fit in" • Takes opinions of others into account • Allows others to make their points • Will not argue aggressively • Democratic and accepting • Selfless and understanding
Dark Side Liabilities	**Dark Side Liabilities**
• Narcissistic and Self-promoting • Harsh/Bullying • Shrewd, self-advancing, and cynical • Too realistic and objective • Non-emotive and non-feeling • No-nonsense and boring • Too direct in dealing with others • Overly emotional and lacking in self-control • Too concerned about pleasing others • Autocratic/Authoritarian • Unwilling to listen to others • Too quick to impose on others • Overly aggressive and demanding • Too quick to act and too hard to hold back • Prone to be outspoken • Discounts the opinions and ideas of others • Can be seen as self-serving • Manipulative • Critical and unwilling to forgive • Harsh in judgment of others • Callous, cold, and overly blunt	• Overly accommodating and obliging • Tendency to avoid interpersonal conflict • Soft • Susceptible and gullible • Can appear as naïve to others • Overly process oriented & not task focused enough • Unwilling to confront others • Willing to adapt to another's argument • Avoids issues, hoping they will get better • Can be manipulated and steamrolled by assertive individuals • Too willing to please • Idealistic • Naïve • Too willing to give others a "second chance" • Overly uncritical • Too forgiving • Too soft on others—unwilling to confront and speak out in the face of opposition • Too timid • Too willing to bend and adapt to a group decision • Defuses an argument by giving too much away

Coaches can gauge clients' likelihood for improvement by understanding how personality traits can predict their likelihood of development. Research suggests that *extraversion, conscientiousness, and agreeableness* are significant predictors of leadership performance at all levels and across industries (Barrick & Mount, 1991). Individuals who score high on *openness to experience and extraversion* are *more likely* to seek coaching and helping interventions (Klockner & Hicks, 2008). Individuals high on these personality factors are generally more willing to take on new challenges and are open to a variety of experiences to enhance learning. As a result, "they are actively involved in their own destiny of the intervention process" (Klockner & Hicks, 2008, p.22).

Abnormal Personality Models

Some individuals are limited by their abilities to benefit from coaching. They have certain personality traits that are extreme enough to be considered *abnormal* and are usually classified within the DSM-IV manual of mental disorders. The categories are prototypes, and a patient with a close approximation to the prototype is said to have that disorder. For nearly half the disorders, symptoms must be sufficient to cause "clinically significant distress or impairment in social, occupational, or other important areas of functioning" (American Psychiatric Association [DSM-IV], 2000).

Figure 1-8 describes the abnormal personality factors that are categorized within the current version of DSM-IV as "personality disorders" but likely affect how the client acts, feels, and behaves within a coaching engagement. It is important to remember that unless you are clinically trained as a coach (e.g., licensed MFT or psychologist), it is always best to seek a consult on how to best deal with these disorders or refer to another colleague with the appropriate training and background to address some of the issues that underlie these disorders.

Figure 1-8

Abnormal Personality Factors and DSM-IV Axis II Personality Disorders[1]

DSM-IV AXIS II DISORDER	PERSONALITY CHARACTERISTICS
Paranoid	+ Insightful on politics
	- Mistrusting/excessively certain
Schizoid	+ Resilient under pressure
	- Non-communicative/lacks empathy/indifferent to others
Schizotypal	+ Creative thinking
	- Erratic decision making
Antisocial	+ Charming and risk taking
	- Manipulative/dishonest/impulsive
Narcissistic	+ Charismatic/confident
	- Can't admit mistakes/sensitive to feedback/lacks empathy
Histrionic	+ Entertaining/emotionally expressive
	- Attention seeking/impulsive/concerned with appearance
Borderline	+ Enthusiastic
	- Emotional outbursts/no clear goals/interpersonal instability
Obsessive Compulsive	+ High standards/detail oriented/perfectionist
	- Difficulty completing tasks/controlling/unwilling to compromise
Avoidant	+ Accurate in work done/independent
	- Risk averse/indecisive/introverted/socially awkward/timid
Dependent	+ Team oriented/considerate
	- Overly concerned to please others/submissive/difficulty in making decisions

[1] The American Psychiatric Association is in the middle of a historic revision to its diagnostic "Bible" the Diagnostic and Statistical Manual of Mental Disorders (DSM), with the latest version redefining the definition and inclusion of the number of "personality disorders" in early 2013. Instead of the old 10 personality types, DSM-V is proposing to simply the system by defining just five: Antisocial/Psychopathic, Avoidant, Borderline, Obsessive-Compulsive, and Schizotypal types. Each type will come with a narrative paragraph description. Additionally, DSM-V will likely add six "trait domains" based on the five-factor personality model (Negative Emotionality, Introversion, Antagonism, Disinhibition, Compulsivity, and Schizotypy).

The Role of Genetics in Personality: Can People Really Change?

Research on behavioral genetics and genetic sociology indicates that up to *50 percent* of personality is genetically determined (Jang et al., 1996; Bouchard & Loehlin, 2001). Studies suggest that character traits are hard-wired from early childhood, but through nurture, they are influenced by our environment and managed throughout our lifespan (Trickey & Hyde, 2009). For example, Arvey and colleagues' research based on twin studies, estimated that about *33 percent* of the variance in *holding leadership roles* (leader emergence) across diverse organizations can be attributed to genetic factors, with environmental factors accounting for the majority of leadership development (Arvey, Zhang, Avolio, & Kreueger, 2007).

In a recent study of 3,412 twins from the U.K. and 1,300 twins from the U.S., researchers examined whether genetic factors were associated with the "Big Five" personality characteristics and the tendency to become an entrepreneur (defined as someone who is self-employed, starting a new business, acting as an owner, or engaging in a start-up process). The researchers found that common genes influenced the correlations between only two personality factors (openness to experience and extraversion) and the tendency to become an entrepreneur (Shane, et al., 2010). These findings support earlier meta-analytic research (Zhao, et al., 2010) exploring personality and entrepreneurial intentions, research found significant correlations between extraversion and entrepreneurial intentions (.16) and between openness to experience and entrepreneurial performance (.21).

Debate continues about whether personality, both normal and disordered, can change significantly or is mainly stable across the life span. Recent longitudinal and cross-sectional aging research has shown that personality traits continue to change *primarily* in young adulthood (Roberts & Mroczek, 2008). Research by Brent Roberts, Professor of

Psychology in the Department of Psychology at the University of Illinois, summarizing over 100 studies of personality suggests that most people become more confident, warm (agreeable), responsible (conscientious), and emotionally stable as they age, especially during young adulthood (ages 20 to 40). In general, although both normal personalities and personality disorders can change to a certain degree, research reveals that they tend to be fairly stable across the life span, and patients in therapy generally experience no more personality change than nonpatients (Ferguson, 2010). Cross-cultural comparisons of personality factors suggested relatively similar levels of personality stability, although personality stability among people in South Pacific nations is slightly lower than among those in the United States, Canada, or European nations.

Although there is much debate about genetic "set points" for personality, we can change, according to new research from Carol Dweck and her colleagues at Stanford University. Dweck's research suggests that people either have fixed beliefs about their personality (it can't be really modified) or they have a malleable set of beliefs that can be developed through efforts and education. Adults (and children) with a malleable viewpoint are more open to learning new things, confronting new challenges, sticking with tough tasks, and demonstrating greater resilience.

Dweck's research suggests that this orientation is trainable and can result in greater performance and other personality related changes (e.g., increased openness to new experiences and sociability). She suggests that by emphasizing and praising traits, we are reinforcing a fixed perspective, and we should really recognize effort or strategies.

Even our level of happiness (subjective well-being) can be changed, despite evidence that at least 50 percent of our happiness is genetically programmed. For example, Ed Diener and his colleagues analyzed data from a 15-year study on marriage transitions and life satisfaction (Diener, et al, 2006). On average, most people moved toward their baseline level of happiness, but interestingly, a large number remained at their baseline, and others stayed below it.

In our own research on happiness with individuals with the auto-immune disease multiple sclerosis (MS), we have seen significant positive changes in work and life satisfaction from early diagnosis of the disease to several months later. We have explored how a comprehensive, 12-week "MS Living Well" program that meets for four hours over 12 consecutive weeks can modify subjective well-being, using our own stress and health risk assessment called StressScan (www.getlifehub.com/stress_scan). We use one scale, in particular called "Psychological Well-Being," which is a global measure of subjective well-being or happiness (questions include aspects of positive affect, engagement and life meaning). We have also replicated this finding with an blended learning online version of this "MS Living Well" program that also demonstrated a significant increase in happiness/psychological well-being over the same 12-week period (Giesser, et al., 2010; Giesser et al., 2007).

It would appear from all the current research that our beliefs about ourselves can change and so can our personality to some extent. Coaches should understand that indeed, people change, but the magnitude of these changes might not be very large. For example, a more recent meta-analysis of 26 longitudinal studies of multi-rater feedback indicated significant but small effect sizes, suggesting that performance improvements will be *practically modest* for even those most motivated and capable of changing behavior over time (Smither, London, & Reilly, 2005). Taken together, the research suggests that people can change when they are motivated and under the right conditions, with the best "fit" coach, but we should be cautious about expecting people to shift from a "competent jerk" to a "lovable star".

Client Coachability

How do you determine if your clients are coachable enough to work with? Goldsmith (2009) identified four indicators for what is considered "uncoachable" within an organizational setting:

1. *"Client doesn't think she has a problem."*
2. *"He is pursuing the wrong strategy for the organization."*
3. *"They're in the wrong job."*
4. *"They think everyone else is the problem."*

While most of your experiences as a coach will be with clients who are on the normal side of the continuum, some of your experiences may be with clients that have significant personality disorders making the client typically "uncoachable." For instance, coaches working with individuals with Borderline Personality Disorder may be dealing with a client that is very challenging or simply "uncoachable". These individuals are characterized by variability of moods and behaviors, chaotic relationships, an extreme fear of abandonment, and accompanying difficulties maintaining a stable and accepting sense of self. Suppose this client is committed one day, and shifts to a completely different mood another day. This "black and white thinking," can interfere in creating or sustaining behavioral change. How does the coach hold this client accountable? In these situations, coaches might seek a consult with a trusted colleague for help or might refer these clients to appropriate clinical practitioners.

As a second example, some highly successful executives may be naturally confident, charming, and exploitative, with an overbearing sense of entitlement that might be diagnostic of a Narcissist Personality

Disorder (American Psychiatric Association [DSM-IV], 2000). Such strengths, however, can often combine with a lack of empathy for others, a failure to recognize shortcomings, and an inability to reflect on mistakes (Mansi, 2009). Coaches may want to think twice before attempting to coach such individuals with extreme cases of low self-awareness and high resistance.

Client's Readiness to Change

Some clients may simply not be *ready* to change. People who smoke realize that this behavior isn't conducive to long-term health, but nobody quits until they are sufficiently motivated to change this difficult, addictive behavior. Simply, people change habits when they are ready to change (Nowack & Heller, 2001). For example, Prochaska, DiClemente, & Norcross (1992) identified specific readiness stages (pre-contemplation, contemplation, preparation, action, maintenance, and relapse) that clients typically go through in order to achieve successful behavioral change. These stages are each associated with techniques and approaches coaches can use to increase motivation to initiate and maintain new behavior over time.

Feedback Orientation of the Client

How do your clients respond to feedback? Your client's receptivity to feedback will vary with each individual. The extent to which clients welcome feedback during coaching has to do with how they process that feedback. Within organizations, the nature and perception of feedback is crucial.

Feedback orientation reflects clients' receptivity to feedback, including their comfort with feedback, tendency to seek feedback and process it mindfully, sensitivity to others' views of oneself, belief in the value of feedback, and feelings of accountability to act on the feedback (Smither, 2002). For instance, coaches that work with highly narcissistic clients may have a difficult time receiving feedback, especially criticism. On the other hand, individuals high on the five-factor personality trait, Openness to experience may have a high feedback orientation that leads them to be less resistant and more open. Consequently, they are likely to be receptive to coaching. The reverse is also true: Good coaching can increase one's feedback orientation.

Chapter 3:

Environmental Factors that Influence Behavioral Change

> **Teamwork is essential – it allows you to blame someone else.**
>
> **ANONYMOUS**

Oftentimes, it is difficult to determine the exact contributing factors of clients' progress. According to Peterson (2010), the relationship between the coach's actions and the client's outcomes are not always clear. There are many other events occurring at the same time as the coaching is taking place, and identifying the exact cause of progress between the coaching activities and the outcomes may be difficult.

In the previous section, we reviewed client factors in the change process, and how each of them can affect the client's optimal change. Suppose all the factors align perfectly: The coach and the client are a great match, the client is coachable and self-directed, and the coach is highly competent and generally effective. What environmental factors can interfere with the client's behavioral change process?

Imagine an individual is being coached to improve his lifestyle and health practices. If this individual is living with a spouse that cooks him food that is highly saturated with cholesterol and fat, wouldn't that interfere with his practice and intention of healthful eating? Similarly, if this individual is trying to quit smoking but lives with people who smoke, it's possible to quit, but it makes the process much more challenging. As another example, it would seem difficult for a patient or client to battle depression when living in a household with constant conflicts, criticisms, and demeaning interactions. Presumably, a client's environment can either support or hinder his or her progress.

For example, a study on religiosity and physical health demonstrated that individuals attending church or spiritual centers have a lower risk for illnesses and are able to recover from illnesses better than those who do not seek spiritual centers (Powell, Shahabi, & Thorensen, 2003). While these authors sought to determine how religiosity and/or spirituality affected an individual's health, they found that those individuals that attended support centers (i.e. church, place of worship) had approximately a 30 percent reduction in risk of diseases. This suggests that the act of attending these support centers may encourage meaningful social roles that provide a sense of self-worth and purpose. The social modeling that these individuals receive through being surrounded by positive healthy behaviors, relationships, and beliefs can increase likelihood for change.

Organization as a Support System

Organizational environment contributes significantly to the coaching process (Kilburg, 2001). If the coach is working in a severely troubled organization (e.g., low engagement, high turnover due to poor leadership practices, extremely high work load and little perceived control by employees), clients may simply not be supported, recognized or reinforced for new skills or behaviors they attempt to practice back on the job (Kilburg, 2001). Research about individual executive development programs indicates that some of the factors that impact the effectiveness of coaching in organizations have much to do with organizational support (McGovern, Lindemann, Vergara, Murphy, Barker, & Rodney Warrenfeltz, 2001). One finding that emerged from the study was that individuals being coached were unable to put adequate time into their professional development plans due to competing workload and pressure.

Individuals that are motivated and enrolled in the change process often need their support system to reinforce and maintain progress. Without the proper support, encouragement and reinforcement of colleagues, management, and work teams, change may become difficult.

Manager-Client Relationship

In a review of the coaching and counseling literature, the single most important factor repeatedly identified as contributing to positive outcomes is a meaningful, lasting, and effective working relationship with the coach, therapist or mentor (Kilburg, 2001). Gregory & Levy (2010) examined the performance coaching relationship formed between the supervisor and direct report. These researchers suggest that the process and the perceived effectiveness of coaching ultimately depend on the relationship between the supervisor and the subordinates. Figure 1-9 shows four dimensions that they describe as critical elements of the coaching relationship, based on the *Perceived Quality of the Coaching Relationship Scale* (PQCR; Gregory & Levy, 2010). When these behaviors are present, leaders are perceived to be better performance coaches, resulting in increased talent engagement, retention, and reduced perceptions of job stress (Nowack, 2006).

Figure 1-9

Perceived Quality of the Managerial Coaching Relationship (PQCR)

DIMENSION	ITEMS
Genuineness of the Relationship	1. My supervisor and I have mutual respect for one another.
	2. I believe that my supervisor truly cares about me.
	3. I believe my supervisor feels a sense of commitment to me.
Effective Communication	1. My supervisor is a good listener.
	2. My supervisor is easy to talk to.
	3. My supervisor is effective at communicating with me.
Comfort with the Relationship	1. I feel at ease talking with my supervisor about my job performance.
	2. I am content to discuss my concerns or troubles with my supervisor.
	3. I feel safe being open and honest with my supervisor.
Facilitating Development	1. My supervisor helps me to identify and build upon my strengths.
	2. My supervisor enables me to develop as an employee of our organization.
	3. My supervisor engages in activities that help me to unlock my potential.

How is Feedback within the Organization Received?

Research suggests that organizational culture and climate impacts a client's resistance or acceptance of feedback (Schilligo, Bogle, Reid, Rivera, Steelman, & Pittman, 2010; McGovern, et al., 2001). Some organizations do not promote open communication and feedback, which, in turn, can be detrimental to an employee's initiative to change. Other organizations provide and support ongoing feedback with the spirit of *feedforward*, in order to initiate successful behavioral change.

Further, some organizations simply punish employees for negative performance and rarely reward or recognize their employees for positive performance. Consequently, these individuals may view the idea of feedback as synonymous with criticism. It is beneficial for employees to have a work climate that has a supportive feedback environment. This type of environment is one that facilitates the constructive exchange and use of job performance feedback between supervisors and employees and among coworkers (Schilligo et al., 2010). Coaches should be aware of their client's organizational culture to determine and ensure effective reception of feedback.

Summary

This chapter is intended for coaches to understand the major contributing elements that impact their clients' progress and ultimately affect successful behavioral change. Coaches should follow ethical guidelines and professional training to be aware of how these factors might influence a coaching engagement. Coaches should be particularly mindful of the factors that can interfere with the best coaching practices. According to the Ethical Principles of and the American Psychological Society's (APA) Code of Conduct, "where differences of age, gender, race, ethnicity, national origin, religion, sexual orientation, disability, language, or socioeconomic status significantly affect psychologists' work concerning particular individuals or groups, psychologists obtain the training, experience, consultation, or supervision necessary to ensure the competence of their services, or they make appropriate referrals." Furthermore, they should be aware of those clients that may be deemed as "uncoachable". Are their personalities extreme enough to be considered a disorder that might require clinical counseling or therapy?

Coaches can also foster professionalism by collaboratively creating and clearly communicating negotiated agreements with their clients. In cases where the coach may not be sure, they should seek consultation to protect the anonymity of their client and/or refer the client to another qualified coach. In fact, some research suggests that coaches should have a shadow consultant or supervising consultant available to them to provide assistance when an assignment develops problems (Kilburg, 2001). This can help them and their clients remain on the path of progressive development.

Key Points

1. The *Enlighten, Encourage* and *Enable* model of individual change serves as a useful model for coaches to understand and use to facilitate successful change in their clients.

2. Three factors are associated with influencing successful behavioral change: 1) Coach factors; 2) Client factors; and 3) Environmental factors.

3. Personality appears to be inheritable and fairly stable over our life span and associated with both meaningful life outcomes and health.

4. There are key principles for *starting* (adopters) new behaviors that may be different from what is required to *maintain* (sustainers) behavior over time.

5. Although self-initiated behavioral change is entirely possible, it's easier if you *have a coach*, mentor, manager, or partner to support you while you attempt a behavioral change.

COACHING EXERCISES

The following section includes various exercises related to the *Factors Influencing Behavioral Change* chapters.

Tips for Getting the Most from the Exercises in the Book

- **Take time to do the exercises.** These exercises are designed to help you and your client to move through the Enlighten, Encourage and Enable stages of successful behavior change.

- **Take time to reflect.** Spend some quality time on each exercise to answer the questions and reflect what they mean for you personally and professionally.

- **Pick and choose the most important exercises to use.** Each of the exercises has been specifically included to support the specific behavior change stage in our model. Some exercises will be more relevant than others for you and your client. However, each has a unique purpose but there is not a need to specifically do all of them or in any order.

- **Share with others.** Consider sharing your thoughts and feelings about one or more of the exercises with a partner, family member, friend or colleague. Seek their impressions and input about your reactions and commitments.

- **Commit to action.** Consider taking specific actions to translate these exercises into goals and new behaviors.

Each of the exercises included in the book and additional ones for each of the *Enlighten, Encourage* and *Enable* behavior change stages can be previewed and printed in a useable format for you and your clients to use for free by visiting our website at: www.envisialearning.com/clueless

COACHING EXERCISE #1

My Coaching Ethical Standards

What ethical standards do you use with your clients? Below is a checklist you can use ensuring them.

❏ Do I collaboratively create negotiated agreements with my clients?

❏ Do I adhere to the ethical guidelines of my relative coaching practice (e.g. *APA Ethical Principles and Code of Conduct* or *International Federation of Coaches (ICF) ethical guidelines*)?

❏ Do I take reasonable precautions to protect against third party disclosure except when required by law or preservation of safety and life?

❏ Do I clearly understand and accurately represent to others my level of professional experience, training, competence and knowledge?

❏ Do I maintain and represent clearly and accurately distinctions between my work and those of others?

❏ Do I take responsibility for clarifying confidentiality with my clients?

❏ Do I keep myself informed of new technologies, legal requirements and standards relative to my profession?

❏ Do I develop and enhance my professional knowledge and competence?

❏ Do I recognize my limits as people and professionals and either renew/extend resources or appropriately refer clients to others who we believe possess them?

❏ Do I monitor the quality of my work and seek ongoing feedback from clients and support from colleagues and other professionals?

❏ Do I keep written notes of my coaching meetings summarizing my impressions and activities?

COACHING EXERCISE #2

How My Clients See My Coaching Style

1. How would my clients describe me as a coach?

2. What are my coaching *strengths and assets*?

3. What knowledge, skills, and abilities do I need to *develop further* as a coach?

COACHING EXERCISE #3

Factors that Influence Your Coaching

Under each of the following categories, think about situations where the following factors influence your coaching success: *Coach Factors* (e.g. culture, gender, theoretical orientation) (2) *Client Factors* (e.g. personality traits, culture, religious beliefs (3) *Environmental or Organizational Factors* (e.g. managerial or organizational support). Write down a situation within each category where a particular factor had an extreme effect on the results of your coaching success.

1. Coach Factors:

2. Client Factors:

3. Environmental or Organizational Factors:

COACHING EXERCISE #4

Case Study—The Competent Jerk

Chris is a 48-year-old International Sales Director for a large, global sales firm. Chris has been with the company for over 11 years and has risen through the ranks based on strong sales performance and demonstrated technical competence. Chris ranks as one of the top producers and manages three multi-national sales teams.

In a recent organizational talent management/succession planning review, senior managers saw little upward mobility and possibility of promotion for Chris, because of strong interpersonal skills deficits. Chris is perceived to be highly arrogant, defensive, and opinionated, and he lacks empathy for others. Chris uses an autocratic style and has little patience for those who are slower to learn or require tremendous feedback about their performance.

Chris is also a "Type A" personality who tends to work tremendously long hours and exhibits poor health habits (rarely exercises, smokes, and weighs too much) that have contributed to his lack of work/life balance and high blood pressure. In the last executive physical, Chris was encouraged to make some immediate changes in eating habits, increase physical activity, and stop smoking.

The CEO of the organization believes Chris can benefit from executive coaching to become a "participative leader" and enhance interpersonal skills that can help build a stronger psychological climate for talent to be even more engaged and productive. The CEO believes Chris should utilize the executive coaching to enhance both leadership effectiveness and physical health. Unfortunately, Chris doesn't really believe a coach will be that helpful but believes politically it would be in his or her interest to work with one for a brief time.

Case Study Questions:

1. What are the presenting issues?

2. What role, if any, might the CEO play in any lifestyle coaching that might take place?

3. How motivated does this client appear to be to make positive health and behavioral changes?

4. If you were asked by the CEO to coach Chris, what steps would you take to contract and clarify your role? What steps might you take to ensure success?

5. How can you measure coaching success with this type of coaching engagement?

6. What knowledge, skills, and experiences would a coach need to have to take this coaching engagement?

7. What potential pitfalls, barriers, or challenges do you see in this situation?

8. What ethical and professional dilemmas do you see in this coaching situation? For example, should companies advocate for the health of their talent?

Coaching References

Amabile, T. & Kramer, S. (2011). The power of small wins. *Harvard Business Review, 89*, 70-80.

American Psychiatric Association: *Diagnostic and Statistical Manual of Mental Disorders*, Fourth Edition, Text Revision. Washington DC, American Psychiatric Association, 2000.

American Psychological Association. *Guidelines for Providers of Psychological Services to Ethnic, Linguistic, and Culturally Diverse Populations.* Retrieved from http://www.apa.org/pi/oema/resources/policy/provider-guidelines.aspx.

Atwater, L. E. & Brett, J. F. (2006). 360-degree feedback to leaders: Does it relate to changes in employee attitudes? *Group & Organization Management, 31*, 578-600.

Arvey, R. D., Zhang, Z., Avolio, B. J. & Kreueger, R. F. (2007). Developmental and genetic determinants of leadership role occupancy among women. *Journal of Applied Psychology, 92*, 693-706.

Barick, M. R. & Mount, M. K. (1991). The big five personality dimensions and job performance: A meta-analysis. *Personnel Psychology, 44*, 1-26.

Bono, J., Purvanova, R. K., Towler, A. J. & Peterson, D.B. (2009). A survey of executive coaching practices. *Personnel Psychology, 62*, 361-404.

Bono, J. & Colbert, A. (2005). Understanding responses to multi-source feedback: The role of core self-evaluations. *Personnel Psychology, 58*, 171-2003.

Bono, J. E. & Judge, T. A. (2004). Personality and transformational and transactional leadership: A meta-analysis. *Journal of Applied Psychology, 89*, 901-910.

Bono, J. E. & Judge, T. A. (2003). Core self-evaluations: A review of the trait and its role in job satisfaction and job performance. *European Journal of Personality, 17*, S5-S18.

Bouchard, T. J. & Loehlin, J. C. (2001). Genes, evolution and personality. *Behavior Genetics, 21*, 243-273.

Costa, P. T. & McCrae, R. R. (1992). The five-factor model of personality and its relevance to personality disorders. *Journal of Personality Disorders, 6*, 343-359.

Deary, I. J., Weiss, A. & Batty, G. D. (2010). Intelligence and personality as predictors of illness and death: How researchers in differential psychology and chronic disease epidemiology are collaborating to understand and address health inequalities. Psychological Science in the Public Interest, *11*, 53-79.

Epidemiology Are Collaborating to Understand and Address Health Inequities. *Psychological Science in the Public Interest, 11*, 53-79.

DeYoung. C. G., Hirsh, J. B., Shane, M. S., Papademetris, X., Rajeevan, N. & Gray, J. R. (2010). Testing predictions from personality neuroscience: Brain structure and the Big Five. *Psychological Science, 21*, 820–828.

Dweck, C. (2010). Can personality be changed? The role of beliefs in personality and change. *Current Directions in Psychological Science, 17*, 391-394.

Diener, E., Lucas, R., & Scollon, C. N. (2006). Beyond the hedonic treadmill: Revising the adaptation theory of well-being. *American Psychologist, 61*, 305-314.

Dolinsky, A., Vaughan, S. C., Luber, B., Mellman, L., & Roose, S. (1998). A match made in heaven? A pilot study of patient-therapist match. *Journal of Psychotherapy Practice & Research, 7*, 119-125.

Ericsson, K. A. (2006). The influence of experience and deliberate practice on the development of superior expert performance. In K. A. Ericsson, N. Charness, R. R., Hoffman, & P. J. Feltovich (Eds.), *The Cambridge handbook of expertise and expert performance* (pp. 683- 703). New York: Cambridge University.

Ericsson, K. A. (1996). *The Road to Excellence: The Acquisition of Expert Performance in the Arts and Sciences, Sports and Games.* Mahwah, (pp.10-11). NJ: Lawrence Erlbaum Associates.

Fiske, V., Simha-Alpern, A. & Sapountzis, L. (2007). When Worlds Collide: Crossing Cultural Divides in Transitional Spaces. *American Psychological Association: Psychologist-Psychoanalyst (Division 39), 27.*

Ferguson, C. J. (2010). A meta-analysis of normal and disordered personality across the life span. *Journal of Personlaity and Social Psychology. 98*, 659-67.

Fleeson, W., Malanos, A. B. & Achille, N. M. (2002). An intraindividual process approach to the relationship between extraversion and positive affect: Is acting extraverted as "good" as being extraverted *Journal of Personality and Social Psychology. 83*, 1409-1422.

Fleschner, S., Walz, G. R. Bleuer, J. C. & Yep, R. K. (2008). Counseling across generations: Bridging the Baby Boomer, Generations X, and Generations Y gap. *American Counseling Association: Counseling Outfitters, 27*, 139-148.

Gardano, A.C. (1996). Multi-Cultural Concerns: General Views About Individualism/ Collectivism. *American Psychological Association: Division 43 (Family Psychology) 13 (1).*

Goldsmith, M. (2002). Try feedforward instead of feedback. Leader to Leader Journal, 25. Retrieved December 2010, from http://www.marshallgoldsmithlibrary.com/cim/articles_display.php?aid=110.

Grant, A., Cavanagh, M. & Parker, H. (2010). The State of Play in Coaching Today: A Comprehensive Review of the Field. *International Review of Industrial and Organizational Psychology, 25*, 125-167.

Grant, A. M., Green, L. & Rynsaardt, J. (2010). Developmental coaching for high school teachers: Executive coaching goes to school. *Consulting Psychology Journal: Practice and Research, 62*, 151-168.

Grant, A., Curtayne, L. & Burton, G. (2009). Executive coaching enhances goal attainment, resilience, and workplace well-being: A randomized controlled study. *The Journal of Positive Psychology, 4*, 396-407.

Grant, A. (2008). Personal life coaching for coaches in training enhances goal attainment, insight and learning. *Coaching: An International Journal of Theory, Research and Practice, 1*, 54-70.

Giesser, B., Coleman, L., Fisher, S. Guttry, M., Herlihy, E., Nonoguchi, S., Nowack, D., Roberts, C. & Nowack, K. (2010). Living Well with Multiple Sclerosis: Comparisons of a 12-Week Blended Learning Versus Direct Classroom Program. Unpublished manuscript.

Giesser, B., Coleman, L., Fisher, S., Guttry, M., Herlihy, E., Nonoguch, S., Nowack, D., Roberts, C. & Nowack, K. (2007). Living Well with Multiple Sclerosis: Lessons Learned from a 12-Week Community Based Quality of Life Program. Paper presented at 17th Annual Art & Science of Health Promotion Conference, March, 2007, San Francisco, CA.

Gilmore, A. (2008). Lifestyle Learning: Improve the Bottom Line with Behavioral Education. *Chief Learning Officer*, 22-27, Interview with Chief Research Officer Kenneth Nowack, Ph.D.

Goldsmith, M. (2009). How to spot the "uncoachables". Retrieved March 35, 2009 from http://blogs.hbr.org/goldsmith/2009/03/how_to_spot_the_uncoachables.html

Green, S., Grant, A. M., & Rynsaardt, J. (2007). Evidence-based life coaching for senior high school students: Building hardiness and hope. *International Coaching Psychology Review, 2*, 24-32.

Green, L. Oades, L., & Grant, A. (2006). Cognitive-behavioural, solution-focused life coaching: Enhancing goal striving and well-being: An exploratory study. *Journal of Positive Psychology, 3*, 185-194.

Gregory, J. B., & Levy, P. E. (2010, April). *Employee coaching relationships: Enhancing construct clarity and measurement*. Poster presented at the 25th Annual Society for Industrial and Organizational Psychology meeting, Atlanta, GA.

Hogan, R. & Hogan, J. (2001). Assessing leadership: A view of the dark side. *International Journal of Selection and Assessment, 9,* 40-51.

Jang, K., Livesley, W. J. & Vemon, P. A. (1996). Heritability of the Big Five Personality Dimensions and Their Facets: A Twin Study. *Journal of Personality, 64,* 577–591.

Judge, T. (2009). Core self-evaluations and work success. *Current Directions in Psychological Science, 18, 58-62.*

Kaiser, R. & Hogan, R. (2011). How to (and how not to) assess the integrity of managers. *Consulting Psychology: Practice and Research, 62,* 216-234.

Kilburg, R. R. (2001). Facilitating intervention adherence in executive coaching: A model and methods. *Consulting Psychology Journal: Practice and Research, 4,* 251-267.

Kilburg, R. R. & Diedrich, R. C. (2007). Facilitating intervention adherence in executive coaching: A model and methods. *The wisdom of coaching: Essential papers in consulting psychology for a world of change,* 241-255.

Klockner, K. & Hicks, R. E. (2008). My next client: Understanding the Big Five and positive personality dispositions of those seeking psychological support interventions. *International Coaching Psychology Review, 3,* 148-163.

Kotter, J. P. (1996). *Leading Change.* Boston: Harvard Business School Press.

Lambert, M. J. & Barley, D. E. (2001). Research summary on the therapeutic Relationship and psychotherapy outcome. *Dean E. Psychotherapy: Theory, Research, Practice, Training, 38,* 357-361.

Landes, S. J. & Sullivan, B. F. (2004, July). Women's therapist selection based on therapist sex and presenting problem. Poster presented at the 2004 American Psychological Association Annual Convention, Honolulu, HI.

Le, H., Oh, I., Robbins, S. B., Ilies, R., Holland, E. & Westrick, P. (2011).Too much of a good thing: Curvilinear relationships between personality traits and job performance. *Journal of Applied Psychology, 96,* 113-133.

Lewis, R. J., Carswell, J., Thussu, S. & O'Brien, J. (April, 2010). Predisposed to Derail: The Personality Correlates of Risk for Derailment. Presented at the 2010 Society of Industrial Organizational Psychology Conference in Atlanta, Georgia.

Lijtmaer, R. M. (2009). The patient who believes and the analyst who does not. *Journal of the American Academy of Psychoanalysis & Dynamic Psychiatry, 37,* 99-110.

Ludeman, K. & Erlandson, E. (2004). Coaching the alpha male. *Harvard Business Review, 9,* 1-10.

Mansi. A. (2009). Coaching the Narcissist: How difficult can it be? *The Coaching Psychologist, 5,* 22-25.

McGovern, J. Lindemann, M. Vergara, M., Murphy, S. Barker, L. & Warrenfeltz, R. (2001). Maximizing the Impact of Executive Coaching: Behavioral Change, Organizational Outcomes, and Return on Investment. *The Manchester Review, (6)* 1.

McCrae, R. R. & Costa, P. T. (1997). Personality trait structure as a human universal. *American Psychologist, 52,* 509-516.

Nave, C., Sherman, R. & Funder, D. (2010). Beyond self-report in the study of hedonic and eudaimonic well-being: Correlations with acquaintance reports, clinical judgments and directly observed social behavior. *Journal of Research in Personality, 42,* 643-659.

Nowack, K. (2003). Executive Coaching: Fad or Future? *California Psychologist, 36,* 16-17.

Nowack, K. & Heller, B. (2001). Making Executive Coaching Work: The Importance of Emotional Intelligence. *Training Magazine trainingmag.com.*

Nowack, K. (2006). Emotional intelligence: Leaders Make a Difference. *HR Trends 17,* 40-42.

Ozer, D. & Benet-Martinex, V. (2006). Personality and the prediction of consequential outcomes. *Annual Review of Psychology, 52,* 401-421.

Peterson, D. B. (2010). Good to Great Coaching: Accelerating the Journey. In G. Hernez-Brome and L. Boyce (Eds.) In *Advancing Executive Coaching,* (pp. 83-103). San Francisco, CA: Jossey-Bass.

Powell, L. H., Shahabi L., & Thorensen, C. E. (2003). Religion and Spirituality. *American Psychologist, 58,* 36-52.

Prochaska, J.O. & Velicer, W. F. (1997). The transtheoretical model of health behavior change. *American Journal of Health Promotion,* 12, 38-48.

Prochaska, J.O., DiClemente, C.C. & Norcross, J.C. (1992). In Search of How People Change: Applications to Addictive Behaviors. *American Psychologist, 47,* 1102-1114.

Roberts, B. W., & Mroczek, D. (2008). Personality trait change in adulthood. *Current Directions in Psychological Science, 17,* 31-35.

Sapountzis, I. (2007). When worlds collide: Crossing cultural divides in transitional spaces. *Psychologist-Psychoanalyst, 27,* 43-44.

Sargent, N. (2011). What's happening in the coaching conversation with an executive at risk of derailing. *International Journal of Evidenced Based Coaching and Mentoring, 5,* 28-39.

Schaffner, A. D. & Dixon, D. N. (2003). Religiosity, Gender, and Preferences for Religious Interventions in Counseling: A Preliminary Study. *Counseling and Values, 48,* 24-33.

Schilligo, J., Bogle, C. A., Reid P., Rivera, I. D., Steelman, L. & Pittman, J. (2010). Antecedents and outcomes of the feedback environment. Presented at the 25th Annual Society for Industrial and Organizational Psychology Conference.

Shane, S., Nicolau, N., Cherkas, L. & Spector, T. (2010). Genetics, the Big Five and the tendency to be self-employed. *Journal of Applied Psychology, 6,* 1154-1162.

Smither, J., London, M. & Reilly, R. (2005). Does performance improve following multisource feedback? A theoretical model, meta-analysis, and review of empirical findings. *Personnel Psychology, 58,* 33-66

Smither, J. W. (2002). Feedback Orientation, Feedback Culture, and the Longitudinal Performance Management Process. *Human Resource Management Review, 12,* 81-100.

Steelman, L. A. & Levy, P. E. (2001, April). The feedback environment and its potential role in 360-degree-degree feedback. Paper presented at the 16th annual meeting of the Society for Industrial/Organizational Psychology, San Diego.

Spence, G. B., Cavanagh, M. J. & Grant, A. M. (2008). The integration of mindfulness training and health coaching: An exploratory study. *Coaching: An International Journal of Theory, Research and Practice, 1,* 1-19.

Spence, G. B. & Grant, A. (2005). Individual and group life coaching: Initial findings from a randomised, controlled trial. In M. Cavamagj. A., Grant, A. & Kemp, T. (Eds.). Evidence based coaching: Theory, research and practice from the behavioural sciences, (pp. 143-158). Brisbance: Australian Academic Press.

Stubbe, J., Poshuma, D., Boomsma, D. & De Geus, J. (2005). Heritability of life satisfaction in adults: A twin-family study. *Psychological Medicine, 35,* 1581-1588.

Trickey, G. & Hyde, G. (2009). A Decade of the Dark-Side. Fighting Our Demons at Work, Retrieved from: http://pcl.live.trunky.net/DarkSideReport.pdf , Accessed 9 November 2009.

Turner, R. A. & Goodrick, J. (2010). The case for eclecticism in executive coaching: Application to challenging assignments. *Consulting Psychology Journal: Practice and Research, 62,* 39-55.

Zhao, H., Seibert, S. & Lumpkin, G. (2010). The relationship of personality to entrepreneurial intentions and performance: A meta-analytics review. *Journal of Management, 36,* 381-404.

PART II:

Enlighten

> "What is necessary to change a person is to change his awareness of himself."
>
> **ABRAHAM MASLOW**

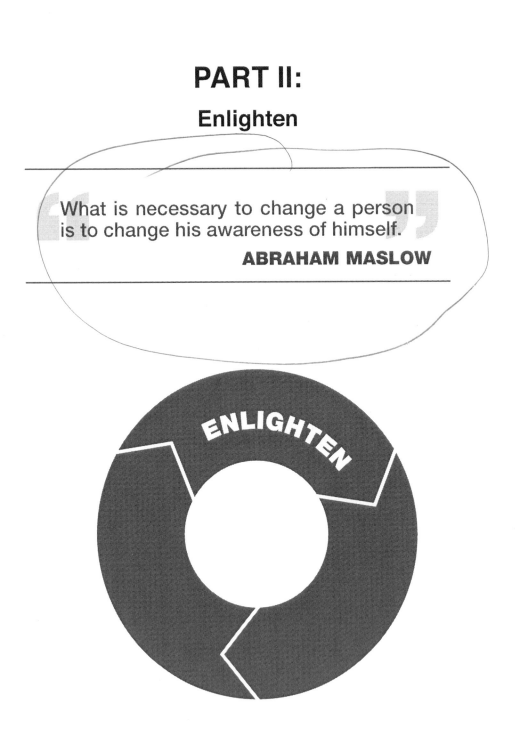

Introduction:
Why Enlightenment is Necessary for Behavioral Change

" The best vision is insight.

MALCOLM S. FORBES

Self-insight or self-awareness appears to be a *fundamental* element and a necessary condition for any successful behavioral change. Many of us may not realize how we are perceived by others or even tune into our own thoughts, feelings or behaviors. Neural circuits are formed after the repeated practice of new behaviors and we shift from being consciously competent to becoming unconsciously competent (e.g., tying our shoe or driving a car). Self-insight is also one of the major building blocks of emotional intelligence (EI), and lack of self-awareness can result in potential career derailment and strained relationships at work and home (Nowack, 2006).

Research shows that the positive benefits of self- awareness are tremendous. For example, self-awareness has been correlated with both individual and team effectiveness (Jordan & Ashkanasy, 2006). There is also a small, but growing, body of empirical literature supporting the idea that as a leader's capacity for self-awareness improves, others are more likely to rate his or her managerial performance as more effective (Kilburg, 2006). Similarly, a lack of self-awareness is one of the main factors contributing to career "derailment" (Hogan, Hogan, & Kaiser, 2011).

Psychologists studying the effects of an intentional self-awareness technique known as "mindfulness" found that trained participants showed a significant improvement in critical cognitive skills (and performed significantly higher in cognitive tests than a control group) after just four days of training for only 20 minutes each day (Zeidan, Johnson, Diamond, David, Goolkasian, 2010). Additionally, deliberate practice of intentional awareness has been shown to reduce rumination (not sure rumination is the word you want here), which, in turn, significantly decreased aggressive behavior towards others (Borders, Earleywine, Jojodia, 2010). For example, in a health-oriented study with cancer patients, mindfulness was shown to significantly decrease negative affect, self-reported pain, and stress (Brown & Richard, 2003). Indeed, being aware of our thoughts, emotions, and behaviors appears to be important for our job success, physical health, and psychological well-being.

Awareness/Insight

One of the major goals of executive, life and career coaching is to increase the level of *accurate self-insight*. Unfortunately, just hearing honest and accurate feedback is not enough. True self-insight takes place when clients deeply *understand* and *accept* the feedback. Once feedback has been accepted, clients are more willing to commit to taking specific actions to facilitate personal and professional development.

The *Enlighten* section of the book discusses how feedback creates awareness of a client's strengths and weaknesses and how they influence different areas of his or her life (e.g. work, family, self, etc.). Particular attention is given to 360-degree or multi-rater feedback systems and their use as useful tools in coaching interventions to facilitate self-insight. When using feedback assessments (e.g., multi-rater or 360-degree feedback), a coach helps the client interpret the meaningfulness of the results and explore the differences between self-perceptions and the perceptions of others.

The coach is also responsible for helping the client manage his or her emotional reactions to feedback. Feedback reactions may range from pleasant surprise to hurt, anger, and even depression (Eisenberger, Lieberman & Williams, 2003). When feedback is given improperly, negative physiological and emotional reactions are more likely to occur. As a result, harmful feedback can lead to defensiveness, rejection of information, and resistance to using the feedback to improve skills and behavior.

Factoid: Meditation and Plasticity of the Brain

Recent research at the Massachusetts General Hospital found that practicing meditation on a daily basis throughout a period of eight weeks resulted in a change in brain structure. Magnetic Resonance Imaging (fMRI) tests showed an increase in grey-matter density in areas of the brain that are associated with memory, self-awareness, empathy, and stress (Hölzel, Carmody, Vangel, Congleton, Yerramsetti, Gard, & Lazar, 2011).

Newer neuroscience research sheds light on why negative feedback could be emotionally harmful. Recent studies confirm that emotional hurt and rejection, whether a part of social interactions or a part of poorly designed and delivered feedback interventions, can actually trigger the same neurophysiologic pathways associated with *physical pain* and suffering (Eisenberger, Lieberman, & Williams, 2003). Additionally, interpersonal judgment and social evaluation tends to elicit strong stress reactions, with cortisol levels in our system being elevated 50 percent longer, when the stressor is interpersonal, versus impersonal (Dickerson & Kemeny, 2004).

When giving feedback, coaches should be aware that its reception will also be influenced by the client's dispositional tendencies. These should be carefully assessed before engaging in the feedback process. As Joo (2005) has pointed out, feedback orientation and the coach's personality directly affect the client's openness to the coach's input, suggestions, and feedback, which can affect the overall effectiveness of an intervention. Research suggests that translating awareness into behavior change may have much to do with how self-aware and ready for change one is to begin with (Nowack, 1999). Such individual differences in reactions to feedback can undermine their effectiveness of setting appropriate goals (Ilies, Judge & Wagner, 2010) for behavior change (Ilies, Judge & Wagner, 2010).

Given the importance of the effects of feedback, coaches need to consider a solid process for facilitating client awareness. First, coaches should select the appropriate means and tools for assessing clients (e.g., 360-degree feedback, personality/style, etc.). Second, coaches should consider the risks and benefits associated with providing feedback. Finally, they should appropriately cope with clients' reactions. The chapters in the *Enlighten* section will thoroughly explore these issues.

Chapter 4:

Different Domains of Assessment

> "Reality is merely an illusion, albeit a very persistent one."
>
> **ALBERT EINSTEIN**

Assessments Used In Coaching

Depending on their client's goals, coaches might utilize diverse types of assessments in interventions. It is not uncommon for many coaches to incorporate their favorite assessments to measure specific aspects of personality, style, skills and abilities, and interests and values with their clients. Assessments used in coaching can be conceptualized as being in four distinct domains, each associated with specific individual and organizational outcomes. Assessment domains often used in coaching assignments include:

- Skills and abilities
- Interests and values
- Personality and style
- Health and well-being

Coaches might focus on one or more of these assessment domains in working with clients and might utilize a variety of approaches, such as interviews, online assessments, card sorts, simulations, interactive exercises, assessment centers, and surveys, to collect and analyze clients' strengths and potential development areas. Figure 2-1 summarizes the major assessment domains and describes what they are most associated with, in terms of specific outcomes of interest to coaching, training, and development interventions.

Figure 2-1
Typical Coaching Assessment Domains and What They Predict

Assessment Domains	What They Predict	Examples of Assessments
Skills and abilities	• Job performance • Career success	• 360-degree feedback • Cognitive ability and general intelligence • In-basket simulations • Assessment centers
Interests and values	• Job satisfaction • Engagement • Retention	• Interest inventories (e.g., Strong Interest Inventory) • Values card sorts • Career inventories (e.g., Career Profile Inventory; The Birkman Method)
Personality and style	• Job performance • Interpersonal skills • Social and relationships • Creativity and risk-taking	• Personality inventories (e.g., Facet5; NEO; Hogan Personality Inventory; Innate Index) • Interpersonal style instruments (e.g., Strength Deployment Inventory; MBTI; FIRO-B; DiSC)
Health and well-being	• Job burnout • Engagement • Absenteeism • Presenteeism • Productivity	• Stress and resilience (e.g., Maslach Burnout Inventory) • Health risk appraisals (e.g., StressScan www.getlifehub.com)

- **Skills and abilities:** These assessments focus on providing feedback on critical skills, competencies, and abilities (e.g., cognitive ability). These assessments have been commonly used in assessment centers because they emphasize the demonstration of competence and performance in specific skill and ability areas. Measures of skills and abilities have the strongest predictive validity with future performance. Some examples include simulations, cognitive ability tests, performance role-plays, and competency-based 360-degree feedback instruments.

When the goal of coaching is to enhance specific skills or a client's performance, assessments measuring specific abilities can be very useful in helping talent increase awareness and facilitate behavioral change. When clients need to better understand how their behavior impacts others, there are no better types of assessments than those comparing self and others' perceptions in the form of 360-degree feedback measures.

- **Personality and style:** In general, personality measures are modest predictors of future performance across all job levels. The two universal predictors of personality that are most predictive of future performance are conscientiousness and emotional stability (two of the "Big Five" factors). Extraversion is highly predictive of performance in jobs or roles that are high in emotional labor (i.e., jobs that depend on high levels of positive interpersonal interactions such as teaching, nursing, etc.). Personality and style tools have been favorites of coaches for many years. Each of us probably has a few that we believe provide talent insight, enabling talent to better understand and manage interpersonal relationships.

Research suggests that conscientious, extraverted, and emotionally stable individuals tend to be the most motivated and successful in the world of work. Further, agreeable and extraverted people are more likely to get along with others and more likely to express the optimistic and positive emotions conducive to effective interpersonal relations (Judge, Picolo, Kosalka, 2009).

Style-based tools are often used to assess specific coaching areas of concern, including decision making, learning, leadership, conflict, and communication. These are the popular "organizational marriage counseling" tools, used frequently to complement other coaching processes, like interviews.

- **Interests/Values:** Although this is counter-intuitive, interests are actually very *poor predictors* of performance and successes. However, they are strongly associated or correlated with job satisfaction, engagement, and retention, so they are important to measure in coaching engagements. Making sure that clients' interests and values are aligned with those of the organization is critical in ensuring clients remain challenged and excited to stay with the organization. There are a number of approaches used to measure interests and values, including card sorts, interest inventories, and other validated career assessments.

- **Health/Well-Being**: One area that has been frequently omitted in the coaches' assessment toolkit is measures of work and life balance, stress, health and resilience. Such issues are common in coaching engagements, and our own research suggests that *40 to 60 percent* of all employees experience a moderately high level of stress on the job (Nowack, 2000; Nowack, 2006; Nowack, 2008). Our work and non-work lives are highly permeable, with most of us taking work stress home and home stress back to our jobs.

We recently explored results from our own validated health risk appraisal, which is called *StressScan* (www.getlifehub.com/stress_scan) to identify what professional working employees reported being stressed about and how that compared to recent findings from the 2010 American Psychological Association *Stress in America* survey of 1,134 adults. *StressScan* measures 14 psychosocial scales and has been shown to be associated with diverse individual (e.g., job burnout, depression, physical health) and organizational (e.g., absenteeism) outcomes (Nowack, 2009).

The APA survey indicated the majority of American workers were living with moderate-to-high levels of work and life stress. Further results indicated that almost half of all adults surveyed (49 percent) reported that job stability was the major source of stress, compared to 44 percent in 2009. At the same time, fewer Americans reported being satisfied with the ways their employers helped them balance work and non-work demands (36 percent in 2010, compared to 42 percent in 2009). Finally, only one-third (32 percent) believed they were doing an excellent or very good job of managing stress.

Our research supports these findings and has implications for coaches in addressing work and life stress and balance issues with their clients. Our stress scale measures self-reported hassles in six distinct areas over a three-month time period including: 1) health issues; 2) work pressure; 3) personal finances; 4) family issues; 5) social obligations; and 6) community or environmental concerns. We analyzed differences by gender across these six scales in a recent sample of 70 women and 79 men working in diverse industries.

In general, women reported significantly higher levels of *overall* work and life stress compared to men. We found only *two of the six stress categories* (financial and family stressors) were rated as *significantly* more challenging by women, compared to their male counterparts, suggesting that women may still perceive that they have two full-time jobs, one at work and the other when they come home.

It's natural to assume that coaches should expect to hear clients share perceptions of some work and family balance challenges and work stressors. It can be argued that helping clients deal more effectively with work and life balance, cope with stress, and build physical health and psychological well-being can be a useful focus in executive, life, career, or health coaching (Palmer, 2003).

Chapter 5:

Multi-Rater/360-Degree Feedback Systems

> Honest criticism is hard to take, particularly from a relative, a friend, an acquaintance, or a stranger.

FRANKLIN B. JONES

The use of multi-rater, or 360-degree, feedback, the process in which managers, direct reports, peers, team members, and customers provide anonymous feedback to others, continues to grow in popularity (Nowack, 2009). Pfau and Kay (2002) suggest that 65 percent of all companies were using this intervention in some manner. Multi-rater feedback systems have proliferated and are being used for diverse purposes and interventions (e.g., executive coaching, performance evaluation, talent management, succession planning, team building, and leadership development). However, what is somewhat atypical is an emphasis on sustaining successful behavioral change over time as a critical outcome of feedback interventions by coaches and consultants using these interventions.

The Growing Popularity of 360-Degree Feedback Assessments

Over the last few years, there has been a dramatic increase in the use of 360-degree assessments within most organizations. Why are so many coaches, consultants, and HRD practitioners using these types of assessment tools? What are the reasons that they have gained so much popularity? The wide use and proliferation of these types of 360-degree feedback assessments can be traced to several trends and developments. Some of these include:

- Online systems that allow data from multiple sources to be easily combined and summarized into feedback reports

- The search for cost-effective alternatives to the administratively complex, yet highly valid, assessment center methodology

- Current organizational process re-engineering, total quality management (TQM) and continuous measurable improvement (CMI) efforts that have emphasized ongoing measurement and improvement of human, technological, and organizational systems

- The increase of career plateauing within all organizations resulting in employees seeking more specific and targeted job-related feedback for on-going professional growth and development

- Professional and career development for talent at all levels

Potential Benefits of 360-Degree Feedback

The primary benefit of 360-degree feedback is that it provides the participant with an opportunity to learn how others perceive him or her, leading to increased self-awareness (Nowack, Hartley & Bradley, 1999). When done well and adhering to "best practices," 360-degree feedback interventions can help increase the understanding of behaviors required to improve both individual and organizational effectiveness and facilitate successful individual and team behavioral change.

Despite the widespread use of multi-rater feedback, coaches still seem to ignore some of the potential issues, challenges, and evidence-based research highlighting the possible risks and dangers of this type of intervention for coaching. The next section will review some of the limitations and potential harm associated with using 360-degree feedback systems.

The Neurobiology of Feedback

"*Sticks and stones can break my bones, but words can never hurt me*" is a famous anonymous saying we have heard, but what if we were tell you that it is absolutely false. Think about a time when someone you love and admire gave you critical or negative feedback. Did you feel hurt and defensive? Newer neuroscience research sheds interesting light on why some perceived feedback can be emotionally harmful.

It is important to note that we are biologically "wired" to react to perceived harm and danger, and this "fight or flight" response occurs within *one-fifth of a second* before we become consciously aware of it (Rock, 2008). Rock's SCARF model provides *five interpersonal perceptions* and situations that automatically activate our primary threat and reward circuitry eliciting our natural tendency to approach or avoid them:

- **Social Status**: Perceptions of social inequity, rank, or even power can elicit our defensive response, and this is one of the most significant determinants of overall health and longevity, even when we control for income and education. Status, perceived importance, or pecking order can influence both our reward circuitry (dopamine levels) and threat response. For example, even when someone offers to give you feedback, it might evoke a status threat, a desire not to be perceived as less than the other individual and when we are threatened, we might react defensively to minimize the perceived pain of a drop in status in our own minds.

- **Certainty**: Lack of certainty about the future tends to trigger our activating response in the part of the brain called the orbital frontal cortex.

- **Autonomy**: Perceptions of having little or no control have long been associated with increased cortisol, blood pressure, and feelings of helplessness. Individuals who believe that their actions impact future outcomes (internal locus of control) appear to be healthier both physically and psychologically than those who believe that no matter what actions they take, the outcomes are primarily due to luck, fate, or chance.

- **Relatedness**: The perception of someone being a friend or foe immediately elicits a response either toward the individual for further engagement or toward avoidance, sensing potential harm or danger. Our threat circuitry fires immediately when we perceive someone as a foe, as well as our ability to be compassionate, empathetic, and caring toward the other individual.

- **Fairness**: Perceptions of treatment by others, as well as whether decisions at work are perceived to be fair and equitable, strongly influence our primal threat response and even our health. A recent prospective study of 6,442 male British civil servants explored the relationship between perceived justice (supervisory practices) and coronary heart disease (CHD) in these workers. Employees who perceived that their supervisors treated them fairly had 30 percent lower CHD incidents after adjustment for other risk factors

(Kivimäki, Ferrie, Brunner, Head, Shipley, Vahtera, & Marmot, 2005).

For over 25 years, researchers have reported that an individual's ability to make decisions about how they work and use their skills is associated with physical illness and psychological distress, with individuals experiencing less job control being more likely to have a poorer health status (Smith, Mustard, & Bondy, 1997; Belkic, et al., 2000).

Feedback May be Harmful to Your Health

Feedback perceived to be hurtful, evaluative or critical might actually be harmful to your health. In a study by Naomi Eisenberger and her colleagues at UCLA (2003), functional magnetic resonance (fMRI) was used to look into the brains of individuals who were involved in a ball-toss video game projected on special goggles while undergoing fMRI was designed to provoke feelings of social isolation and rejection (Eisenberger, Lieberman & Williams, 2003). The imaging technique takes advantage of the magnetic properties of blood to measure brain activity as a function of blood flow where the greater the flow, the greater the neural activity. While each research participant believes the game of virtual toss ("cyberball") involves two additional participants, it actually engages the subject directly against a computer program. The first game is equitable, but the second round moves into a frustrating game of "keep away" with the participant literally being "left out" and socially rejected. Research participants reported subjectively being "hurt" and being left out from the social interaction simulation they had experienced.

The study concluded that when we feel isolated or socially rejected, we experience this feeling in the same part of the brain associated with *physical pain* (dorsal anterior cingulate cortex).

Subsequent studies by the same research group also found that subjects with higher proinflammatory cytokine levels (IL-6) also reported more subjective distress and more brain activity associated with pain during social rejection. Our body produces these cytokines to fend off pain by causing disease-fighting inflammation with accompanying fatigue, fever and sickness behaviors that encourage social withdrawal.

Current findings also suggest that people report higher levels of self-reported pain and have diminished performance on a cognitively demanding task after reliving a past socially painful event than after reliving a past physically painful event (Chen, Williams, Fitness, & Newton, 2008). Social and emotional pain is real and, apparently, is the physiological equivalent of physical pain. To "have a broken heart" may be a poetic phrase, but it is one that we now know is rooted in a neurobiological reality.

Factoid: The Neurobiology of Pain Relief

In a study of 256 patients with chronic arm pain (rating of at least three on a 10-point scale), 133 were treated with inert sugar pills (once a day for eight weeks) and the other patients were treated with fake acupuncture (twice a week for 6 weeks). 25 percent of the fake acupuncture group experienced side effects, including 19 who felt pain, while 31 percent of the placebo pill group experienced dizziness, restlessness, nausea, dry mouth, and fatigue. After 10 weeks, the pill group reported significant decreases in pain (average 1.50 points), and after eight weeks, those receiving fake acupuncture reported a drop of 2.64 points. The fake acupuncture had a greater effect than the placebo sugar pill on self-reported pain.

DeWall et al. (2010) also conducted experiments that extended this initial research on the neurobiology of emotional and social pain. In the first experiment, individuals took 1000 milligrams of a pain reliever acetaminophen or placebo pill every day and reported their social pain. Those who took acetaminophen showed a *significant decrease* in social pain and hurt feelings. In a second experiment, individuals took acetaminophen or placebo daily for three weeks. At the end of the three-week period, those individuals played the same ball toss computer game designed to elicit social rejection. While playing the game, researchers monitored brain activity with functional magnetic resonance imaging (fMRI). They found that acetaminophen actually reduced neural responses to social rejection in the brain regions associated with the distress of social pain, as well as the emotional component of physical pain (the dorsal anterior cingulate cortex and anterior insula). This study provides further evidence that the physical and social pain centers in the brain rely on some of the same behavior and neural mechanisms.

It is not at all uncommon for clients to experience strong emotional reactions to both the quantitative and qualitative sections of 360-degree feedback reports generated by organizations or vendors selling these assessments (Illgen & Davis, 2000; Kluger & De Nisi, 1998; Wimer & Nowack, 1998). Feedback to others might be purposefully untrue, skewed to be overly critical or flattering, accurate but hurtful or vague, or of limited value for desired behavioral change. As an example, Smither and Walker (2004) analyzed the impact of upward feedback ratings, as well as narrative comments, over a one-year period for 176 managers. They found that those who received a small number of unfavorable behaviorally-based comments improved more than other managers, but those who received a large number relative to positive comments *significantly declined* in performance more than other managers.

In one of the most cited social science research studies, Kluger and DeNisi (1998) conducted a meta-analysis that reviewed over 3,000 published and unpublished analyses on performance feedback (607 effect sizes, 23,633 observations). They found that although there was a significant effect for feedback interventions, *one third of all studies showed performance declines.* The authors speculated that performance feedback sometimes led to an actual decline in performance, because it led to individuals feeling hurt, disengaged and emotionally upset.

People *do* change following feedback, but the *magnitude* of change can sometimes be quite small and practically insignificant. For example, in a review of 24 longitudinal 360-degree feedback studies by Smither (2005), feedback was significantly associated with positive behavioral change but the effect sizes were relatively small (.05 for peers and .15 for supervisors and direct reports). Atwater, Waldman, Atwater, and Cartier (2000) reported that improvement following an upward feedback intervention only resulted for 50 percent of the supervisors who received it. Even a "glass half-full" interpretation of this finding is not something that coaches should be satisfied with as the ultimate goal of feedback is to help translate awareness into successful behavioral change.

Taken together, these findings suggest that with respect to the behavioral change of leaders and others in organizations, "zebras don't easily lose their stripes." Despite the complexity of successfully creating behavioral change, it is important for coaches to understand and accept that *all of us likely have skill and ability "set points" that may provide an upward ceiling to growth and development for many of our clients.* Therefore, coaches should be mindful of the potential risks, emotional harm and negative emotional reactions that can be associated with using 360-degree feedback interventions and keep in mind that in some circumstances, feedback might actually be emotionally hurtful and even harmful to one's health.

What Vendors Won't Tell You: Limitations and Challenges in Using 360-Degree Feedback Systems

Cigarettes in the United States all come with health warning labels. Perhaps vendors should do the same when marketing and selling the 360-degree feedback assessments that are so commonly used by coaches, consultants, and organizational practitioners. These same cautions apply to multi-rater assessments developed "in house" by many organizations using their own competency models. At least five important factors should be considered when using and interpreting 360-degree feedback interventions.

1. Ratings *Between* Rater Groups Are Only Modestly Correlated With Each Other

It seems intuitive to expect differences in perspectives between rater groups, such as *direct reports, peers, supervisors, self, and others*. However, research has shown that the ratings *between* individuals are not as highly associated with each other as commonly assumed (Conway & Huffcutt, 1997; Harris & Schaubroeck, 1988; Facteau & Craig, 2001; Woehr, Sheehan, & Bennett, 2005; Nowack, 1997). In general, direct reports tend to emphasize and filter interpersonal and relationship behaviors into subjective ratings, whereas superiors tend to focus more on "bottom-line" results and task-oriented behaviors (Conway, Lombardo, & Sanders, 2001; Nowack, 2002; Porr & Fields, 2006). Research by Oh & Berry (2009) suggests that, at least for leaders, peer reports are *more reliable* than the ratings of direct reports.

At a practical level, this means that clients might have a difficult time understanding how to interpret observed differences by rater groups and whether to decide to focus their developmental "energy" on managing upward, downward, or laterally in light of these potentially discrepant results. Coaches should help clients understand the meaning of potential differences between rater groups and what actions to take to address these perceptual gaps.

2. Ratings *Within* Rater Groups Are Only Modestly Correlated With Each Other

Suppose the client has three direct reports. Two of them give very high ratings, and one gives a very low rating. How do the coach and client interpret this? Greguras and Robie (1995) explored within-source variability in a study of 153 managers using 360-degree feedback. Researchers analyzed the number of raters and items required to achieve adequate reliability in practice. These researchers suggested that if a 360-degree feedback assessment has an average of five questions to measure each competency, it would require at least four supervisors, eight peers, and nine direct reports to achieve acceptable levels of reliability (.70 or higher).

Because clients rarely can find that one "all knowing and candid" rater to provide them with specific and useful feedback, the report suggests that having an adequate representation and a larger number of feedback sources is critical to ensuring accurate and reliable data. Given these findings, vendors who do not provide a way for participants to evaluate within-rater agreements may increase the probability that average scores used in reports may be inaccurate or used inappropriately for development purposes.

3. Perceptual Distortions by Participants and Raters Make the Interpretation of 360-Degree Feedback Results Challenging

A triad of positive illusions that we all tend to possess to remain psychologically healthy and that would appear to be important moderators of multi-rater feedback interventions has been previously posited by Taylor & Brown (1988) that would appear to be important moderators of multi-rater feedback interventions:

- People tend to inflate perceptions of their skills and abilities
- People typically exaggerate their perceived control over work and life events
- People generally express unrealistic optimism about the future

The prevalence of self-enhancement is not hotly debated, but there is continued controversy about whether it is essentially *adaptive* or *maladaptive*. This has important implications for understanding and interpreting 360-degree feedback. If self-enhancement is conceptualized as seeing one's self generally *more positively* than others, then the outcomes (performance, health, career, and life success) are frequently more favorable, but if it is defined as having higher self-ratings than the others who provide feedback, then the outcomes are frequently less than favorable (Sedikides & Gregg, 2003; Taylor & Brown, 1988). Coaches should keep in mind that people generally forget negative feedback about themselves, specifically in the areas that matter most to them, and they typically remember performing more desirable behaviors than other raters can later identify (Gosling, John, Craik, & Robins, 1998).

4. **Feedback Combined with Structured Follow-Up and Coaching Leads to Better Outcomes**

All too often, vendors and practitioners espouse the "diagnose and adios" approach to 360-degree feedback, hoping that self-directed insight alone will result in motivated behavioral change efforts (Nowack, 2007). As previous research suggests, this approach could actually contribute to more negative affect and behavioral disengagement. In one of the few empirical studies recently conducted on the impact of executive coaching, Smither, London, Flautt, Vargas, and Kucine (2003) reported that after receiving 360-degree feedback, managers who worked with a coach were significantly *more likely* to set measurable and specific goals and solicit ideas for improvement, and subsequently they received improved performance ratings.

In addition, Olivero, Bane, and Kopelman (1997) found that feedback and coaching for two months increased productivity over the effects of a managerial training program (80 versus 22.4 percent) for 31 participants. Finally, a recent doctoral dissertation that evaluated the effectiveness of 360-degree feedback interventions on 257 leaders found that over 65 percent expressed a strong interest in an online follow-up tool used to measure progress and facilitate individual behavioral change (Rehbine, 2007). These coaching evaluation studies all emphasize the importance of supportive, coach-driven, follow-up activities to help clients translate insight into deliberate practice.

Chapter 6:

Mirror, Mirror, on the Wall: Matching Feedback to an Individual's Self-Insight

> There are three things extremely hard: steel, a diamond, and to know one's self.
>
> **BENJAMIN FRANKLIN**

Often, clients perceive themselves differently from how others experience them. According to much 360-degree feedback research, leaders, in particular, are more likely to have inflated views of their skills and abilities (Nowack, 2009; 1997). We know that this is true for both male and female leaders and it is even more pronounced as leaders move up the corporate hierarchy or have a longer tenure with the organization.

In one recent national survey of 1,854 leaders, 92 percent rated themselves as excellent or as good as a manager (Rasmussen Reports, 2006). Unfortunately, only 67 percent of direct reports agreed with them and at least 10 percent rated their bosses as performing poorly. Leaders are not alone. In a survey at one company, 42 percent of a group of engineers ranked themselves in the top five percent of that group, often referred to as the "better-than-average effect". These biased self-evaluations could easily impede motivation to improve further (Ehrlinger, 2008).

Negative Effects of Misperceptions

Unfortunately, effectiveness on the job tends to decrease as self and other ratings are misaligned (Atwater, Ostroff, Yammarino, and Fleenor, 1998). Other researchers found that managers who rated themselves higher than others had more negative reactions to the feedback process and lower motivation to improve. They were significantly less likely to show improvement when they were reassessed (Brett and Atwater, 2001).

Factoid: Clueless Leaders

A global survey of executives and leaders by Korn Ferry International involving respondents from over 70 countries revealed that only 27 percent of respondents thought their boss was doing the job better than they could! In this survey, 11 percent rated the performance of their current boss as poor, 14 percent rated it as below average, and 23 percent rated it as "average." Forty-two percent did perceive their manager as either performing either above average or "excellent.

One aspect of "emotional intelligence" is the accurate perception of one's own skills, strengths, and impact on others. The concept of self-awareness is described as one of the four parts of Daniel Goleman's concept of Emotional Intelligence (EI), which includes four key areas: 1) Self-Awareness; 2) Social Awareness; 3) Self-Management; and 4) Relationship Management (Cherniss, 2010).

Figure 2-2

The Four Parts of Emotional Intelligence

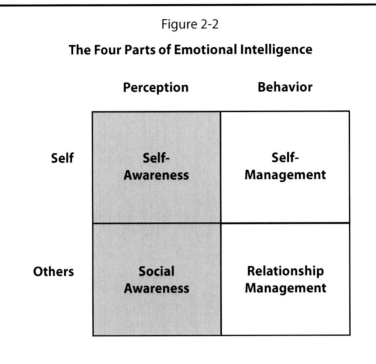

A growing amount of research literature suggests that emotional intelligence and emotional and social competence are *significantly associated* with job performance with positions requiring frequent customer and interpersonal interactions, even when mental ability and personality variables are controlled (Cherniss, 2010). Current research on emotional intelligence suggests that, highly conscientious employees who lack social and emotional intelligence perform significantly more poorly than those high in conscientiousness and emotional intelligence (Nowack, 2006).

The highest performing managers and leaders are perceived to have significantly more "emotional and social competence" than other managers. Poor social and emotional intelligence (e.g., over-estimation of strengths relative to other raters) is often a predictor of executive and management "derailment" and failure in one's job.

Using the "Gap" Between Self and Others' Perceptions to Identify Developmental Opportunities

The alignment between self and others' perceptions on a 360-degree feedback assessment can serve as a proxy for insight and self-awareness. In other words, this perceptual gap can serve as a metric and an approximation for self-awareness. It is theoretically possible that both the participants and raters aren't accurate in their perceptions and ratings of skills, personality traits and behaviors.

Whenever a number of raters are in disagreement with an individual's self-perception, the coach's role is to bring the client closer to reality. Coaches can analyze these misperceptions to find strengths weaknesses, and developmental opportunities. As an example, EIV360 includes a process by which the gap between self-ratings and the ratings of others is apparent graphically.

This validated, 360-degree feedback emotional intelligence assessment includes competencies that are shown in four quadrants by each rater category, indicating the extent to which self-ratings are aligned with other ratings. Self-awareness can be categorized in four distinct ways:

- Potential Strengths (low self-ratings and high other ratings)
- Confirmed Strengths (high self-ratings and high other ratings)
- Potential Development Areas (high self-ratings and low other ratings)
- Confirmed Development Areas (low self-ratings and low other ratings)

Figure 2-3

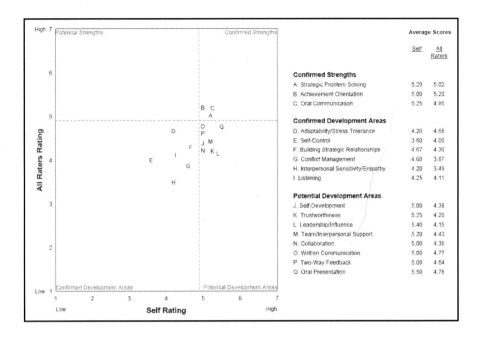

These four quadrants, which are based on the Johari Window (Luft & Ingham, 1955), provide a convenient way to conceptualize a proxy of self-insight by directly comparing self and other ratings on each of the competencies measured in the 360-degree feedback assessment.

Confirmed Strengths vs. Confirmed Development Areas

Confirmed Strengths represent competencies in which the individual's self-ratings are relatively high and matched by how others experience and perceive their behavior. Similarly, *Confirmed Development Areas* represent those competencies where both self and others agree that some improvement or development might be required. An individual with a majority of competencies falling within the quadrants defined as confirmed strengths or confirmed development areas might be interpreted as someone who has relatively high insight and awareness about his or her behavior. In general, coaches can expect less defensiveness and challenge in coaching sessions with clients who appear to have a greater congruence between self and other ratings.

Potential Strengths & Potential Weaknesses

Potential Strengths represent competencies in which the individual's self-ratings are lower than the ratings from other rater groups. Some personality research suggests that these "under-estimators" can be described as highly self-critical, perfectionist, and highly achievement oriented. They may have very high standards for themselves and others and may lack confidence. As a result, these individuals are often less inclined to leverage their strengths and seem to be focused more on their weaknesses or developmental opportunities.

Potential Development Areas represent competencies in which the individual's self-ratings are higher than those of others. Research by Kruger & Dunning (1999) suggests that over-estimation occurs, in part, because people who are unskilled in particular areas reach erroneous conclusions about actual abilities, and this incompetence robs them of the meta-cognitive ability to realize it. In four separate studies, the authors found that participants scoring in the bottom quartile on tests of humor, grammar, and logic grossly overestimated their actual performance and ability. Although their test scores put them in the 12th percentile, they estimated themselves to be in the 62nd.

Interestingly, improving the skills of the participants, thus increasing their meta-cognitive competence, helped the participants recognize the limitations of their abilities. The more skilled that you are, the more practice you have put in, the more experience you have, and the better you can compare yourself to others. On the other hand, the less skilled that you are, the less practice you have put in, and the fewer experiences you have, the worse you are at comparing yourself to others on certain tasks. Over-estimation due to lack of experience is often referred to as the *Dunning-Kruger effect* and should be something that coaches are aware of as a possible explanation for these self-other differences in 360-degree feedback assessments.

Additional research suggests that individuals who have an inflated view of their own behaviors, relative to others providing them with feedback, are significantly more likely to experience potential career derailment (Brett & Atwater, 2001). These "overestimators" are likely to display more resistance and defensive reactions to feedback in coaching sessions. Coaches and facilitators can help clients with this over-estimator profile to identify strategies to help others better appreciate their skills, efforts and accomplishments. The can also constructively challenge clients about the meaning of these perceived rating differences and how these more critical perceptions might influence relationships and career goals.

Chapter 7:

Best Practices for 360-Degree Feedback

> In his later years, Pablo Picasso was not allowed to roam an art gallery unattended, for he had previously been discovered in the act of trying to improve on one of his old masterpieces.
>
> **UNKNOWN**

Multi-rater or 360-degree feedback is a critical component of most coaching, training, and talent-development programs. Research on 360-degree feedback suggests some "Best Practices" that, when followed, maximize the use of feedback for future behavioral change. This section will provide suggestions and recommendations for consideration in the implementation of any 360-degree feedback process, based on our own research and practice (Nowack, 2005; 2009).

What is the Purpose of the 360-Degree Feedback Process?

It is important to emphasize that *360-degree feedback is not an end in itself.* It is a process to help individuals become more aware of their strengths and potential development areas in order to facilitate behavioral change. It is important to keep in mind that *feedback* is a necessary, but not sufficient, condition for successful behavioral change. Helping clients understand and accept feedback will be essential in order to enable clients to commit to development goals and actions to enhance their skills and performance on the job. A successful 360-degree feedback intervention involves a series of specific steps that start with why such an intervention should be done and culminate in increased awareness and a commitment to translate this insight into deliberate practice. Let's take a look at the eight steps common to most 360-degree feedback projects.

Figure 2-4

The Eight Steps of a Typical 360-Degree Feedback Process

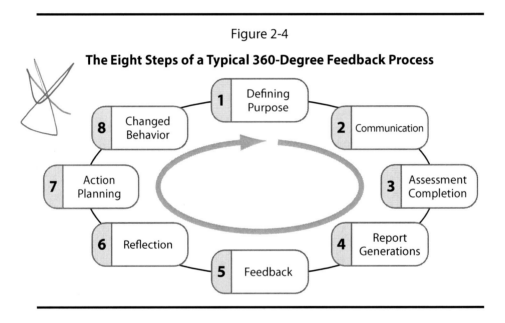

Look at the typical process illustrated above. What 360-degree feedback does is formalize the natural *feedback* process (Step 1). People observe each other all the time, often unconsciously and unsystematically. They gain impressions, some of which are remembered, and some of which are forgotten. These perceptions are formed continuously in any relationship and result in an impression of a client's style and effectiveness. The formalization comes from *communication* to the participant and his or her invited raters (Step 2)

to think about the participant in a conscious and structured way, usually by completing some form of *360-degree feedback assessment* (Step 3). The data obtained is then processed into a formal feedback *report* (Step 4) containing raters' perceptions expressed in numerical, graphical, and narrative form, which is then presented as *feedback* (Step 5).

The key issue is what a client will do with the information once they have received it, and that part of the process does not start until Step 6 *(Reflection)*. Reflection involves several activities, including self-analysis by the client; discussions with a coach, mentor, or supervisor; sharing feedback with others; clarifying things that came as a surprise; and validating things the client is already aware of. Only when this has been done can the client translate this data into a meaningful and practical *action plan* (Step 7), which will result in successful *behavioral change* (Step 8).

Factoid: Follow Me, I'll make you Miserable

It has been estimated that 65 to 75 percent of employees in any given organization report that the worst aspect of their job is their immediate boss. In fact, estimates of the base rate for managerial incompetence in corporate life range from 30 to 75 percent, with the average level of poor leadership hovering at about 50 percent (Hogan & Kaiser, 2005).

"Best Practices" in Using 360-Degree Feedback: Q&A

This section reviews common questions in the purpose of feedback; the type of assessment or competencies to use; and the implementation, interpretation, and leveraging of 360-degree feedback interventions. Figures 2-5 through 2-8 summarizes these questions in the following categories: 1) The Purpose and Goals of the 360-degree feedback project, 2) Assessment & Competencies, 3) Process and

Implementation of the 360-degree feedback intervention, and 4) Interpreting the Results and Leveraging the impact of 360-degree interventions. These questions and answers should be helpful for coaches and other users of 360-degree feedback in order to understand and apply some of the latest research and "best practices" to ensure successful interventions.

Figure 2-5

Best Practices in Using 360-Degree Feedback: Q&A

Purposes / Goals

1. What are some of the major features of 360-degree feedback?
2. What is the purpose of doing 360-degree feedback?
3. What are the benefits of 360-degree feedback?
4. What are the possible negative effects?
5. Does 360-degree feedback work?
6. Should 360-degree feedback ever be used for performance appraisal or compensation?
7. What if the organizational culture isn't ready for 360-degree feedback?
8. Is 360-degree feedback ever inappropriate?
9. How do you ensure the success of 360-degree feedback?

PURPOSES AND GOALS

1. *What are some of the major features of 360-degree feedback?*

The idea behind 360-degree feedback is to gather information from key stakeholders who can share perceptions and observations about one's skills, abilities, personality, and behavior. This information can be compared to the participant's own self-rating and used for developmental planning purposes. There are many features that describe multi-rater or 360-degree feedback including:

- It typically measures specific behaviors and competencies associated with job performance and success
- It provides a confidential process for obtaining feedback from others who work closely with the individual
- It focuses on observed behaviors that can be modified
- It provides graphical, numerical, and open-ended information to be used for developmental purposes in the form of a summary feedback report
- It provides clarity about one's strengths and insight about potential areas of improvement and development
- It provides a process for improving individual or team performance by continuously providing ongoing feedback when administered over time
- It typically has a development focus without being used for personnel decisions
- Feedback is always anonymous, except for the manager
- Feedback assesses perceptions and not reality
- It is comprehensive and behaviorally focused

2. *What is the purpose of doing 360-degree feedback?*

Feedback in the form of multi-rater systems can be used in a wide variety of human resources systems and interventions ranging from information only to personnel decision making. The most common uses of 360-degree feedback for coaching and development (Nowack, 1999a) include:

- Executive coaching

- Supervisory and management training
- Team building/Team development
- Compensation/Salary increases
- Performance appraisal/evaluation
- Leadership development
- Identification of high potential talent and development
- Training needs assessment
- Talent management and succession planning
- Personnel selection

3. *What are the benefits of 360-degree feedback?*

Since it is not possible to know the one person in the organization who is totally accurate and candid about the perceived knowledge, skills, and abilities of others, 360-degree feedback provides a snapshot of perceptions from various stakeholder perspectives. The use of this intervention can help increase formal and informal communication, open up difficult performance discussions, increase insight and learning, encourage targeted goal setting, highlight specific skills and competencies associated with job performance, and improve performance and productivity. Some additional benefits and advantages of 360-degree feedback include:

- Providing the participant with an opportunity to learn how others perceive them, leading to increased self-awareness
- Encouraging self-development
- Helping increase understanding of the behaviors required to improve both individual and organizational effectiveness
- Promoting an open culture where giving and receiving feedback is an accepted norm
- Increasing communication within an organization

- Clarifying supervisory and managerial expectations
- Being a powerful initiator for individual and team change

4. *What are the possible negative effects of 360-degree feedback?*

At an *organizational* level, poorly constructed and delivered 360-degree feedback systems can be time consuming and costly to develop and can increase disengagement and poor employee morale. At an *individual level*, feedback, when delivered poorly and perceived as critical, evaluative, or judgmental, can cause stress, social pain, and emotional distress, which is physiologically identical to physical pain, at least at a neurobiological level (Eisenberger, Lieberman & Williams, 2003).

Alternately, feedback can be brutally honest and accurate, creating the same negative affect; too positive; or not truthful, creating ambiguity and confusion about how to interpret the information given by invited raters. Brett and Atwater (2001) found that managers who rated themselves higher than others rated them (over-estimators) reported significantly more negative reactions to the multi-rater feedback process. They noted specifically that "negative feedback (i.e., ratings that were low or that were lower than expected) was not seen as accurate or useful, and it did not result in enlightenment or awareness but rather in negative reactions such as anger and discouragement.

5. *Does 360-degree feedback work?*

In general, research on the impact of 360-degree feedback generally supports the idea that it has more positive than negative impact on performance and development (Nowack, 2009; Kluger & DeNisi, 1996). For example, Reilly, Smither, and Vasilopoulos

(1996) evaluated the impact of an upward feedback program for two-and-a-half years and found evidence of performance improvement unrelated to the number of times managers received feedback and not entirely due to regression to the mean.

Additionally, a more recent meta-analysis of 26 longitudinal studies of multi-rater feedback indicated significant performance improvements (Smither, London, & Reilly, 2005). Atwater, Waldman, Atwater, and Cartier (2000) reported an improvement following an upward feedback intervention for 50 percent of the supervisors who received it. Taken together, there is supporting evidence that feedback is a necessary and important condition for successful behavioral change and most useful for those with low levels of self-insight and performance.

6. Should 360-degree feedback ever be used for performance appraisal and compensation?

In a recent 2009 survey of over 50 companies by the 3D group, 32 percent reported using 360 degree feedback for administrative as well as development purposes and 68 percent reported using it only for development. Only 16 percent reported that 360-degree feedback was directly linked to pay increases. 360-degree feedback can support performance appraisal systems but should cautiously be linked to remuneration and compensation systems (Fleenor, Taylor & Chappelow, 2008). For example, the generation of an individual performance development plan is typically a strategic part of most performance-appraisal systems. The use of 360-degree feedback assessment as part of developmental planning can strengthen existing performance-management and appraisal systems. When 360-degree feedback is used in compensation, it is difficult to know which rater group to use (e.g., manager ratings are significantly higher than direct reports) and how to evaluate within-rater agreement. The type of rating and response scale should also be appropriate for the intended purpose (e.g., not using a potential scale for compensation decisions).

7. *What do you do if the organizational culture isn't ready for 360-feedback interventions?*

Not all organizations are ready to use 360-degree feedback systems, or the time such a feedback system is introduced may not be optimum to ensure success. For example, it is not recommended to introduce a 360-degree feedback process in the middle of a very large organizational change. It is highly recommended that 360-degree feedback systems should be piloted by a willing stakeholder or a group that is open to giving and receiving feedback. Often, the use of a "180-degree feedback" process between an employee and his or her manager is a wonderful way to softly introduce the benefits of a full-blown, 360-degree feedback to the organization. In order to succeed, employees need to feel comfortable with the feedback process, and they need to believe they will be given honest, constructive, and useful feedback. Finally, 360-degree feedback processes should be used to solve real business needs. In this way, such feedback is introduced as a solution for improving leadership effectiveness or team building. Some key questions to ask to determine if your culture is ready for the successful introduction and use of 360-degree feedback interventions include:

- Is employee engagement high enough to support a feedback intervention?
- Is the organization supportive of talent development and coaching?

- Do managers get trained, rewarded, and compensated if they act as performance coaches?

- Do employees feel comfortable giving feedback without reprisal?

- Has your organization had a bad experience with a prior 360-degree feedback intervention?

- Is talent motivated to use the feedback it receives for its own professional growth and development?

- Does your organization have resources, training, and other support in place to help talent create and implement professional development plans as a result of the feedback?

- Will talent be held accountable to discuss the results of feedback with bosses and to create a development plan?

8. *Is 360-degree feedback ever inappropriate?*

Use caution in going forward with 360-degree feedback processes under the following situations: 1) if the person participating in 360-degree feedback is very new to the organization, 2) if there are not enough respondents who truly understand the full scope of the individual's responsibilities, 3) if you are in a time of major organizational change or a transition, such as just before or after a merger or acquisition, and 4) if you are in an organizational culture, climate, or environment where there is a high degree of mistrust.

9. *How do you ensure 360-degree feedback success?*

Current research on "best practices" in the use of 360 degree feedback (Nowack, 2009) suggests that results can be optimized if you understand the following principles: 1) Hold the participant and line manager accountable for creating, implementing and completing a development plan, 2) Provide individual coaching to assist in interpreting the multi-rater feedback, 3) Link the 360-degree feedback intervention to a performance-management process, 4) Target competencies for 360-degree feedback interventions related to strategic business needs; and 5) Build in mechanisms to evaluate progress of both the completion of development plans and effectiveness of newly practiced behaviors/skills.

Figure 2-6

Best Practices in Using 360-Degree Feedback: Q&A

Assessment/Competencies

10. What competencies should be measured?
11. How independent are competencies?
12. How do you go about developing competencies for a 360-degree feedback assessment?
13. What type and how many raters should be included?
14. Do ratings between rater groups agree with each other?
15. Do ratings within rater groups agree with each other?
16. What is the optimum length of a 360-degree assessment?
17. What kind of response scale should you use?
18. How many rating points should be on a 360-degree rating scale?
19. How do you label response scales in 360-degree feedback?
20. Do the 360-degree feedback questions and competencies have adequate reliability and validity?
21. Is a customized 360-degree feedback assessment better than a vendor's off-the-shelf assessment?
22. How do I write good behavioral statements?
23. How many behavioral statements should I have in each competency?

ASSESSMENT AND COMPETENCIES

10. *How many and what competencies should be measured?*

The type and number of competencies measured for a 360-degree feedback assessment should be based on a theoretical model, a particular job level, or the core, strategic competencies required of an organization to be successful in its competitive market. It is also important to consider the ability of raters to make reliable and discriminate judgments about behaviors they are rating. In general, there is tremendous overlap between vendor job level competency models based on interviews, focus groups, and survey approaches in identifying job-related skills, abilities, and success factors.

In a meta-analytic review of the criterion-related validity of assessment centers by Arthur et al. (2003), the mean number of competencies measured by raters was 10.60. The authors emphasize that a much smaller number of competencies may adequately explain the variance in performance outcomes. It is important to note that in assessment centers, raters (assessors) are typically carefully selected, motivated and trained to evaluate observed performance without ever knowing the participant. In 360-degree feedback processes, raters might not be fully motivated or skilled at making behavioral ratings suggesting that minimizing the overall number of competencies to be evaluated might actually enhance reliability and accuracy of ratings although little research exists to determine the optimum number of competencies to be measured. The exact number of competencies being measured might be less of an issue if they are job relevant and the items being measured are behaviorally based and clear to the rater.

For example, the competency model behind the Envisia Learning, Inc. *EV360* assessment was based on job analysis interviews with senior level executives from several diverse industries, resulting in a total of 22 competencies grouped into four areas associated with executive success: 1) performance leadership, 2) change leadership, 3) interpersonal leadership, and 4) intrapersonal leadership. This executive competency model appears to be useful for executive coaching, talent/succession planning and training programs focused on enhancing one or more competencies.

11. *How independent are competencies?*

Research studies on 360-degree feedback have consistently shown high intercorrelations *among* competencies, and as such, there may be some justification for research purposes to combine all competencies into an overall outcome measure (e.g., leadership). However, for developmental or coaching purposes, it is desirable to maintain the competency architecture and the model behind the assessment to support the feedback and developmental planning process, in light of findings that the overlap in competencies, although significant, only accounts for about 50 percent of the variance. At a practical level for coaching and developmental purpose, treating each competency separately can be supported.

12. *How do you go about developing competencies for a 360-degree feedback assessment?*

Competencies are those KSAOs (knowledge, skills, abilities, and other attributes) that differentiate between high and low performers (McClelland, 1961). However, the term competencies is often confused with other terms, including dimensions, KSAOs, success factors or profiles, leadership traits, and core competencies. Several approaches to competency-model development include:

- Analyzing company information
- Utilizing existing competency models
- Conducting incumbent or subject matter expert (SMEs) interviews and focus groups
- Conducting job and family KSAO surveys

Competency modeling steps typically include the following:

1. *Performance criteria:* defining the criteria for superior performance in a role, position, or job level.

2. *Criterion sample:* choosing a sample of people performing the role for data collection and/or SMEs.

3. *Data collection:* collecting sample data about behaviors that lead to success.

4. *Data analysis:* developing hypotheses about the competencies of outstanding performers and how these competencies work together to produce desired results.

5. *Validation:* validating the results of data collection and analysis.

6. *Application:* applying the competency models in human resource systems.

13. *What type and how many raters should be included?*

The type of raters that should provide feedback to participants will depend on a number of factors, including the purpose of the 360-degree feedback process, the job level of the participant, the competencies being assessed, and the relevant stakeholders who have had an opportunity to provide constructive feedback. In general, individual-based 360-degree feedback includes the participant's manager, direct reports, team members participants collaborate with that might be at different job levels, peers at the same job level, internal and external customers, or volunteers outside the organization.

How many raters are necessary to provide meaningful and accurate 360-degree feedback? The answer, of course, is only one rater, but we simply don't know who is all-knowing and perfectly accurate in his or her observations. Ideally, we should get a sampling of data from those around the participant who can provide a complete view of the participant's strengths and potential development areas.

The following analogy demonstrates this; Sitting down with a child to solve a puzzle with them and asking the question, "How many puzzle pieces do you need to assemble to have confidence that what you are making resembles the picture on the cover?" as a way to answer how many raters do you need in 360-degree feedback. The more puzzle pieces we assemble correctly, the more confident we become that we are seeing the image that is also on the cover of the box. But we don't need to assemble all of the pieces to verify this. All we need is a "critical mass" of puzzle pieces to be assembled to trust we are seeing the true picture of the puzzle. Like making puzzles, when we ask a large group of raters for feedback, we begin to see our behavior with more confidence and clarity. In fact, there is some research that suggests what this "critical mass" of feedback is in order to reach a level of confidence that others are accurately experiencing our behavior and can identify signature strengths and development opportunities.

Reguras and Robie (1995) suggest that the optimum number of raters involved in most 360-degree feedback projects would require at least four supervisors, eight peers, and nine direct reports to achieve acceptable levels of reliability (.70 or higher). Of course, this statistical standard may not be practical in circumstances where leaders have only a few direct reports or one manager they have worked for many years.

Recent research suggests that as many as 26 percent of companies report that when two or fewer respondents provide data for a given group and these small sample sizes may be inadequate for reliable measurement (3D Group, 2009).

These findings do suggest that inviting more, rather than fewer, raters would be helpful in ensuring accuracy and a large enough rater pool to make the 360-degree feedback findings relevant and useful. Inviting and having too few raters in each rater category may limit the meaningfulness and accuracy of the feedback for professional and personal development.

14. *Do ratings* between *rater groups agree with each other?*

Self-ratings weakly to moderately often correlate weakly to moderately to other rater perspectives, with a greater convergence between peer and supervisor ratings (Nowack, 1992). It seems intuitive to expect that some differences in perspectives will occur across rater groups. In general, direct reports tend to emphasize and filter *interpersonal* and relationship behaviors into subjective ratings, superiors tend to focus more on performance-oriented behaviors, and peers tend to be most accurate at predicting *future leadership potential* (Nowack, 2002; 2009).

These meaningful rater group differences might also be a point of confusion in the interpretation of 360-degree feedback for clients trying to use these results to determine specific behaviors to modify and which stakeholder to target. This possible ambiguity in understanding and interpreting multi-rater feedback is important in light of recent research suggesting that people who are even mildly neurotic report *more distress* by uncertainty within oral and written feedback than when given even direct negative feedback (Hirsh, & Inzlicht, 2008). At a practical level, this means clients might be challenged to understand how to interpret differences observed by rater groups and asked to decide whether to focus efforts on managing upward, downward, or laterally in light of these potentially discrepant results. Coaches should be cognizant of the moderate correlations *between* different rater groups and help their clients to fully understand and interpret the meaning of such differences.

15. *Do ratings* **within** *rater groups agree with each other?*

In earlier meta-analytic study by Conway & Huffcutt (1997), the average correlation between two supervisors was only .50. Between two peers, it was .37, and between two subordinates, it was only .30. As such, agreement *within* rater groups appears to be an important issue to discern for clients in the interpretation of their 360-degree feedback reports. Vendors who do not provide a way for participants to evaluate within-rater agreement in feedback may increase the probability that average scores used in reports can be easily misinterpreted—particularly if they are used by coaches to help clients focus on specific competencies and behaviors for developmental planning purposes.

For example, Envisia Learning, Inc., provides up to *three separate measures* of rater agreement within each feedback report, including a range of scores that measure the distribution of ratings on most and least frequent behaviors and a statistical metric of rater agreement, based on standard deviation. These within-rater agreement metrics help clarify outliers and clarify how to possibly interpret polarized scores on specific questions and competencies.

16. *What is the optimum length of a 360-degree feedback assessment?*

In general, 360-degree feedback questionnaires should be targeted and contain relevant questions. They should be long enough to accurately measure the competencies they are attempting to assess, but not too long as to decrease the motivation to complete them. It takes, on average, between 30 and 60 seconds to answer each question, and if a respondent is asked to complete questionnaires on a number of people, it is important that respondent fatigue doesn't set in. Typically, 360-degree feedback questionnaires contain between 40 and 70 items along with several open-ended questions. They often can be completed in 10-15 minutes. In a recent 2009 survey of over 50 companies by the 3D group (3D Group, 2009 Benchmark Study) the "sweet spot" for the number of questions in a 360-degree feedback questionnaire appeared to between 11 to 40 (33 percent) and 41 to 69 (42 percent). A total of 16 percent of the 50 companies surveyed had questionnaires that had 70 or more questions.

17. *Which response scale is best for 360-degree feedback?*

Many studies suggest that response scales have a large impact on the 360-degree feedback data and some response scales seem to be preferable to others.

For example, Bracken and Rose (2011) suggest that commonly used frequency scales (e.g., never to always) are inferior to others but are quick to point out that the majority of research has focused on the anchors themselves and additional research is needed to identify optimal response choices and anchor format.

A recent meta-analysis by Heidemeier and Moser (2009) suggests that social comparison scales (scales with relative rather than absolute anchors) wer able to reduce leniency in self-ratings and they suggest they should be employed much more often than in the past.

Common rating scales used by vendors in most 360 assessments include:

- Effectiveness
- Potential
- Ranking/Comparison
- Frequency

Effectiveness scales ask participants and raters to provide judgments about how effectively the individual demonstrates specific competencies and underlying behaviors. Potential scales are commonly used for succession planning systems and ask raters to predict how well the participant might perform in the future or what potential the participant has to succeed. Ranking scales typically ask raters to compare the participant to some type of standard (e.g., evaluate the participant compared to the most effective leader the rater has experienced within his or her organization). Frequency and extent scales typically ask how often the participant has demonstrated or expressed specific behaviors. Kaiser and Overfield (2011) suggest the use of "too little/too much" frequency rating scales to distinguish when managers do an appropriate amount of a behavior from when a person may overdo it. Their findings suggest that raters are able to make these distinctions and are a reliable and valid method for measuring strengths overused.

The goal of any 360-degree feedback assessment is to provide targeted feedback on critical success factors that will be included as part of a coaching, training, or development program. If the program is successful, it can be hoped that talent will be more effective in practicing and demonstrating specific technical, leadership, task/project management, or communication competencies and behaviors. Feedback that is less ambiguous and more behaviorally-oriented will be most helpful to the talent using the 360-degree feedback process.

When questions measuring competencies are written to reflect effective or desired behavior, frequency or extent scales provide more clarity about what strengths should be leveraged and the potential areas for improvement. In general, response or rating scales are important to consider when developing customized 360-degree feedback assessments and interpreting off-the-shelf tools available from vendors.

18. *How many rating points should be on a 360-degree feedback rating scale?*

There is no definitive agreement in the literature about the optimal number of response categories that should be used in order to get the most reliable data. However, there is a general range provided in the 360-degree feedback literature that suggests the number of response categories to use. For example, Bandalos and Enders (1996) found that the *reliability* was highest for scales having five to seven points. Preston and Colman (2000) examined response categories ranging from two to 11, and found that *test-retest validity* was lowest for two to four point scales, was highest for seven to 10 point scales, and decreased for scales with more than 10 response categories. Later research by Lozano, Garcia-Cueto, and Muniz (2008) also looked at the reliability and validity of scales ranging from two to nine response options with four different sample sizes and found that the optimum number statistically favored response scales with between *four and seven options* with current findings from the 2009 Benchmark study of the 3D Group suggesting that the most popular is a 5-point scale (76 percent) followed by a 7-point scale (16 percent).

19. *How do you best label 360-degree feedback rating scales?*

An important issue for response scales is considering how to best label the response scale anchors. Weng (2004) analyzed the *reliability* of Likert-type rating scales and found that scales with all response options clearly labeled yielded higher test-retest reliability than those with only the end-points labeled. This suggests that having all of the points on a scale clearly labeled helps reduce ambiguity. Cools, Hofmans, and Theuns (2006) found that a scale with five response options was the least prone to context effects and that the use of extreme answer categories on the left and right ends of the scale *did not* improve the psychometric properties of the scale. Viswanathan, Bergen, Dutta, and Childres (1996) in studying the optimal number of response categories and appropriate category descriptors found that the right number of categories was important, so that there was not a mismatch between participants' natural responses and the response categories.

Leniency effects (negative skew or low variability) in scale ratings are fairly common in 360-degree feedback. Few raters use the entire rating scale range, and most scores tend to be inflated, independent of the scale being used. Recent research suggests that the use of *positively worded* scales can result in *lower mean scores and increased variability*, relative to typical, anchored scales (English, Rose, & McClellan, 2009) Positive-worded scales are comprised of anchors with a larger number of positive verbal qualifiers and should be considered for coaches, consultants, and organizations creating their own customized 360-degree feedback assessments.

Example of a Traditional Frequency Scale

1: To a very small extent
2: To a small extent
3: To a moderate extent
4: To a large extent
5: To a very large extent

Example of a Positively-Worded Response Scale

1: Almost never
2: Sometimes
3: Frequently
4: Almost always
5: Always

20. *Do the 360-degree feedback questions and competencies have adequate reliability and validity?*

There are many different types of reliability and validity. Ideally, a customized 360-degree feedback questionnaire should have established scale reliability (e.g., Cronbach's alpha greater than .70) to ensure that the questions are accurately measuring a single concept. It would also be useful to know whether the customized questionnaire had acceptable test-retest reliability.

Validity is also important for 360-degree feedback questionnaires. There are many different types of validity, so it is easy to be confused when someone says that his or her 360-degree feedback tool is valid. Minimally, a customized questionnaire should have "face validity," so that participants and raters tend to believe the questions and competencies are relevant to the purpose and goals of the feedback process.

It is possible to establish face validity by running a focus group with a representative group from within your organization or by piloting the 360-degree feedback questionnaire before a wider roll-out. It is important to establish whether the 360-degree feedback questions are clear and can be answered, whether the questionnaire itself is relevant to the individuals participating in the 360-degree feedback project, and whether all of the organization's key competencies are being measured.

Other kinds of validity that should be considered in the development of a customized 360-degree feedback assessment include criterion-related validity (does the customized instrument actually predict anything meaningful like performance?) and convergent or divergent validity (does the customized instrument correlate with like and dislike measures?). Whether you create and develop your own or purchase a vendor's assessment, you should make sure of the following basic psychometric properties:

1. Test-retest reliability (scores remain stable over a very short period of time when administered again)

2. Internal consistency reliability (the competencies or scales have items that are highly interrelated with each other)

3. Face validity (the competency model and questions appear to make sense for the job level or purpose of the assessment at a face level)

4. Criterion-related validity (scores on the assessment are correlated at a significant level with a relevant outcome like job performance or satisfaction)

5. Convergent and divergent validity (the assessment scale or competency is associated with scales that are similar and not associated with scales that are different).

21. *Is a customized 360-feedback assessment better than a vendor's off-the-shelf assessment?*

Not necessarily. Well-designed and psychometrically-sound off-the-shelf 360-degree feedback questionnaires (such as those available from Envisia Learning, Inc.) can be used effectively if the behaviors are all relevant. If behaviors are not relevant to the organization, then completing the 360-degree feedback questionnaire could be difficult and will not give you the results you are looking for. A customized 360-degree feedback assessment can be useful if designed to fit your exact needs or to support unique organizational competency frameworks or strategic development objectives and initiatives.

22. *How do I write good behavioral statements to be used in 360-degree feedback assessments?*

Writing good behavioral statements for a customized 360-degree feedback assessment is critical to ensure that what is being measured is accurate and useful for developmental purposes. Here are some recommended tips to ensure your questions are specific, behavioral, and useful:

- Ask only one thing in each question
- Ask something that can be observed by others
- Write in a clear language and avoid terms that may not be obvious, such as jargon or technical terms
- Double check that the item is relevant to the competency area
- Verify that the wording of the question matches the scale
- Utilize Envisia Learning, Inc.'s, *Custom View 360 Library* online system to select from an extensive item pool of over 2,000 questions

23. *How many behavioral statements should I have in each competency?*

To ensure reliability of a scale, a general rule of thumb is to have a *minimum of three* behaviors in a 360-degree assessment. In general, the more questions you have for each scale, the more internal consistency and reliability increases. However, it is important to make sure you have written questions to measure the full scope of the competency you are trying to measure, without increasing the length to such an extent that compliance to complete the assessment is diminished or your questions are redundant.

Figure 2-7

Best Practices in Using 360-Degree Feedback: Q&A

Process/Implementation

24. Who should receive feedback from the assessments?
25. Who should select raters? Does it matter?
26. What kind of communication should be shared with participants, managers, and raters?
27. How should the feedback be given?
28. How do you ensure the confidentiality of raters?
29. Should HR have the ability to identify raters selected and track their progress?
30. Should participants be told who has completed questionnaires?
31. Are there differences between written and online assessments?
32. How do you best roll out a 360-degree feedback initiative across an entire company or job level?
33. Can open-ended questions be damaging emotionally to participants?
34. Should you edit or delete critical or non-helpful open-ended comments?
35. Does a 360-degree feedback report require debriefing?
36. Should a 360-degree feedback report contain a mix of graphs, charts, and open ended questions to maximize understanding?
37. What should you do if raters don't agree in their ratings?
38. How should the 360-degree feedback data be collected?
39. Should participants share their reports with others?
40. Do you need an external coach to debrief and interpret 360-degree feedback reports?
41. Can 360-degree feedback be used alongside personality and style assessments?
42. What is a typical 360-degree feedback project time schedule?
43. Should new employees be included in a 360-degree feedback process?
44. Should participants inform respondents that they have been invited to give feedback?

PROCESS AND IMPLEMENTATION

24. *Who should receive feedback from the 360-degree assessments?*

The goal of all 360-degree feedback processes is to provide clear information for professional development in a manner that motivates individuals to make specific behavioral changes, leading to enhanced effectiveness. The feedback from 360-degree assessments can be shared with the program participant, his or her manager, and others within or outside the organization. The 360-degree feedback research suggests that the motivation for behavioral change is increased when feedback is perceived to be confidential and used for developmental purposes (Nowack, 2005).

Participants and raters who believe that feedback will be shared with others or believe that the process is not anonymous tend to inflate ratings or "game the system," making the information less objective and candid. However, what is most critical is to communicate and clarify the limits of confidentiality and anonymity and who will be receiving the actual results from any 360-degree feedback before the project is initiated.

25. *Who should select raters as part of a 360-degree feedback process?*

Selection of raters is important to ensure "buy in" and acceptance of the feedback results by participants because current research suggests that rater source factors explain (much) more variance in 360-degree feedback ratings whereas general performance explains (much) less variance than was previously believed (Hoffman, Lance, Bynum, & Gentry (2010). Typically, raters can be selected by program participants or they can be selected by management, or it can be a collaborative process between the participant and management. In a recent study reviewing 360-degree feedback use in over 50 North American companies by the 3D Group (2009 Benchmark Study), 61 percent had participants select their own raters with manager approval, 31 percent allowed participants to select their own independently, 4 percent had human resources select raters, 2 percent had managers select raters and 2 percent reported some other process. When used for developmental purposes, research suggests that allowing participants to select their own raters may enhance feedback acceptance *without* reducing rater accuracy (Nieman-Gonder, 2006). Of course, for some purposes, such as performance appraisal or talent and succession planning, having human resources or managers select raters might be prudent and even recommended.

26. *What kind of communication should be shared with participants, managers, and raters?*

It is important to communicate clearly to all stakeholders involved in a 360-degree feedback process. Communication can take place face-to-face or via email and should cover such things as the purpose of the 360-degree feedback intervention, the deadline dates to collect data, confidentiality, who will receive the feedback report, and whom to contact for technical and administrative questions. It is desirable to meet with all participants, if possible, to discuss questions that they might have about the assessment and what raters they might want to invite for feedback.

Managers of the participants should be contacted about their role and responsibilities and about whether they will receive a copy of the feedback report or not. Raters should be informed about what type of feedback is being sought by participants, with assurances about anonymity and the volunteer nature of their participation. If possible, it would be desirable to model the type of open-ended comments that are desirable (behaviorally-based, specific, non-evaluative) for the raters and to encourage raters to use the "Not Applicable" or "Not Observable" rating if they truly do not have enough information to accurately provide feedback to the participant.

27. *How should the 360-degree feedback be given?*

It is important that participants in a 360-degree feedback process be given a chance to interpret the final report in a manner that enhances the motivation to change behavior. Typically, feedback reports are returned to individuals during workshops or individual meetings, rather than simply mailed or e-mailed without facilitated discussion. In a large, corporate 360-degree evaluation study conducted by Envisia Learning, Inc., observed behavior change was greatest when feedback reports were facilitated by either an internal or external consultant (Nowack, 2005).

Research suggests that feedback should be facilitated by either internal or external facilitators or the participant's manager to ensure that the report is clearly understood and any potential negative reactions are managed. The use of internal or external facilitators can help focus on specific developmental areas and highlight specific training and developmental activities that might be most useful for the participant, based on the results and findings of the 360-degree feedback process.

28. *How do you ensure the confidentiality and anonymity of raters?*

Confidentiality is an important aspect of 360-degree feedback for both participants and respondents. It is necessary to ensure that everyone participates and feels able to answer honestly and candidly. If there are any doubts around confidentiality, then people will feel anxious about completing the questionnaire, and they'll be unsure of the purpose of the 360-degree feedback process or the use of the data. If respondents are not guaranteed that their 360-degree feedback responses are anonymous, then they may not provide accurate responses. In fact, research suggests that ratings are inflated when raters do not perceive their input is anonymous.

One approach that Envisia Learning, Inc., uses to ensure anonymity and confidentiality is called *Anonymity Protection (AP)*. On each project, the coach, consultant, or organization using our assessments can set the minimum number of raters in each specific rater group required in order for data from invited raters to be included in the summary feedback report. It is fairly common that data from a participant's manager will be shared openly, and the results from other rater groups are combined to ensure confidentiality. The *Anonymity Protection* level is often set on specific 360-degree feedback projects for direct reports, peers, and others at two to three, but this level depends on the size of the staff and team and the preferences of the coach or organization using the 360-degree feedback assessment.

29. *Should human resources or executives have the ability to identify the raters selected and track their progress?*

Human resources or executives might find it valuable to identify and select raters for particular goals in using 360-degree feedback, often for purposes of performance evaluation or talent management and succession planning. In most cases, 360-degree feedback sponsors should have the ability to track and monitor which raters participants have invited if they are empowered to select their own and to determine how many raters have completed the 360-degree assessments to ensure that the feedback results will include as many raters as possible. Envisia Learning, Inc., provides an administrative tracking Web site for coaches, consultants, and human resources to monitor and track all 360-degree feedback projects and to help maximize the success of each feedback intervention.

30. *Should participants be told who has completed questionnaires?*

Much research verifies that when raters are held accountable or identified, they tend to inflate ratings on 360-degree feedback assessments, because they are concerned about the repercussions of low ratings. Thus, the anonymity of raters does appear to ensure more accurate ratings (Morgeson, Mumford, & Campion, 2005). Participants typically do know the responses of their own manager, but this is expected even in developmentally-oriented 360-degree feedback processes, because bosses typically provide evaluation of direct reports during performance reviews. At Envisia Learning, Inc., we share *how many* raters have completed the assessments but not *who* has completed the assessments to ensure the anonymity of raters providing feedback to each participant in a project. With this information, participants can send out reminders to all invited raters to increase participation or contact our organization for us to send out reminder e-mails to all raters who have not yet completed the assessment by a specific due date assigned on the project.

31. *Are there differences between handwritten and online assessments?*

The two most popular approaches for data collection are online or paper-and-pencil surveys. However, the majority of vendors and companies today utilize Internet-based administration systems, and several studies have verified that there is *equivalence* in using online methods, despite the ease of faking and response distortion that might be more easily controlled with the older paper-and-pencil approach (Penny 2003; Smither, Walker & Yap, 2004). However, the issues often raised of faking and response distortion, although still relevant, are less important, given that the majority of 360-degree feedback interventions are used for developmental purposes. It is important to keep in mind though that 360-feedback assessments are largely used for developmental purposes and should not be constructed and administered as if they were a personnel test (e.g. making the questions transparent, linking questions to the competencies they measure, etc.).

32. *How do you best roll out a 360-degree feedback initiative across an entire company or job level?*

Ideally, it would be best to start at the most senior level that is sponsoring the leadership or talent development intervention to model the process and help facilitate leaders becoming better performance coaches. Without senior leadership support, most 360-degree feedback initiatives are doomed to fail, because participants are not held accountable for translating this feedback into development plans that can be reinforced by leaders in the organization (Nowack, 2009).

In large organizations, it is also important to consider the burden of completing large numbers of 360-degree feedback assessments at one time that might create rater fatigue, lack of candor, or diminished motivation to provide specific feedback. In these cases, organizations should consider "cascading" their 360-degree feedback project, so that small groups within departments or the organization begin the process at different times.

33. Can open-ended questions be emotionally damaging to participants?

The usefulness of having qualitative comments in 360-degree feedback interventions is not widely debated. In fact, before online administration of 360-degree feedback assessments was even possible, most coaches and consultants relied on summarizing interviews with key stakeholders to share feedback themes with participants. Typically in either vendor developed 360 assessments or customized ones designed in-house, open-ended questions are typically included voluntarily and confidentially answered by raters.

Of course, narrative comments can possibly be evaluative, overly critical, or negative, having an adverse impact on acceptability. For example, Smither and Walker (2004) analyzed the impact of upward feedback ratings, as well as narrative comments, over a one-year period for 176 managers. They found that those who received a small number of unfavorable, behaviorally-based comments improved more than other managers, but those who received a large number relative to positive comments significantly declined in performance more than other managers. Like quantitative results, open-ended comments can create strong emotional reactions that can interfere with the acceptance of feedback and lead to diminished engagement and productivity.

In most 360-degree feedback interventions, invited raters are often not given any type of training or guidance to maximize the usefulness of their written comments. Ideally, invited raters should be communicated with early on to describe the purpose of the 360-degree feedback intervention, how their ratings will be used, who will have access to them, and how to make them as behavioral, constructive, and useful for the participant as they can possibly be. This type of communication and training can be helpful to reduce both leniency and strictness errors and other forms of rating biases.

34. *Should you edit or delete critical and non-helpful open-ended comments?*

Participants generally find comments from open-ended questions useful and a great way of clarifying the sometimes confusing quantitative scores (e.g., when rater agreement is low but average scores are moderate or moderately high). Open-ended comments do have some potential downsides, as they take more time to complete and require more effort on the part of raters to make them more behavioral and useful. Open-ended comments might also reveal the raters, diminishing anonymity in the feedback process.

Some vendors may decide to remove critical comments to minimize potentially negative reactions, and others believe they have an unwritten contract with raters to allow them to share any recommendations, suggestions, and observations they have as part of the 360-degree process. Some vendors might also build in the capacity to correct spelling of rater comments and allow for multiple languages to be collected (Envisia Learning, Inc. has this feature in its customized 360 engine).

The determination of what constitutes "non-helpful" comments is challenging for those arguing that highly critical, judgmental, or hurtful comments should be eliminated before the report is shared with the participant. Most coaches follow ethical guidelines that value not harming participants emotionally in some way with the feedback interventions they are using. However, the decision to remove or delete potentially hurtful comments might be a decision that is left at the coach or consultant level and not one that a vendor should ever be involved in deciding. If the feedback to a participant is quite negative, finding a way to deliver the message in a way that minimizes defensiveness and emotional pain while enhancing acceptance can be quite challenging for most coaches or consultants.

35. *Does a 360-degree feedback report require debriefing?*

"Best practices" in 360-degree feedback processes suggest that the greater transfer of learning and goal setting occurs when a manager or coach helps participants understand and debrief their reports (Nowack, 2009). All too often, vendors and some practitioners espouse the *"diagnose and adios"* approach to multi-rater feedback, hoping that self-directed insight alone will result in motivated behavior change efforts.

In one of the few empirical studies recently conducted on the impact of executive coaching, Smither, et al., (2003) reported that after receiving 360-degree feedback, managers who worked with a coach were *significantly more likely* to set measureable and specific goals and solicit ideas for improvement. They subsequently received improved performance ratings. Thatch (2002) found that in six weeks of executive coaching following multi-rater feedback, performance increased by 60 percent, and in a much cited study in the public sector, Olivero, Bane, and Kopelman (1997) found that employee feedback and coaching for two-months increased productivity above the effects of a managerial training program (22.4 versus 80.0 percent) for 31 participants. These coaching studies support the importance of supportive follow-up after feedback is received to facilitate developmental action planning and the practice of targeted behaviors.

Some limited support for other approaches to structured follow-up comes from a recent doctoral dissertation study evaluating the effectiveness of 360-degree feedback interventions in 257 leaders in diverse organizations (Rehbine, 2007). In this study, over 65 percent of those surveyed expressed a strong interest in utilizing some type of an online follow-up tool to measure progress and facilitate their own individual behavior change efforts. Taken together, additional research would appear useful to further investigate the use of such online developmental planning and reminder systems to help translate the awareness from multi-rater feedback into deliberate practice facilitated with internal or external coaches, as well as the participant's manager.

36. *Should a 360-degree feedback report contain a mix of graphs, charts, and open-ended questions to maximize understanding?*

Little research exists to provide definitive answers as to the best way to present 360-degree feedback results. However, it is intuitive that participants have different learning styles, and some may prefer to favor the interpretation of either qualitative versus quantitative presentations of results. One study that does give some insight about what presentation style might maximize the acceptability, understanding, and interpretation of 360-degree feedback results comes from Atwater and Brett (2003). These researchers compared several different report presentations to participants and concluded that:

1. Individuals appear to be significantly less positive and less motivated after receiving text feedback than after receiving numeric feedback.

2. Individuals appear to prefer numeric scores and normative feedback in multi-rater interventions.

Some but not all vendors offer choices in report presentation options. The ability to provide multiple options in feedback reports appears to be helpful for participants to understand and accept feedback and ultimately decide to focus on one or more competency areas for development efforts. For example, Envisia Learning, Inc., provides the following free options for each feedback report, based on coach, consultant, organizational preferences, and the purpose of the 360-degree feedback presentation (www.360online.net/reportOptions):

- Graphical presentation of results (color-coded graphs) comparing self-ratings to those of others
- Summary tables showing all 360-degree feedback assessment questions by rater categories
- Comparison results using vendor norms, organizational norms, or average scores
- Standardized norms presented in graphs, using t-scores or z-scores. Most/least frequent behaviors with rating distributions by each rater category

- Johari Window printing preference, showing a four-box grid comparing self assessment ratings to those of others for each rater category, providing an index of self-insight or self-awareness

- Multiple methods to access *rater agreement*, such as a range of scores and a statistical measure of rater agreement based on standard deviation to help participants understand and interpret outliers and polarized perceptions
- Open-ended questions categorized by rater group or randomly presented

37. *What should you do if raters don't agree on their ratings?*

Current research suggests that rater agreement will indeed vary in 360-degree feedback assessments largely because feedback research shows that different rater sources provide unique, performance-relevant information (Nowack, 2009; Lance, Hoffman, Gentry & Barankik, 2008). Given these findings, vendors who do not provide a way for participants to evaluate within-rater agreement in feedback may increase the probability that average scores used in reports can be easily misinterpreted, particularly if they are used by coaches to help participants using 360-degree feedback assessment focus on specific competencies and behaviors for developmental planning purposes.

Participants should reflect on why specific behaviors might be perceived and experienced positively by some raters and negatively by others. A large discrepancy by raters often suggests a polarized perspective and one that might require additional information gathering to truly understand the meaning of within-rater differences on the 360-degree feedback behavior in question.

38. *How should the 360-degree feedback data be collected?*

Today, almost all 360-degree feedback is collected using online surveys (although handwritten assessments may still be required in special circumstances). Previous research (Smither, Walker & Yap, 2004) demonstrates the equivalence of handwritten and online assessments. However, it is also recommended, when possible, to supplement online surveys and assessments with selected interviews or focus groups to ensure a greater specificity and clarity of feedback responses.

39. *Should participants share their report with others?*

In most 360-degree feedback processes used for developmental purposes, the participant is the only person who gets to keep a copy of the individual summary feedback report. In some cases, the report might be made available to an internal or external coach the participant is working with or a trainer or facilitator who is conducting an organizational workshop. It is typical for talent management and succession planning purposes that a copy of the feedback report might also be made available to one's manager or the human resources department. Of course, a participant who has a good relationship with his or her manager and engages with the manager as a performance coach will be expected to openly share his or her feedback report, whether formally part of a 360-degree feedback intervention or not.

40. *Do you need an external coach to debrief and interpret 360-degree feedback reports?*

"Best practices" in using 360-degree feedback suggest that having *someone* debrief the report is important to manage potential negative emotions surrounding the data, increase the understanding of rater differences, and facilitate developmental planning (Nowack, 2005). However, the process of discussing feedback results appears to be more important than *who* facilitates the discussion assuming the manager, coach, or client has an understanding of the 360-degree feedback assessment, the competencies being measured, and basic helping skills. Sometimes, having managers facilitate discussion of the results can have a distinct advantage in helping translate insight into developmental planning to support job performance and career growth (Rehbine, 2007).

41. *Can 360-degree feedback be used alongside personality and style assessments?*

In general, 360-degree feedback assessments provide data on how participants are perceived by others, while personality and style assessments provide insights about *why* people might behave as they do. Including a personality-and-style-based tool along with a 360-degree feedback assessment is common for many coaches, consultants, and organizations involved in leadership and talent management training or development interventions. Most coaches have their own favorite personality-and-style-based tools as part of their coaching toolkit. Together, these two types of assessments can help facilitate a deeper awareness, an understanding of the participant's strengths that can be leveraged, and blind spots to focus on for further development.

42. *What is a typical 360-degree feedback project time schedule?*

Most 360-degree feedback processes share a common timeline. The recommended process below will give you an idea of how long each step in a complete 360-degree feedback process might take, although it is highly dependent on the company culture, the purpose of the 360-degree intervention, and the availability of raters.

- Communication of 360-degree feedback process (one to two weeks, if in-house meetings are conducted with participants, invited raters, and managers)
- Selecting raters (one to two weeks, if participants discuss their rater pool with their manager)
- Distribution of online questionnaires (one week)
- Completion of online questionnaires (two to four weeks, but this depends on the nature of the project and organization)
- Processing of 360-degree feedback reports (one to two days)
- Feedback meetings (one two hours for each participant)
- Completion of development plan (one to two weeks)
- Reassessment (12-18 months)

43. *Should new employees be included in the 360-degree feedback process?*

The goal of 360-degree feedback is to provide useful, accurate, and constructive information to employees to leverage their strengths and focus on potential development areas. If employees are too new to a job role or organization, then raters are unlikely to have enough opportunity for specific feedback. Depending on the purpose of the 360-degree feedback intervention and the competency model being used, care should be taken if including employees with less than six months' tenure in a role or position in a 360-degree feedback process.

Most vendors provide "not applicable" or "unable to observe" as options on their typical response rating scale, so if a relatively new employee is included in a 360-degree feedback initiative, raters who don't have opportunities to observe the employee and provide useful feedback can utilize these response choices. In such cases, the use of *open-ended* comments might be more useful for the initial impressions created by new employees to solicit and analyze or to help target important competencies and behaviors for developmental purposes.

44. *Should participants inform respondents that they have been invited to give feedback?*

In general, it is highly recommended that participants communicate to those they invite to be raters about the nature of the 360-degree initiative they are participating in, how the data will be used, what specific feedback would be most useful to the participants, and when they would like the feedback to be completed. Communication about the purpose of the 360-degree feedback assessment process and confidentiality with invited raters is likely to increase compliance and cooperation and reduce rater bias, especially if the participant is specific about the type of feedback that would be most helpful to him or her.

Figure 2-8

Best Practices in Using 360-Degree Feedback: Q&A

Interpreting/Leveraging

45. How can development be facilitated?
46. When are average scores misleading?
47. Should you use average or normative scoring?
48. What is the best standardized score to use?
49. How can you measure whether raters agree with each other?
50. Which rater group should you focus on for development?
51. Under what conditions does 360-degree feedback work best?
52. How often should you repeat a 360-degree feedback process?
53. How can you leverage the impact of 360-degree feedback to ensure successful behavior change?
54. Does personality impact how people respond to 360-degree feedback?
55. How do you manage the feedback of under-estimators?
56. How do you manage the feedback of over-estimators?
57. How do you evaluate the impact of 360-degree feedback?
58. Are raters providing unique feedback?
59. Which participants are most motivated to accept feedback?
60. What kind of training or certification is required to help participants understand and interpret their 360-degree feedback reports?
61. Are there cultural differences to be considered in the use of 360-degree feedback?
62. How many goals should be included to maximize success in the development planning process?
63. What are the advantages of "mini-surveys" when used to measure development progress?
64. What can coaches do to make the interpretation and use of 360-degree feedback more effective?

INTERPRETING AND LEVERAGING IMPACT

45. *How can professional development be facilitated?*

Multi-rater or 360-degree feedback systems that have an action plan linked to them have been shown to be more successful than those that do not. "Best practices" suggest that program participants and their managers should meet to discuss results and to implement a development plan for behavior change (Nowack, 2009). This professional development plan should be included as part of the ongoing evaluation system to ensure that it is monitored and reviewed.

Note that the feedback results should not be used as part of any overall evaluation rating or compensation decisions, only as one part of the developmental planning process). The professional development plan should be specific about additional training, on-the-job activities, or developmental resources that the talent will focus on. Finally, it is recommended that the professional action plan be written and implemented using a current Web-based goal planning and evaluation system (e.g., using the online coaching system called *Talent Accelerator* and *Coach Accelerator* available through Envisia Learning, Inc.) to facilitate monitoring and tracking progress by an internal or external coach.

Figure 2-9

SET GOALS FOR YOUR DEVELOPMENT AREAS   ADD DEVELOPMENT AREAS

Development areas can be broken down into smaller, specific and measurable goals. For example, if you choose to work on "Oral Presentation" as a development area, you can create one or two specific behavioral goals that can lead to an improvement in your presentation style. You might create a goal to "Limit the text in the use of PowerPoint in my next presentation" or "Insert a personal story at the very the beginning of my presentation that is relevant to the topic to cultivate audience interest and enthusiasm."

Click the "SET A NEW GOAL" next to the development areas you have selected to begin the process. We have a handful of suggested goals for you to choose for each or you may wish to create your own that are specific, behavioral, measurable, observable, attainable, and time specific.

ENGENDERS TRUST   SET A NEW GOAL   ✕ REMOVE

SELF-CONTROL   SET A NEW GOAL   ✕ REMOVE

MY GOALS   REVIEW REFLECTIVE QUESTIONS | ADD DEVELOPMENT AREAS

SELF-DEVELOPMENT   SET A NEW GOAL

Ask and Request More From Others When Frustrated
Due in 29 days.

Eliminate Defensiveness
Due in 29 days.

ADAPTABILITY/STRESS TOLERANCE   SET A NEW GOAL

Monitor and Modify Dysfunctional Self-Talk
Due in 19 days.

46. *When are average scores within 360-degree feedback reports misleading?*

Average scores are typically used by vendors in 360-degree feedback reports. However, without a way to discern outliers, polarized scores and rater agreement, the interpretation of average scores can be quite misleading in reports. For example, if a vendor provides a table of most and least frequent behaviors, it is not uncommon to use average scores to present these results. It is important that vendors provide a metric to determine whether these average scores reflect homogeneity of rater responses or enough dispersion to make the average score difficult to practically use for developmental planning efforts.

For example, in each of the 360-degree feedback reports produced by Envisia Learning, Inc., there is a section at the end that provides a summary table containing average competency and item scores by each rater group, as well as an overall average of all raters, excluding self ratings. Each item or question measuring specific competencies is grouped under its appropriate competency to assist in the interpretation of the results. A feature of this section is the *Index of Rater Agreement,* shown in parentheses after the average scores for each rater group. This *Index of Rater Agreement* ranges from 0 to 1.0 and is based on a statistical measure of dispersion or spread by raters, called standard deviation. This index is derived by subtracting 1 from the calculated standard deviation divided by a scale-specific divisor.

An agreement index score of 0.0 suggests little or no rater agreement among those answering a specific question. An agreement score of 1.0 suggests uniform and consistent ratings by all raters providing feedback. Agreement index scores *less than .50* might suggest a greater diversity, inconsistency, and spread among the raters.

Figure 2-10

Example Behavior Summary Table with the
Index of Rater Agreement in Parentheses

Questions	Self	Manager	Peer	Direct Report	Team Member	Average
Written Communication	**5.60 (0.84)**	**2.80 (0.67)**	**2.60 (0.69)**	**4.00 (0.24)**	**2.50 (0.56)**	**3.00 (0.47)**
Uses appropriate grammar, tense & language in written communications	6.00 (1.00)	4.00 (1.00)	3.00 (0.67)	4.50 (0.17)	3.50 (0.83)	3.71 (0.47)
Uses written communications effectively & appropriately.	6.00 (1.00)	4.00 (1.00)	2.50 (0.50)	4.00 (0.33)	2.50 (0.50)	3.14 (0.42)
Writes in a logical & organized manner.	6.00 (1.00)	2.00 (1.00)	2.50 (0.83)	3.50 (0.50)	3.00 (1.00)	2.86 (0.67)
Writes in a clear, direct & concise manner.	5.00 (1.00)	2.00 (1.00)	2.50 (0.83)	4.00 (0.33)	2.00 (1.00)	2.71 (0.54)
Writes technical information in an easily understood manner.	5.00 (1.00)	2.00 (1.00)	2.50 (0.83)	4.00 (0.00)	1.50 (0.83)	2.57 (0.36)
Administrative Control	**5.20 (0.61)**	**2.40 (0.66)**	**2.60 (0.66)**	**3.90 (0.45)**	**2.70 (0.74)**	**2.97 (0.56)**
Establishes effective mechanisms to monitor & ensure that work is done on time & with quality.	6.00 (1.00)	4.00 (1.00)	2.50 (0.83)	4.00 (0.67)	2.50 (0.83)	3.14 (0.67)
Develops systems and procedures to monitor individual, team and organizational progress on projects, tasks and assignments	4.00 (1.00)	3.00 (1.00)	2.50 (0.50)	4.00 (0.33)	3.00 (0.67)	3.14 (0.48)
Develops systems to monitor budgets, costs, & expenses.	5.00 (1.00)	1.00 (1.00)	2.00 (0.67)	4.50 (0.50)	3.50 (0.83)	3.00 (0.47)
Follows-up with employees to monitor quality & effective performance.	7.00 (1.00)	2.00 (1.00)	3.50 (0.83)	3.00 (0.33)	2.50 (0.83)	2.86 (0.58)

It is not uncommon to misinterpret average scores represented on graphic comparisons as being accurate. However, when the *Index of Rater Agreement* is less than .50, it might suggest caution in interpreting these average scores. In reality, some raters might have a very positive bias in responding to the questions, whereas other raters might have a very negative bias in responding, creating a polarized view of the respondent. The *Rater Agreement Index* can be calculated at both the item and competency level. At the item level, it indicates the amount of rater agreement in answering each 360-degree feedback question.

47. *Should you use average or normative scoring in reports to facilitate interpretation?*

All vendors tend to aggregate results from different rater groups in 360-degree feedback reports in some manner to facilitate the interpretation, understanding, and acceptance of data. Most commonly, aggregate data is presented as *average* scores across all raters in a particular category. Average scores simply allow comparison of all raters within a category to self-assessment scores, based on mathematical calculations of the mean scores of the raters.

Some vendors also provide *normative*, or benchmark, scoring based, on global, industrial, or company-specific groups within a database that can be used for external or internal comparison. For example, Envisia Learning, Inc., has extensive North American, European, and global norms for all of its off-the-shelf validated 360-degree feedback assessments. Each year, the norm groups are analyzed and updated to ensure that they represent the most up-to-date benchmark. Additional details are also made available to characterize the norm group by gender, age, ethnicity, tenure, job level, and industry, so that greater understanding will occur if such norms are used within 360-degree feedback reports.

The use of norms in a 360-degree feedback report can be represented by several *standardized statistics* to enable the understanding of differences between self-perception and others' perception of the participant, relative to the specific norm group used. For example, Envisia Learning, Inc., provides a choice of two standardized norm presentations that can be used in feedback reports: 1) z-scores (standardized score with a mean of 0 and standard deviation of 1) or 2) t-scores (standardized scores with a mean of 50 and standard deviation of 10).

Figure 2-11

Examples of Standardized Scores in 360-Degree Feedback Reports

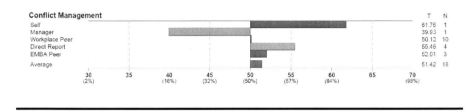

Standardized t-scores are very common in psychological assessments. They standardize the mean to be 50 and the standard deviation to be 10 (approximately 68 percent of everyone in the database will have t-scores between one standard deviation above and below the mean).

Figure 2-11

Examples of Standardized Scores in 360-Degree Feedback Reports

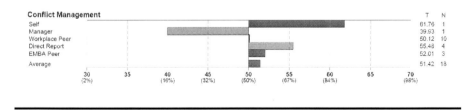

Standardized z-scores are less common in psychological assessments. They standardize the mean to be 0.0 and the standard deviation to be 1 (approximately 68 percent of everyone in the database will have a z-score between one standard deviation above and below the mean).

In Envisia Learning, Inc., reports using standardized scores, we will also present the *percentile* equivalent score at the bottom of both graphs.

The use of norms in 360-degree feedback reports should not be taken lightly as a report preference, despite the size or representation of the norm group being used. In some cases, simple average score comparisons are best to help facilitate the understanding of self-other differences. In other cases, having an internal or external normative benchmark might be useful and desirable in comparing how self-others differences compare to these normative groups.

48. *What is the best standardized score to use?*

Some coaches, consultants, and organizations might prefer to use one type of standardized score over another in feedback reports. For example, z-scores often result in scores that are *negative* if they are below the mean, which could create an emotional reaction on the part of participants interpreting their results. It is important to keep in mind that all standardized scores (e.g., sten scores, percentiles, t-scores, z-scores) are representing the same data to the participant. However, some might be easier to interpret and understand. Coaches, consultants, and organizations should use vendors that provide for the same flexibility in the use of standardized scores within 360-degree feedback reports as we do at Envisia Learning, Inc., to maximize acceptance and understanding.

49. How can you measure if raters agree with each other?

Dispersion, agreement, or variance *within* rater groups is important to measure and report back to participants in 360-degree feedback reports (Nowack, 2009). At Envisia Learning, Inc., we provide up to three *different* types of metrics of rater agreement within each of our reports including:

1. The range of scores (indicates a band of responses, from the highest to lowest scores on a specific competency by all raters)

Figure 2-12

Vision/ Goal Setting	Avs	N
Self	6.00	1
Manager	4.40	1
Peer	5.33	3
Direct Report	5.70	4
	5.40	8

2. The distribution of scores (indicates a visual way to discern the *spread* of scores by raters on specific questions)

Figure 2-13

Least Frequent Behaviors	Competency	Average Score	1- To an Extremely Small Extent	2- To a Very Small Extent	3- To a Small Extent	4- To a Moderate Extent	5- To a Large Extent	6- To a Very Large Extent	7- To an Extremely Large Extent
Creates opportunities to be innovative & create new ideas & concepts.	Problem Analysis	3.0	0	0	1	0	0	0	0
Considers alternatives & generates contingency plans when making decisions & solving problems.	Problem Analysis	3.0	0	0	1	0	0	0	0

145

3. The statistical measure of rater agreement, based on standard deviation from 100 percent agreement to no agreement; any agreement *less than 50 percent* statistically is meaningful and indicates enough variability within raters to suggest that the average score could be misleading if used to highlight strengths or potential development areas.

50. *Which rater group should you focus on for development?*

Differences between raters on 360-degree feedback assessments are common, and research suggests that the different rater groups are often only moderately associated with each other (Nowack, 1992). However, these meaningful rater group differences might also be a point of confusion in the interpretation of data for participants trying to use the results to determine specific behaviors to modify and which stakeholder to target.

At a practical level, this means that participants might be challenged to understand how to interpret observed differences by rater groups and asked whether to decide to focus their developmental "energy" on managing upward, downward, or laterally in light of these potentially discrepant results. Research suggests that raters tend to use specific *filters* when completing 360-degree feedback assessments (Nowack, 2009). For example, superiors tend to focus more on performance, output, and task-oriented behaviors (Nowack, 2002).

In our research, we find that managers tend to reflect on three things when they complete 360-degree feedback assessments: 1) bottom-line performance (does the employee meet or exceed his or her performance objectives?), 2) technical competence (does the employee technically know what he or she is doing?), and 3) "burr in the saddle effect" (has the employee created situations or problems that require the manager to investigate further or try to spend time resolving internal or external customer complaints?). Employees who are viewed by managers as getting work done with quality, as possessing strong technical competence, and as minimizing extra work on the part of the manager to resolve internal or external political issues are generally rated higher on 360-degree feedback assessments.

In general, direct reports tend to emphasize and filter *interpersonal and relationship* behaviors into their subjective ratings, whereas peers tend to be fairly accurate in actually predicting future leadership potential (although it is unclear exactly what qualities, competencies, personality attributes, or other behaviors they might be weighing when they complete 360-degree assessments). Based on these rating filters, observational opportunities, and job-role relationships with participants, it seems that peer ratings might be interpreted as an important message about *moving ahead*, whereas direct report ratings might be interpreted as an important message about *getting along*. Participants should consider both the source and the congruence between various rater groups in determining which one they might target as a part of their developmental planning.

51. *Under what conditions does 360-degree feedback work best?*

Generally, 360-degree feedback processes, in order to be effective, depend on the participant, the coach, and organizational factors to support the receptivity, acceptance, and leveraging of feedback for enhanced insight and behavioral change. Several studies by Envisia Learning, Inc., have suggested some "Best Practices" that should be followed including those outlined below

(Nowack, 2005; 2009). When the organizational culture is conducive to giving and receiving feedback and not under some major change effort, the implementation of a 360-degree feedback intervention is most likely to be met with success that is consistent with its goals.

1. Define and communicate clearly about the purpose of the 360-degree feedback intervention, including the limits of confidentiality and anonymity
2. Provide individual coaching to assist in interpreting and using the 360-degree feedback results
3. Hold the participant and manager accountable to create and implement a professional development plan
4. Track and monitor progress on the completion of the development plan
5. Link the 360-degree feedback intervention to a human resources performance management process
6. Use 360-degree feedback assessments with sound psychometric properties
7. Target competencies for 360-degree feedback interventions that are related to strategic business needs

52. *How often should you repeat a 360-degree feedback process?*

Given that people need time to make meaningful behavioral change and then time for that change to be seen by others, we recommend that somewhere between 12 to 24 month intervals are most appropriate for repeating a 360-degree feedback process. This allows people to work through their development and action plans to create change. For example, Envisia Learning Inc. provides a *time series 360-degree feedback report* that combines and summarizes results from the first and subsequent administrations of 360-degree feedback to show change in scores over a time period. Of course, it is also highly recommended to periodically evaluate the impact of the participant's goal setting and development plan progress. For example, Envisia Learning Inc. has a goal evaluation system called *ProgressPulse* which can be administered at any time following coaching or training that asks invited raters to evaluate progress on specific participant goals (i.e., whether they are improving, staying the same or even getting worse). This feedback is combined into a brief report to help provide accountability and measure learning transfer.

53. *How can you leverage the impact of 360-degree feedback to ensure successful behavioral change?*

Organizations that implement a systemic approach to talent development with support from a manager and follow up development activities tied to performance improvement will have the most effective outcomes in leadership development (Nowack, 2009). A better understanding of the role of the manager as an important internal coach and how organizational culture influences promoting and sustaining new behavior is in need of greater exploration. The manager can reinforce and support the implementation of the development plan of the participant. This is important in light of recent findings suggesting that effect sizes for transfer of management training interventions are generally low (particularly when seen by direct reports and peers) but can be improved significantly with opportunities for structured and deliberate practice (Taylor, Taylor, & Russ-Eft, 2009).

Use of newer online goal setting and development planning/ reminder systems like *Talent Accelerator* by Envisia Learning, Inc. (www.envisialearning.com) can facilitate goal planning and follow-up in order to leverage multi-rater feedback interventions. In a recent unpublished one-year longitudinal study using this online coaching system with a major university medical center, significant behavioral change was observed by managers, direct reports, and peers on a post-program assessment (Nowack, 2011). This finding suggests that performance can be practically enhanced by using a 360-degree feedback process involving managers as "performance coaches" and holding participants accountable for creating and implementing a development plan based on 360 results.

54. *Does personality impact how people respond to 360-degree feedback?*

Personality does indeed influence how participants react to 360-degree feedback, how motivated they will be to act on the suggestions and observations of others, and how likely they will be to implement and sustain new behaviors to become more effective. Research by Smither, London, and Richmond (2005) explored the relationship between leaders' personalities and their reactions to and use of 360-degree feedback. Leaders high in emotional stability were more likely to be rated by a psychologist as motivated to use the feedback results for professional development. Additionally, leaders high in extroversion or sociability were more likely to have sought additional feedback six months later, while leaders high in conscientiousness were more likely to have engaged in developmental behaviors. These researchers also found that extroverted leaders who are open to experience were more likely to perceive and view negative feedback as valuable and were most likely to seek further information about their feedback.

In general, individuals with high self-esteem reported more favorable attitudes toward the 360-degree feedback than those with low self-esteem. Feedback recipients who rate themselves highly on receptivity and the desire to make a good first impression were also perceived by feedback providers as having more positive reactions to feedback (Atwater, Brett, and Charles, 2007). Research by Bono and Colbert (2005) suggests that the motivation to change behavior following 360-degree feedback is related to a personality concept called core self-evaluations (CSE). Specifically, they found that individuals with high levels of core self-evaluations (those with high self-esteem, generalized self-efficacy, internal locus of control and low neuroticism) will be most motivated to change behavior when they receive discrepant feedback, while those with low levels of core self-evaluations will be most motivated when others' ratings are most similar to their own. These results suggest the potential value of coaching to assist individuals to understand potentially complex feedback and to increase the motivation to set developmental goals. In general, leaders with an internal locus of control (i.e., those who believe they have some control over what happens to them) tend to react to peer and subordinate feedback more favorably, with a greater intention to improve their skills.

Goal orientation may influence whether an individual views feedback as a development opportunity or a challenge to his or her self-rating. Individuals with a learning goal orientation tend to hold a view of ability as modifiable and believe they are capable of improving their level of abilities (Brett and Atwater, 2001). These researchers found that those with a learning goal orientation believed the feedback was more useful than those with a performance goal orientation.

Taken together, it seems people are most motivated to use 360-degree feedback for development when they are conscientious or extroverted and when they had high self-efficacy, an internal locus of control, and low anxiety. As a result, coaches should assess the personality and style of their clients and reflect on how this might impact the receptivity and use of the 360-degree feedback results.

55. *How do you manage the feedback of under-estimators?*

One form of "cognitive distortion" that is common in 360-degree feedback processes occurs when the participant rates him or herself significantly lower than how they are perceived and rated by others. These "under-estimators" are actually viewed as possessing strengths but not recognizing or acknowledging them relative to others giving them feedback.

At Envisia Learning, Inc., we have looked at this "leveraging strengths" concept from an interesting angle in the last few years. In our use of 360-degree feedback assessments, we have an interpretation based on the Johari Window concept that shows self-ratings compared to others who provide feedback in a graphic manner. We can classify individuals into four types, based on the profile that emerges from self-other ratings. We have polite labels for these quadrants that include:

- *Potential Strengths*: the under-estimation of self-ratings compared to others
- *Confirmed Development Areas:* both self and other ratings are low
- *Confirmed Strengths:* both self and other ratings are high
- *Potential Development Areas:* self-ratings are inflated relative to others

"Under-estimators" (about 25 to 30 percent of those taking our assessments) have a substantial number of competencies appearing in the "Potential Strengths" quadrant, and our feedback meetings with them are predictable. Individuals with this type of cognitive distortion are particularly fascinating, and when you sit down to debrief a 360-degree feedback report, we consistently find the following characteristics and behaviors:

- Highly perfectionist
- Expect high performance for themselves and others
- Often express a history of one or more depressive episodes in their adult lives
- Focus on their weaknesses and look for fault, criticism, and potential deficits in their feedback from others
- Ignore and gloss over any feedback suggesting strengths as being too complimentary

In short, these participants tend to blow off all of the strengths seen by others and dwell on anything that isn't perfect in their summary feedback report. No matter what we try to do, these clients won't leverage their strengths as seen by others. All they want to do is focus on what they see as their developmental opportunities or weaknesses.

In a recent Harvard Business Review article, Kaplan and Kaiser (2009) show that it is just as detrimental to overdo strengths as it is to under-do them. Those expressing the right amount of strength showed an association with a measure of leadership success. As the authors point out, leveraging and emphasizing strength might lead to actually interfering with being flexible and adopting new behaviors. If you receive feedback that you are admired for your perseverance in the face of ambiguity and challenge, you might find that "letting go" and backing off won't come easily, even if it is clear that repeatedly banging your head against the wall creates a dent in the wall and a possible concussion that further impairs your reasoning and thinking.

It is important for coaches to do their best to help under-estimating clients see their feedback in balance and prepare for the likelihood that they will accentuate and focus on the negative, despite feedback from others that they are actually performing strongly or possess high competence in particular skills and abilities being rated.

56. *How do you manage the feedback of over-estimators?*

It has been estimated that 65 to75 percent of the employees in any given organization report that the worst aspect of their job is their immediate boss. In fact, estimates of the base rate for managerial incompetence in corporate life range from 30 to 75 percent, with the average level of poor leadership hovering at about 50 percent (Hogan, R. & Kaiser, R., 2005). Many of these leaders tend to have inflated views of their skills and abilities, and this appears fairly common in 360-degree feedback research (Nowack, 1992).

Over-estimation is the type of distortion that occurs when talent and leaders rate themselves more highly on specific assessments of skills and abilities than how others experience them. The bigger the distortion and gap between self and other ratings, the greater the likelihood these individuals will find feedback challenging to accept and use for development purposes. As a result, over-estimators are prone to exhibit defensive behavior in feedback meetings and look for ways to dismiss findings or find fault with the 360-degree feedback instrument, the raters who provided feedback, or the process itself.

If you were to take a look at the common psychological definitions for the *Narcissistic Personality Disorder*, you might see many of these manifested in talent and leaders who highly over-estimate their skills and abilities, including:

1. Having a grandiose sense of self-importance
2. Being preoccupied with fantasies of success, power, etc.
3. Believing they are unique and can only be understood by other high-status people (or institutions)
4. Infrequently acknowledging mistakes or weaknesses
5. Requiring excessive admiration, praise, and recognition
6. Having a sense of entitlement
7. Possibly being interpersonally manipulative to achieve their own goals
8. Lacking empathy and being unwilling or unable to demonstrate true caring about the feelings of others
9. Demonstrating arrogance

Our own unpublished research suggests that talent and leaders who have this perception of themselves when looking in the mirror might not only be high risk to derail in their careers but also might be at risk for getting sick. Some limited evidence suggests that over-estimators might also utilize a repressive coping style, which has been shown to be associated with both immune suppression and cardiovascular activation. The over-estimators tend to be challenging in feedback meetings and will often be at risk to potentially derail and ignore the feedback they receive, despite the fact that this distortion would appear to be useful for these individuals to pay attention to.

57. *How do you evaluate the impact of 360-degree feedback?*

The initial 360-degree feedback provides a benchmark and baseline for the talent. It is hoped that the results of the 360-degree feedback program will result in enhanced performance and effectiveness. One important metric in evaluating this type of training intervention is to compare change over time on the key competencies being measured through the 360-degree feedback assessment. This ensures that the 360-degree feedback process focuses on individual change, rather than being a one-time event. This is frequently seen within many organizations.

"Best Practices" suggest that the 360-degree feedback process be repeated 12 to 18 months following the initial administration of feedback to facilitate the effectiveness of the training program and monitor individual progress on individual development plans (Nowack, 2005; 2009; Nowack, Hartley, & Bardley, 1999). Surveys and focus groups can also be used to evaluate the process, as well as the outcomes with targeted stakeholders.

58. *Are raters providing unique feedback?*

As mentioned earlier, different raters do appear to be applying *different* observational filters that bias and reflect on the behaviors they are rating (Nowack, 2009). As such, ratings from managers appear to be performance-oriented, ratings from direct reports are more interpersonally oriented, and ratings from peers are focused on future leadership potential. At a practical level, this suggests that results from 360-degree feedback do prompt unique feedback from the different rater groups involved in such processes. As such, each rater group provides important but somewhat unique feedback to interpret and decide how to use in each 360-degree feedback process.

59. *Which participants are most motivated to accept feedback?*

Limited research suggests that two factors play a role in who is most likely to be the most motivated and respond the most favorably to 360-degree feedback (Atwater & Brett, 2006). The findings suggest that:

- Individuals who have higher levels of organizational commitment are more motivated to change, regardless of the nature of the feedback.

- Individuals who hold more positive attitudes toward the feedback process are also more motivated to change and report more follow-up activities than those who held less positive attitudes.

Smither, Brett, and Atwater (2008) examined some of the factors that influence the accessibility of feedback and subsequent improvement in performance. First, participants are more likely to recall *positive*, rather than negative, feedback from others. Second, participants are more inclined to recall feedback that relates to their performance orientation but not as likely to recall feedback that concerns their capacity to develop subordinates. Third, participants were more inclined to recall feedback that alluded to specific, tangible behaviors, rather than global, abstract traits. Finally, participants were more likely to recall feedback from supervisors and subordinates than from peers.

60. *What kind of training or certification is required to help participants understand and interpret their 360-degree feedback reports?*

Most researchers support the idea that some level of training is required to professionally and ethically provide feedback using multi-rater systems. Exactly what experiences, academic degrees, or certifications should be required is not very clear. Some vendors require certification training as a requirement to purchase and use 360-degree feedback assessments, and others provide relevant training manuals and resources to purchasers for free. Coaches and consultants may have very diverse backgrounds (Nowack, 2003) and academic degrees, but familiarity with assessments in general would generally be useful to professionally utilize 360-degree feedback systems (Nowack, 2003). Current research on coaching differences by education and traing has found taht psychologists are more likely to meet face-to-face, contract for fewer sessions, and are more likely to use 360-degree assessments in their practice (Bono, et al., 2009).

Minimally, coaches and consultants should be familiar with vendor reports; be able to interpret the graphs, tables, and data presented; be competent in handling negative feedback and strong emotional reactions of clients; be capable of discussing results; and be able to help formulate specific developmental plans. Additionally, coaches and consultants should have some background and understanding of the basic psychometric properties of assessments, including the various types of reliabilities and validities, different standardized norms that can be used, and issues surrounding the uses of normative data for interpretation of results. Finally, all coaches and human resource practitioners involved in 360-degree feedback interventions should adhere to accepted professional practices and ethical standards to ensure the best interests of their clients.

61. *Are there cultural differences to be considered in the use of 360-degree feedback?*

There is an increasing use of 360-degree feedback in different cultures and countries particularly as multi-national companies use it throughout their organization. Differences in 360-degree feedback rating and interpretation should be expected to some degree in other cultures. Some dimensions that appear to be important include individualism versus collectivism, power distance, and gender egalitarianism. Atwater and her colleagues (2009) explored self and subordinate ratings of leadership in 964 managers from 21 countries, based on assertiveness, power distance, and individualism or collectivism. Self and other ratings were more positive in countries characterized as high in assertiveness and power distance. In the U.S., lack of self-awareness predicts performance, but this metric was less useful in five European countries (U.K., Germany, Denmark, Italy, and France). In European countries, only others' ratings of leadership predicted managerial effectiveness.

Cultural relevance was compared across five countries (US, Ireland, Israel, The Philippines, and Malaysia), and this supported the overall effectiveness of the 360-degree feedback process but also revealed important differences (Shipper, Hoffman, & Rotondo, 2007). This study suggested that the 360-degree feedback process is relevant in all cultures but most effective in those low on power distance with individualistic values (e.g., United States versus Philippines). Eckert, Ekelund, Gentry, and Dawson (2010) investigated self-observer rating discrepancies on three leadership skills on data from 31 countries. Finally, research on 360-degree feedback across 17 countries by Robie, Kaster, Nilsen, and Hazucha (2000) suggests that, overall, there were more similarities than differences across countries. For example, the ability to solve complex problems and learn quickly appears to be universally predictive of effectiveness for leaders.

A recent study by Ng et al. (2011) explored the role of power distance and individualism-collectivism on 172 leaders which included 1,447 superiors, peers and subordinates who provided feedback. Subordinates demonstrated the most rating leniency (i.e., higher overall ratings) relative to superiors and peers. The effects of power distance on leniency and halo ratings were significantly stronger for subordinates than for peers or superiors. The effects of collectivism on leniency were stronger for subordinates and peers than for superiors and the effects of halo ratings were stronger for subordinates than superiors, but these effects did not differ for subordinates and peers. These findings suggest that raters, particularly subordinates and peers with high power distance and collectivistic values are most prone to rating bias than superiors. Rater training might be useful to help improve the quality of feedback from all raters. In addition, raters providing consistently high ratings across questions might be prompted by online 360 feedback systems to alert raters of their most current responses.

Taken together, these studies suggest that cultural values and differences such as power distance, individualism-collectivism might significantly affect self-other ratings. Coaches should consider cultural values and such differences when helping clients and raters interpret and use 360-degree feedback systems to minimize potential rating biases.

62. *How many goals should be included to maximize success in the development planning process?*

Behavioral change efforts are often not linear but tend to be progressive, regressive, or even static. It seems intuitive that focus on a single behavioral change goal is easier to initiate and sustain, but, surprisingly, multiple simultaneous efforts (e.g., behaviors planned to improve multiple competencies at the same time) tend to be equal or even more effective, because they reinforce quick benefits (Hyman, Pavlik, Taylor, Goodrick, & Moye, 2007). Of course, it is important for clients to be successful, so making sure that not too many challenging or unrealistic goals are set is something a coach can discuss with their client.

In our online coaching and goal-setting/evaluation system called *Talent Accelerator*, we allow participants to select as many competencies as they would like to *begin* their development plan. At any point, they can add new competencies and specific tasks, activities, and actions to enhance effectiveness. The system is flexible enough to allow coaches working with their clients to target new competencies and goals throughout the entire coaching engagement.

63. *What are the advantages of "mini-surveys" to measure development progress?*

Tracking and monitoring progress on development plans is essential for sustaining new behavior over time. It is important to continuously seek feedback from others to see how a participant is progressing in their targeted goal. Research by Goldsmith (2006) on 8,208 leaders over an 18-month period shows the importance of follow-up with others (e.g., direct reports, peers and their managers):

- 53 percent of the leaders who did not follow-up were rated as unchanged or less effective
- 66 percent of the leaders who did "a little follow-up" showed improvement

- 95 percent of the leaders who did "a lot of follow-up" were rated as dramatically improved

Sometimes it is too early to conduct another full 360-degree feedback assessment or not feasible to do so. In such cases, the use of "mini-surveys" can be quite helpful in gathering quick feedback about whether others see clients improving, staying the same, or even getting worse on targeted competencies that have been a part of their development plan.

At Envisia Learning, Inc., we offer for each of our assessments a *mini-survey* assessment called *ProgressPulse* that allows participants to gather information about their progress one or more of their developmental goals, using an effectiveness scale targeted to a specific competency. We allow participants to go out and solicit feedback from the original 360-degree rater pool or add new raters. These raters are simply asked to evaluate how effective the participant is on the competency being evaluated, as well as providing an open-ended comment to support the rating:

During the last few months since you provided earlier feedback, how effective is the person on the competency defined below?

-2: Much Less Effective

-1: Slightly Less Effective

 0: Unchanged

+1: Slightly More Effective

+2: Much More Effective

NO: Not Observable

Comment: What could this person do more, less, or differently to continue becoming effective in the competency they have attempted to work on?

The results from the *ProgressPulse* are summarized in a brief online report that provides a useful metric of effectiveness or improvement on the participant's developmental goals. Such feedback can be useful for additional development planning efforts.

64. *What can coaches do to make the interpretation and use of 360-degree feedback more effective?*

An interesting study by Robert Hooijberg and colleagues, looked at what makes coaching effective, surveyed 232 managers from diverse organizations (Hooijberg, & Lane, 2009). One of the key questions asked was: "What did your coach do that you found most effective?"

From the view of the client or participants, three major categories determined feedback success: 1) interpreting results (34.8 percent), 2) inspiring action (27.5 percent), and 3) professionalism (23.3 percent). The majority of clients thought the best coaches were those who analyzed strengths and weaknesses, helped assimilate feedback, and made concrete developmental recommendations.

This study seems to contradict much of the coaching literature and suggests that participants using 360-degree feedback expect and want their coach to take a more active role in interpreting their results and making developmental recommendations. This finding *is* consistent with the concept of "feedforward," developed by Marshall Goldsmith, who suggests letting us know what we can be doing more, less, or differently in the future to become better and more successful.

Eight Tips for Facilitating Constructive 360-Degree Feedback

1   **Be careful not to argue about the feedback with the participant.** Keep in mind that over-estimators are likely to be more defensive and resistant to negative feedback than other raters.

2   **Balance between self-views and other-views.** Make sure the goal of the feedback process is for your client to see the data in balance. Whenever possible, reduce the gap between the different perceptions to bring clients closer to reality.

3   **Balance between strengths and weaknesses.** Be aware that under-estimators will tend to focus on their weaknesses, despite being viewed quite positively by others. These clients will have the most difficult time seeing their results in balance and will typically dwell on the few neutral or constructively critical results that they can find.

4   **Promote a setting for honest and open communication.** Contract clearly about the nature of the 360-degree feedback process and communicate with all parties involved about how the report will be debriefed, who will get a copy, and what is expected once participants receive feedback.

5   **Provide Specific and Behavioral Feedback.** If you can't be specific and behavioral with your feedback, it's just dumb luck that participants will figure out what to do more, less, or differently to be effective on the job. Remember, just one small behavior change that is successful can make the difference between success on the job and future derailment.

6   **Encourage Reflection.** Ask participants to summarize how they are being experienced or perceived by others as a result of your coaching intervention. By testing for awareness, you can be sure that at least the participant truly understands what others experience and perceive about his or her style that is productive and/or challenging.

7   **Utilize Self-Monitoring.** Ask the participant to keep a journal or track the number of times during the day or week when he or she is aware of acting or behaving in a particular way and whether others find the behavior either productive or challenging. Such self-monitoring will, in and of itself, become a useful intervention to increase the self-awareness required for behavior change efforts.

8   **Utilize Follow-Up Messages.** Frequent follow-up telephone calls or e-mail messages that remind participants to focus on a developmental task are invaluable in enhancing awareness of what need to be changed. Good coaches are also "professional nags" in helping participants stay focused and motivated to translate understanding from 360-degree feedback reports to implementing specific development tasks and activities targeting one or more competencies.

Summary

Enlightenment is about how individuals become aware of their strengths and weaknesses in order to develop. Assessing clients can involve a wide variety of approaches and tools, each with different predictors of future success and performance. Coaches should carefully consider what outcomes they are trying to achieve and select the assessment that best matches their goals. Multi-rater feedback systems are powerful and common tools for feedback and *must* be used with caution. If not, your clients' behavioral change can be more harmful than beneficial.

For example, clients often face the challenge of having views of themselves and their performance that are completely contrary to the views of their raters. For this reason, it is important for coaches to consider feedback tools that provide a theoretical foundation and are limited by reliability issues. Also, it is important for coaches and practitioners to be familiar with and use "Best Practices" when using 360-degree feedback interventions. The next section of the book provides exercises for all types of individuals who wish to increase self-insight and self-awareness.

Key Points

1. Coaches and consultants should understand the major assessment domains of skills and abilities, personality and style, interests and values, and health and well-being and what outcomes these domains are most strongly associated with in talent development.

2. Social and interpersonal stress causes the stress hormone to be elevated 50 percent longer, and social pain appears to use the same neurobiological pathways as physical pain.

3. The use of 360-degree feedback for the development of talent can be enhanced by following "Best Practices" in defining the purpose; designing and acquiring a psychometrically sound 360-degree feedback assessment; implementing a process to ensure confidentiality, trust, and anonymity; providing feedback in a manner that increases understanding and acceptance; and leveraging the feedback for successful behavioral change.

4. Keep in mind the *three tenets* of 360-degree feedback:

   - *Feedback is important:* Most of us don't wake up each morning and spontaneously change behavior.

   - *You can't always get what you want*: Feedback doesn't always result in enhanced performance.

   - *Be realistic:* Don't expect 360-degree feedback to modify "competent jerks" into "lovable stars".

ENLIGHTEN EXERCISES

The following section includes various exercises related to the *Enlighten* chapters.

Tips for Getting the Most from the Exercises in the Book

- **Take time to do the exercises.** These exercises are designed to help you and your client to move through the Enlighten, Encourage and Enable stages of successful behavior change.

- **Take time to reflect.** Spend some quality time on each exercise to answer the questions and reflect what they mean for you personally and professionally.

- **Pick and choose the most important exercises to use.** Each of the exercises has been specifically included to support the specific behavior change stage in our model. Some exercises will be more relevant than others for you and your client. However, each has a unique purpose but there is not a need to specifically do all of them or in any order.

- **Share with others.** Consider sharing your thoughts and feelings about one or more of the exercises with a partner, family member, friend or colleague. Seek their impressions and input about your reactions and commitments.

- **Commit to action.** Consider taking specific actions to translate these exercises into goals and new behaviors.

Each of the exercises included in the book and additional ones for each of the *Enlighten, Encourage* and *Enable* behavior change stages can be previewed and printed in a useable format for you and your clients to use for free by visiting our website at: www.envisialearning.com/clueless

ENLIGHTEN EXERCISE #1

Who Am I?

Complete the following intrapersonal questions, designed to answer the question, "Who am I?"

1. What physical or cognitive limitations might affect my ability to pursue my passions?

2. What limitations might affect my ability to manage my career?

3. What do I care deeply about?

4. What is my complete potential that allows me to be creative in all parts of life?

5. What are the elements that allow me to be fully creative in all parts of life?

6. What motivates and guides me through life?

7. What is my calling in life? Have I listened for it?

8. What am I meant to be doing in life?

9. What activities would give me a driving sense of purpose?

10. What am I doing that makes a difference to me?

11. What builds meaning and satisfaction for me?

12. When I look back, what impact do I want to have made on the world?

ENLIGHTEN EXERCISE #2

How Do Others See Me?

Complete the following intrapersonal questions designed to answer the question, "How do others see me?"

1. How do others perceive my style, strengths, and development areas?

2. How accurate are my perceptions about my strengths and development areas, compared to the perceptions of others?

3. In what ways am I misunderstood?

4. How do the ways I act and behave contribute to the impressions I create?

5. How might my supporters view me?

6. How might my critics view me?

7. What strengths of mine, when overused, could be perceived to be liabilities by others?

8. How would I describe my interpersonal style or personality?

9. In what areas would I like to learn more about how others perceive me?

ENLIGHTEN EXERCISE #3

My Personal Balance Sheet

A balance sheet is used in business, but you can also apply this concept to evaluating yourself. Use the form below to create your own Personal Balance Sheet.

My Assets	My Liabilities
My signature strengths (skills and abilities I do well, and others agree I do them well).	My weaknesses (skills and abilities I don't do very well).
My potential strengths (skills and abilities I could develop further).	My development opportunities (skills and abilities I am motivated to improve).
My personality strengths (traits, styles, and habits that help me to be successful).	My personality liabilities (traits, styles, and habits that sometimes can get in the way of my success or, if overused, become liabilities).

ENLIGHTEN EXERCISE #4

My Success Scorecard

This scorecard is a way to look at personal and life success from a more balanced perspective. These four areas form the basic structure of what people try to gain through the pursuit and enjoyment of success. What actions will you take to maximize each of the four below?

Happiness: Feelings of pleasure and positive emotions and the absence of negative emotionality and acceptance of current work and life situations.	**Achievement**: Identifying and deploying signature strengths and a sense of meaningful accomplishment at work and life activities.
Relationships: Maximizing positive social exchanges with meaningful others in your life and giving back to community, family, and others.	**Legacy and Meaning:** Defining your personal mission, values, and meaning in life.

ENLIGHTEN EXERCISE #5

Organizational Assessment:
What Are My Options?

Complete the following interpersonal questions designed to answer the question, "What are my options within or outside the organization?"

1. What pace of work do I prefer?

2. Who can I turn to for advice, mentoring, coaching, and honest feedback?

3. What type of work environment is the most satisfying to me?

4. How would I describe our organizational culture (norms and acceptable behaviors)?

5. What external threats exist to the future of the organization?

6. What are the technological or social trends influencing the organization that may create changes in personnel, policies, and procedures in the future?

7. How can my manager or others help me in my career?

8. What community and volunteer opportunities can I get more involved in?

9. What training and development opportunities exist within and outside the organization?

10. What opportunities exist for me to enhance specific skills and acquire new knowledge?

11. What are the positions that are most interesting to me

ENLIGHTEN EXERCISE #6

Do It Now

"Someday, I'd like to do this…" is a common mantra for many of us. "Someday, I will hike Half Dome." "Someday, I will start my own business." "Someday, I will take a class to improve my skills."

Life isn't a dress rehearsal. Live each day as if it is your last, for one day, it will be.

Exercise:

List five things you have been procrastinating about doing and plan to take some action on at least one of them this week:

1.

2.

3.

4.

5.

ENLIGHTEN EXERCISE #7

My Life 10 Years From Now

Think about yourself 10 years in the future. Visualize what your work and life will be like at that time.

In 20____, I will be _____ years old.

If I am working, I am:

The friends, family members, and people I will be close to are:

My biggest accomplishments and the things I am most proud about are:

My recreation, leisure, and fun activities in a typical week include:

My health would be described as:

My friends would describe me in the following way:

Things I am doing to help others:

My goal(s) for the next 10 years are:

174

ENLIGHTEN EXERCISE #8

How I Cope with Work and Life Stress

All of us react to stress based on the situation and our personality or style. Use the questions below to summarize how you typically respond to work and life stress, pressure, and challenge. Which techniques do you typically use when you are under stress (*check all that apply to you)?*

Positive Appraisal

❏ Look at things optimistically, rather than pessimistically.

❏ Use humor in the situation to lessen the impact of the stress.

❏ Emphasize the advantages, benefits, and consequences.

❏ Focus on happier times and situations.

❏ Use positive self-talk and avoid catastrophic thinking.

Negative Appraisal

❏ Focus on the worst-case scenario.

❏ Blame and criticize yourself.

❏ Bring it up and talk about it excessively without closure.

❏ Blame and criticize the situation or others for the problem.

❏ Avoid dealing with the situation all together.

❏ Shut out and repress emotions to avoid the hurt and pain.

Problem-focused Coping

❏ Get exercise to clear my mind and get energized.

❏ Seek social support to express my feelings and emotions.

❏ Take charge of the things I can control.

❏ Seek spiritual guidance or use my beliefs to get through the stressful situation.

❏ Seek information to better understand my issues and challenges.

❏ Get adequate sleep to energize my battery.

❏ Give gratitude for what I have in life.

❏ Practice forgiveness with others.

ENLIGHTEN EXERCISE #9

Focus on the Now

"Live each day as if it is the last, for one day, it will be." - Anonymous

1. Multiply your age times 365 days (*your age in number of days*):

2. Subtract that number from 27,421 days (*average life span*[1]):

I have about _____ days left.

[1]Center for Disease Control estimate of the average life span in the U.S. is 77.9 years (both sexes)

ENLIGHTEN EXERCISE #10

My Ethical Core

How would you describe your ethical core (which drives the way you work and live)? What choices do you make each day when nobody is around that provide a sense of your level of honesty, integrity, and ethics?

Ethics Questions:

1. You come to a four-way stoplight very late night. It is taking a long time to change. No one is coming in any of the directions as far as you can see. What do you do?

2. You are at an ATM at 11 p.m. No one is around at all. You request $60 from your account. You receive $100, but your receipt shows only the requested $60.00. What do you do?

3. You are an air cargo pilot. There has been a tragic industrial chemical spill 450 miles away from where you are in a remote location. You have been asked to deliver the only known antidote to the location. It must be delivered in 2 hours, or hundreds of workers will die. You are on route and less than an hour away from your destination when you receive a phone call. Your 10-year-old child has been in a terrible accident. You are the child's only known source of blood supply. The doctors at the scene give the child less than three hours to live without your blood donation. Do you continue on or do you turn around? (There are no other options).

Enlighten References

Arthur, W., Day, E. A., McNelly, T. & Edens, P. (2003). A meta-analysis of the criterion related validity of assessment center dimensions, *Personnel Psychology, 56,* 125-153.

Atwater, L., Ostroff, C., Yammarino, F. & Fleenor, J. (1998). Self-other agreement: Does it really matter? *Personnel Psychology, 51,* 577-598.

Atwater, L. A., Waldman, D., Atwater, D. & Cartier (2000). An upward feedback field experiment. Supervisors' cynicism, follow-up and commitment to subordinates. *Personnel Psychology, 53,* 275-297.

Atwater. L., Wang, M., Smither J. & Fleenor J. (2009). Are cultural characteristics associated with the relationship between self and others' ratings of leadership? *Journal of Applied Psychology, 94,* 876-886.

Atwater, L. & Brett, J. (2006). 360 degree feedback to managers: Does it result in changes in employee attitudes? *Group & Organizational Management, 31,* 578-600.

Atwater, L., Brett, J. & Charles, A. (2007). Multisource feedback: Lessons learned and implications for practice. *Human Resource Management. 46,* 285-387.

Bandalos, D. L. & Enders, C. K. (1996). The effects of non-normality and number of response categories on reliability. *Applied Measurement in Education, 9,* 151-160.

Belkic, K., Landsbergis, P., Schnall, P., Baker, D., Theiorell, T., Siegrist, J., Peter, R. & Karasek, R. (2000). Pscyhosocial factors: Review of the empirical data among men. *Occupational Medicine: State of the Art Reviews, 15,* 24-46.

Bono, J. E., Purvanova, R. K., Towler, A. J. & Peterson, D. B. (2009). A Survey of Executive Coaching Practices. *Personnel Psychology, 62,* 361-404.

Bono, J. & Colbert, A. (2005). Understanding responses to multi-source feedback: The role of core self-evaluations. *Personnel Psychology, 58,* 171-203.

Borders, A., Jajodia, A. & Earleywine, M. (2010). Could mindfulness decreaseanger, hostility, and aggression by decreasing rumination? *Aggressive Behavior, 36,* 28-44.

Bracken, D. W. & Rose, D. S. (2011). When does 360-degree feedback create behavior change? And how would we know it when it does? *Journal of Business and Psychology, 26,* 183-192.

Brett, J. & Atwater, L. (2001). 360-degree feedback: Accuracy, reactions and perceptions of usefulness. *Journal of Applied Psychology, 86,* 930–942.

Brown, K. W. & Richard, M. (2003). The benefits of being present: Mindfulness and its role in psychological well-being. *Journal of Personality and Social Psychology*, 84, 822-848.

Chen, Z., Williams, K., Fitness, J. & Newton, N. (2008). When hurt will not heal.Exploring the capacity to relive social and physical pain. *Psychological Perspectives, 19*, 789-795.

Cherniss, C. (2010). Emotional intelligence: Toward a clarification of a concept. *Industrial and Organizational Psychology Perspectives on Science and Practice, 3*, 110-126.

Conway, J. M., Lombardo, K., & Sanders, K. C. (2001). A meta-analysis of incremental validity and nomological networks for subordinate and peer ratings. *Human Performance, 14*, 267–303.

Cools, W., Hofmans, J., & Theuns, P. (2006). Context in category scales: Is "fully agree" equal to twice agree? *European Review of Applied Psychology, 56*, 223-229.

Conway, J. & Huffcutt, A. (1997). Psychometric properties of multi-source performance ratings: A meta-analysis of subordinate, supervisor, peer and self-ratings. *Human Performance, 10*, 331–360.

Dewall, C. N., MacDonald, G., Webster, G. D., Masten, C. L., Baumeister, R. F., Powell, C., Combs, D., Schurtz, D. R., Stillman, T. F., Tice, D. M. & Eisenberger, N. I. (2010). Acetaminophen reduces social pain: Behavioral and neural evidence. *Psychological Science, 21*, 931-937.

Dickerson, S. & Kemeny, M. (2004). Acute stressors and cortisol responses: A theoretical integration and synthesis of laboratory research. *Psychological Bulletin, 30*, 355-391.

Dweck, C. & Leggett, E. (1988). A social-cognitive approach to motivation and personality. *Psychological Review, 95*, 256-273.

Eckert, R., Ekelund, B., Gentry, W. & Dawson, J. (2010). I don't see me like you see me but is that a problem? Cultural differences in rating discrepancy in 360-degree feedback instruments. *European Journal of Work and Organizational Psychology, 19*, 259-278.

Ehrlinger, J. (2008). Skill level, self-views and self-theories as sources of error in self-assessment. *Social and Personality Psychology Compass, 2*, 382-398.

Eisenberger, N. I., Lieberman, M. D. & Williams, K. D. (2003). Does rejection hurt? An fMRI study of social exclusion. *Science, 302*, 290–292.

English, A., Rose, D. & McClellan, J. (2009). Rating Scale Label Effects on Leniency Bias in 360-degree Feedback. Paper presented at the 24th Annual Meeting of the Society for Industrial Organizational Psychologist. New Orleans, LA.

Facteau, J. D. & Craig, S. B. (2001). Are performance appraisal ratings obtained from different rating sources comparable? *Journal of Applied Psychology, 86,* 215–227.

Fleenor, J., Taylor, S. & Chappelow, C. (2008). Leveraging the Impact of 360-degree Feedback. New York: John Wiley & Sons.

3d Group (2009). *Current practices in 360-degree feedback: A benchmark study of North American Companies.* 3D Group Technical Report #8326. Berkeley, CA: Data Driven Decisions, Inc.

Goldsmith, M. (2006). The Impact of Direct Report Feedback and Follow-Up on Leadership. Unpublished manuscript. www.marshallgoldsmith.com/articles

Gosling, S. D., John, O. P., Craik, K. & Robins, R. W. (1998). Do people know how they behave? Self-reported act frequencies compared with on-line codings by observers. *Journal of Personality and Social Psychology, 74,* 41–61.

Greguras, G. J. & Robie, C. (1995). A new look at within-rater source interrater reliability of 360-degree feedback ratings. *Journal of Applied Psychology, 83,* 960–968.

Harris, M. & Schaubroeck, J. (1988). A meta-analysis of self-supervisor, self-peer, and peer-supervisor ratings. *Personnel Psychology, 41,* 43–62.

Heidemeier, H. & Moser, K. (2009). Self-other agreement in job performance ratings: A meta-analytics test of a process model. *Journal of Applied Psychology, 94,* 353-370.

Hirsh, J. B. & Inzlicht, H. (2008). The devil you know: Neuroticism predicts neural response to uncertainty. *Psychological Science, 19,* 962-967.

Hoffman, B., Lance, C. E., Bynum, B. & Gentry, W. (2010). Rater source effects are alive and well after all. *Personnel Journal, 63,* 119-151.

Hogan, J., Hogan, J. & Kaiser, R. (2011). Management derailment. *APA handbook of industrial and organizational psychology,* 3: Maintaining, expanding, and contracting the organization, APA Handbooks in Psychology (pp. 555-575).

Hogan, R. & Kaiser, R. (2005). What we know about leadership. Review of *General Psychology, 9,* 169-180.

Hölzel, B., Carmody, J., Vangel, M., Congleton, C., Yerramsetti, S., Gard, T. & Lazar, S.W. (2011). Mindfulness practice leads to increases in regional brain gray matter density. *Psychiatry Research Neuroimaging, 191,* 36-43.

Hooijberg, R. & Lane, N. (2009). Using multisource feedback coaching effectively in executive education. *Academy of Management Learning & Education, 8,* 483-493.

Hyman, D. J., Pavlik, V. N., Taylor, W. C., Goodrich, G. K. & Moye, L. (2007). Simultaneous versus sequential counseling for multiple behavioral change. *Archives of Internal Medicine, 167,* 1152-1158.

Kaiser, R. B. & Overfield, D. V. (2011). Strengths, strengths overused, and lopsided leadership. Consulting Psychology Journal: Practice and Research, 63, 67-88.

Kivimäki, M., Ferrie, J., Brunner, E., Head, J., Shipley, M., Vahtera, J. & Marmot, M. (2005). Justice at Work and Reduced Risk of Coronary Heart Disease Among Employees: The Whitehall Study. Archives of Internal Medicine, 165, 2245-2251.

Kluger, A. N. & DeNisi, A. (1996). The effects of feedback interventions on performance: A historical review, a meta-analysis, and a preliminary feedback theory. Psychological Bulletin, 119, 254-284.

Ilgen, D. & Davis, C. (2000). Bearing bad news: Reactions to negative performance feedback. Applied Psychology: An international Review, 49, 550-565.

Ilies, R., Judge, T. A. & Wagner, D. T. (2010). The influence of cognitive and affective reactions to feedback on subsequent goals: Role of behavioral inhibition/activation. European Psychologist, 15, 121-131.

Joo, B. (2005). Executive Coaching: A conceptual framework from an integrative review of practice and research. Human Resource Development Review, 4, 462-488.

Jordan, P. J. & Ashkanasy, N. M. (2006). Emotional Intelligence, emotional Self-Awareness, and Team Effectiveness. In V. U. Druskat, F. Sala and G. Mount (Ed.), Linking Emotional Intelligence and Performance at Work: Current Research Evidence with Individuals and Groups (pp. 145-163). Mahwah, New Jersey: Lawrence Erlbaum Associates.

Judge, T., Picolo, R. & Kosalka, T. (2009). The bright and dark sides of leader traits: A review and theoretical extension of the leader trait paradigm. The Leadership Quarterly, 20, 855-875.

Judge, T. A. & Ilies, R. (2002). Relationship of personality to performance motivation: A meta-analytic review. Journal of Applied Psychology, 87, 797-807.

Kaplan, R. & Kaiser, R. (2009). Stop overdoing your strengths. Harvard Business Review. February 2009, 100-103.

Kaptchuk, T. J., Stason, W. B., Davis, R. B., Legedza, A. R., Schyer, R., Kerr, C. E., Stone, D. A, Nam, B. H., Kirsch, I. & Goldman, R. H. (2006). Sham device versus inert pill: a randomized controlled trial comparing two placebo treatments for arm pain due to repetitive strain injury. British Medical Journal, 332, 291-297.

Kilburg, R. (2006). Wisdom Mapping I: Self and Family Awareness. Executive Wisdom: Coaching and the emergence of virtuous leaders. The Psychologist-Manager Journal, 10, 145-167.

Kluger, A. & DeNisi (1996). The effects of feedback interventions on performance: A historical review, meta-analysis and preliminary feedback theory. *Psychological Bulletin, 119,* 254-285.

Koo, M. & Fishbach, A. (2010). Climbing the goal ladder: How upcoming actions increase level of aspiration. *Journal of Personality and Social Psychology, 99,* 1-13.

Kruger, J. & Dunning, D. (1999). Unskilled and unaware of it: How difficulties in recognizing one's own incompetence lead to inflated self-assessments. *Journal of Personality and Social Psychology, 77,* 1121-1134.

Lance, C. E., Hoffman, B. J., Gentry, W. & Baranik, L. E. (2008). Rater source factors represent important subcomponents of the criterion construct space, not rater bias. *Human Resources Management Review, 18,* 223-232.

Lozano, L. M., Garcia-Cueto, E. & Muniz, J. (2008). Effect of the number of response categories on the reliability and validity of rating scales. *European Journal of Research Methods for the Behavioral and Social Sciences, 4,* 73-79.

Luft, J. & Ingham, H. (1995). The Johari window, a graphic model of interpersonal awareness. Precedings of the western training Laboratory in group development. Los Angeles, UCLA.

McClelland, D. C. (1961). The Achieving Society. NY: Van Nostrand.

Morgeson, F. P., Mumford, T. V. & Campion, M. A. (2005). Coming full circle: Using research and practice to address 27 questions about 360-degree feedback programs. *Consulting Psychology Journal: Practice and Research, 57, 3,* 196-209.

Ng, K. Y., Koh, C., Kennedy, J. & Chan, K. Y. (2011). Rating leniency and halo in multisource feedback ratings: Testing cultural assumptions of power distance and individualism-collectivism. *Journal of Applied Psychology,* 96, 1033-1044

Nieman-Gonder, J. (2006). The effect of rater selection on rating accuracy. Poster presented at the 21st Annual Conference of the Society for Industrial and Organizational Psychology, May 2006, Dallas, TX.

Nowack, K. (1992). Self-assessment and rater assessment as a dimension of management development. *Human Resources Development Quarterly, 3,* 141–155.

Nowack, K. (1993). 360 Degree feedback: The whole story. *Training & Development Journal, 47,* 69-72.

Nowack, K. (1997). Congruence Between Self and Other Ratings and Assessment Center Performance. *Journal of Social Behavior and Personality, 12,* 145-166.

Wimer, S. & Nowack, K. (1998). Thirteen common mistakes in implementing multi-rater feedback systems. *Training and Development, 52,* 69-80.

Nowack, K. (1999a). 360 Degree feedback. Intervention: 50 Performance Technology Tools San Francisco, Jossey-Bass, Inc., 34-46.

Nowack, K., Hartley, J. & Bradley, W. (1999b). Evaluating results of your 360-degree feedback intervention. *Training and Development, 53,* 48-53

Nowack, K. (2000). Occupational stress management: Effective or not?. In P. Schnall, K. Belkie, P. Landensbergis, & D. Baker (Eds.), Occupational Medicine: State of the Art Reviews, (pp. 231-233). Hanley and Belfus, Inc., Philadelphia, PA.

Nowack, K. (2002). Does 360 Degree Feedback Negatively Effect Company Performance: Feedback Varies With Your Point of View. HR Magazine, 47 (6).

Nowack, K. (2003). Executive Coaching: Fad or Future? *California Psychologist, 36,* 16-17.

Nowack, K. (2005). Longitudinal evaluation of a 360 degree feedback program: Implications for best practices. Paper presented at the 20th Annual Conference of the Society for Industrial and Organizational Psychology, Los Angeles, March 2005.

Nowack, K. (2006). Optimising Employee Resilience: Coaching to Help Individuals Modify Lifestyle. *Stress News, International Journal of Stress Management, 18,* 9-12.

Nowack, K. (2006). Emotional intelligence: Leaders Make a Difference. *HR Trends, 17,* 40-42.

Nowack, K. (2007). Why 360-Degree Feedback Doesn't Work. *Talent Management, 3,* 12.

Nowack, K. (2008). Coaching for Stress: StressScan. Editor: Jonathan Passmore, Psychometrics. In Coaching (pp. 254-274). Association for Coaching, UK.

Nowack, K. (2009). Leveraging Multirater Feedback to Facilitate Successful Behavioral Change. *Consulting Psychology Journal: Practice and Research, 61,* 280-297.

Nowack, K. (2011). Talent Accelerator Case Study: Leveraging the Impact of 360 Feedback. *Unpublished Manuscript, Santa Monica, Envisia Learning. Inc.*

Oh, I. & Berry, C. M. (2009). The five-factor model of personality and managerial performance: Validity gains through the use of 360 degree performance ratings. *Journal of Applied Psychology, 94,* 1498-1513.

Olivero, G., Bane, D. & Kopelman, R. (1997). Executive coaching as a transfer of training tool: Effects on productivity in a public agency. *Public Personnel Management, 26,* 461–469.

Palmer, S. (2003). Health coaching to facilitate the promotion of healthy behaviour and achievement of health-related goals. *International Journal of Health Promotion & Education, 41,* 91-93.

Penny, J. (2003). Exploring differential item functioning in a 360-degree assessment: Rater source and method of delivery. Organizational Research Methods, 6, 61-79

Pfau, B. & Kay, I. (2002). Does 360-degree feedback negatively affect company performance? *HR Magazine, 47*, 55-59.

Porr, D. & Fields, D. (2006). Implicit leadership effects on multi-source ratings for management development. *Journal of Managerial Psychology, 21*, 651–668.

Preston, C.C. & Colman, A.M. (2000). Optimal number of response categories in rating scales: Reliability, validity, discriminating power, and respondent preferences. *Acta Psychologica, 104*, 1-15.

Rehbine, N. (2007). *The iimpact of 360-degree feedback on leadership development. Unpublished doctoral dissertation, Capella University.*

Rock, D. (2008). SCARF: A brain based model for collaborating with and influencing others. *Neuroleaderhip Journal, 1*, 1-9.

Rehbine, N. (2007). The impact of 360-degree feedback on leadership development. *Unpublished doctoral dissertation, Capella University.*

Reilly, R. R., Smither, J. W. & Vasilopoulos, N. L. (1996). A longitudinal study of upward feedback. *Personnel Psychology, 49*, 599-612.

Robie, S., Kaster, K., Nilsen, D. & Hazucha, J. (2000). The right stuff: Understanding cultural differences in leadership Performance. *Unpublished Manuscript, Personnel Decisions, Inc.*

Sedikides, C. & Gregg, A. (2003). Self-enhancement: Food for thought. *Perspectives on Psychological Science, 3*, 102–116.

Shipper, F., Hoffman, R. & Rotondo, D. (2007). Does the 360 feedback process create actionable knowledge equally across cultures? *Academy of Management Learning & Education, 6*, 33-50.

Siefert, C., Yukl, G. & McDonald, R. (2003). Effects of multisource feedback and a feedback facilitator on the influence of behavior of managers toward subordinates. *Journal of Applied Behavior, 88*, 561-569.

Smith, P., Mustard, F. & Bondy, S. (2007). Examining the relationship between job control and health status: A path analysis approach. Journal of *Epidemiology & Community Health, 62*, 54-61.

Smither, J., London, M. & Reilly, R. (2005). Does performance improve following multisource feedback? A theoretical model, meta-analysis, and review of empirical findings. *Personnel Psychology, 58*, 33–66.

Smither, J., London, M., Flautt, R., Vargas, Y. & Kucine, I. (2003). Can working with an executive coach improve multisource feedback ratings over time? A quasi-experimental field study. *Personnel Psychology, 56*, 23–44.

Smither, J., London, M. & Richmond, K. (2005). The relationship between leaders' personality and their reactions to and use of multisource feedback: A longitudinal study. Group & Organizational Behaviors, 30, 181-210.

Smither, J. & Walker, A. G. (2004). Are the characteristics of narrative comments related to improvement in multi-rater feedback ratings over time? *Personnel Psychology, 89*, 575-581.

Smither, J. Walker, A. & Yap, M. (2004). An examination of web based versus paper and pencil upward feedback ratings. *Educational and Psychological Measurement, 64*, 40-61.

Smither, J., Brett, J. & Atwater, L. (2008). What do leaders recall about multi- source feedback? Journal of Leadership and Organization Studies, 14, 202-218.

Taylor, S. E. & Brown, J. D. (1988). Illusion and well-being: A social psychological perspective on mental health. *Psychological Bulletin, 103*, 193–210.

Taylor, P., Taylor, H. & Russ-Eft, D. Transfer of management training from alternate perspectives. *Journal of Applied Psychology, 94,* 104-121.

Thach, E. (2002). The impact of executive coaching and 360-feedback on leadership effectiveness. *Leadership and Organization Development Journal, 23*, 205–214.

Weng, L. (2004). Impact of the number of response categories and anchor labels on coefficient alpha and test-retest reliability. *Educational and Psychological Measurement, 64*, 956-972.

Viswanathan, M., Bergen, M., Dutta, S. & Childres, T. (1996). Does a single response category in a scale completely capture a response? *Psychology & Marketing, 13*, 457-479.

Woehr, D. J., Sheehan, M. K. & Bennett, W., Jr. (2005). Assessing measurement equivalence across rating sources: A multitrait–multi-rater approach. *Journal of Applied Psychology, 90*, 592–600.

Zeidan, F., Johnson, S. K., Diamond, B. J., David, Z. & Goolkasian, P. (2010). Mindfulness meditation improves cognition: Evidence of brief mental training. *An International Journal,* 2, 597-605.

PART III:

Encourage

Things do not change, we change.

HENRY DAVID THOREAU

ENCOURAGE

Introduction:

Now That I Know Who I Am—Am I *Really* Ready for Change?

In the previous *Enlighten* section, we introduced a variety of exercises and techniques individuals can use to become more aware of their interpersonal style, personality, interests, values, social support, signature strengths, and potential development areas. As we have discussed, self-insight/self-awareness is a *necessary, but not sufficient, condition* for behavioral change. Too many times, we have been given feedback by others only to view it as incorrect, biased, judgmental, unfair, or simply inaccurate. In these cases we tend to react defensively and have little or no motivation to want to modify our own behaviors. Unless there is willingness and motivation to translate awareness into the deliberate practice of new behaviors, feedback only helps us to become more enlightened if we truly understand and accept the information shared with us. For example, we may learn that our blood pressure is dangerously high, but modifying our diet and exercising may not be something we are really committed to practice on a daily basis.

This *Encourage* section is about the process by which clients' motivation to change behavior is assessed and influenced to enable greater *readiness* to modify existing habits and patterns. During this stage, the coach determines whether the client is ready to move forward and the amount of effort he or she is willing to exert. In addition to assessing motivation, determining a client's readiness to change should also include a consideration of any personality factors that could potentially derail the behavioral change process.

The coach also encourages motivation by helping the client envision the benefits of successful behavioral change, sometimes called a "What's-In-It-For-Me" (WIFM) approach by using a coaching technique called *Motivational Interviewing (MI)*. Motivational Interviewing is a structured approach that coaches can use to enhance client motivation and commitment to action. MI describes techniques for discussing the differences between the personal outcomes that can be achieved by the client's current behaviors and those that can be achieved by his or her ideal behaviors. In that sense, it is a means of exploring the WIFMs, as well as exploring the obstacles to achieving the client's goals. One of the advantages to MI is that it is a collaborative, non-directive approach and is therefore more likely to lead to sustained behavioral change efforts (Passmore, 2007).

Another technique used in the *Encourage* stage is to utilize an individual *change model or theory* to help the client better understand the typical stages that individuals progress through in a behavioral change effort. Once the coach and client have chosen an appropriate method, they can provide a structured process for reviewing the feedback, ask reflective questions that increase motivation, and identify one or more competencies or specific actions to further develop. In order to accomplish this, coaches must be able to connect with their clients in a manner that motivates and inspires behavioral change. One simple approach to establishing this rapport is to tell relevant stories and link them back to an individual behavioral change model. For example, in my own coaching practice, clients are particularly motivated when they can relate to someone who has successfully overcome similar work and life challenges and obstacles.

Once coaches have assessed readiness and motivation levels, they can help the client identify next steps in the development journey (i.e., translating goal intentions to actual implementation). At this point, coaches and clients must reach an agreement in order to proceed with goal implementation stage. If the client is not ready to change behavior, coaching might not be totally effective or even appropriate, unless the terminal goals are entirely to enhance insight and self-awareness. With unmotivated clients, coaches have to ask some important questions before they move ahead with the behavioral change intervention, such as:

- Does the client possess an adequate environmental support system?
- Would another coach be more effective to motivate the client?
- Is the client's personality contributing to resistance, defensiveness, a lack of confidence to change, or an inability to handle ambiguity and challenges along the way?
- Does the client have a record of prior failure in the behavioral goal they are tackling that might lead to diminished self-esteem and self-efficacy (e.g., weight loss)?

Whatever the reason, it may be necessary to come to terms with the situation *before* attempting to proceed with a potentially frustrating and futile process of behavioral change coaching. So, let's take a look at ways to assess the motivation to change in our clients and then how to move them along a readiness continuum to the actual implementation of specific and measurable development goals.

Factoid: New Year's Resolutions by the Numbers

1. Nearly four out of 10 adults will make one or more resolutions for the New Year, according to a study done by the University of Scranton.

2. After the first week of carrying out the goal, about 75 percent of people maintain their goal.

3. After week two, nearly 70 percent of people will maintain their goal.

4. After one month, about 64 percent will stick with their resolution.

5. After six months, about 46 percent of people are still on track with their goal.

Norcross, Mrykalo & Blagys, (2002)

Chapter 8:

Assessing Readiness to Change Behavior

"A man is but the product of his thoughts. What he thinks, he becomes.

MAHATMA GHANDI

People only change behavior when they are sufficiently *motivated* to do so. The challenge, of course, is how to help clients who aren't motivated in the first place to increase their level of *readiness* to change and for those who are somewhat motivated to enhance their commitment to specific goals and actions.

One useful model that focuses specifically on the continuum of individual motivation to change behavior is called the Transtheoretical model of behavioral change (TTM). It offers some insight and suggestions for coaches about how to move client's from a state of being completely unmotivated to a commitment of action as well as a client's decision making processes.

Transtheoretical Model of Readiness to Change

In order to assess whether clients are ready to change, coaches may *first* need to understand the process by which change occurs. Prochaska & DiClemente's Transtheoretical Model (1983) has become a classic way of conceptualizing how individuals initiate change. It takes into account that most individuals do not change in a linear fashion but rather in a spiral in which relapse is fairly common for most complicated behavioral change efforts. The Transtheoretical Model outlines behavioral change as a process involving progress through a series of five "readiness" stages described below:

1. *Precontemplation* is the stage in which people are not intending to take action in the foreseeable future, usually measured as the next six months. People may be in this stage because they are uninformed or under-informed about the consequences of their behavior, or they may have tried to change a number of times and become demoralized about their ability to change. Both groups tend to avoid reading, talking, or thinking about their high-risk behaviors. They are often characterized in other theories as resistant or unmotivated, or as not ready for health promotion programs. The fact is, traditional health promotion programs are often not designed for such individuals and are not matched to their needs.

2. *Contemplation* is the stage in which people are intending to make some behavioral change efforts in the next six months. They are more aware of the pros of change but are also acutely aware of the cons. This balance between the costs and benefits of change can produce profound ambivalence that can keep people stuck in this stage for long periods of time (chronic contemplation or behavioral procrastination). These people are also not ready for traditional, action-oriented programs.

3. *Preparation* is the stage in which people are intending to take action in the immediate future, usually measured as the next month. They have typically taken some significant action in the past year. These individuals have developed a plan of

action, such as joining a health education class, consulting a counselor, talking to a physician, buying a self-help book, or relying on a self-change approach. For example, these are the people that should be easily recruited for action-oriented leadership development, executive coaching, weight loss, or exercise programs.

4. *Action* is the stage in which people have made specific, overt modifications in their lifestyle practices within the past six months. Since action is observable, behavioral change often has been equated with action. But in the Transtheoretical Model, action is only one of five stages. The *action* stage is also the stage where vigilance against relapse is critical.

5. *Maintenance* is the stage in which people are working to prevent relapse, but they do not apply change processes as frequently as do people in action. They are less tempted to relapse and increasingly more confident that they can continue their change efforts over a specific period of time.

6. *Relapse* is often discussed as a distinct stage characterized by lapses and often full-blown relapses back to old behaviors. Some individuals rely primarily on change processes that have to do with contemplation and self-revaluation while they move into the action stage. They try to modify their behaviors by becoming more aware and gaining insight. Other individuals rely primarily on change processes that enable them to take action, without insight and awareness. These individuals may seem ready to change because they are taking action; however their lack of awareness may be likely to lead to temporary change (Prochaska, DiClemente, & Norcross, 1992). Awareness is one of the key elements that are vital for successful behavioral change (Nowack & Heller,

2001). Clients must know what it is about their behavior that is hindering their maximum potential before they can take action.

Figure 3-1
Transtheoretical Model (TTM)

Envisia Learning Change Model	Transtheoretical Model (TTM)	What Happens in This Stage?	What Does the Coach Do?
ENLIGHTEN	Pre-contemplation	Client does not perceive there is a problem.	Coach provides feedback.
	Contemplation	Client becomes aware of the problem.	Coach raises awareness.
ENCOURAGE	Preparation	Client recognizes the problem and intends to change the behavior.	Self-efficacy is nurtured in this stage. Commitment, motivation, and belief in ability to change are present.
ENABLE	Action	Client takes action consistently.	Reinforcement is needed through coaching and mentoring. Successes need to be recognized, even if the success is only an attempt and not yet evident.
	Maintenance	Client maintains behavior for a certain period of time (i.e. three months).	Coach helps client understand what helps him or her maintain behavior in order to keep it going.
	Relapse	Client may return to the old habits due to intrapersonal and environmental stressors and lack of social support.	Coach takes client back to first stage again, until change becomes consistent.

The coach can use the TTM model to set expectations and facilitate the client through the change process. In particular, the TTM *Preparation* stage of this model overlaps with our *Encourage* stage, where the client prepares for goal setting and action.

Decisional Balance Force Field Analysis

One technique coaches can use to evaluate and modify change readiness is using the decisional balance Force Field analysis developed by Kurt Lewin. It states that change results from competition between *driving* and *restraining* forces (Dorn, 2008). It identifies forces that help reach the desired outcome and those that hinder that process. Driving forces can be thought of as problems or opportunities that provide motivation for change within the organization. Restraining forces are the various barriers to change.

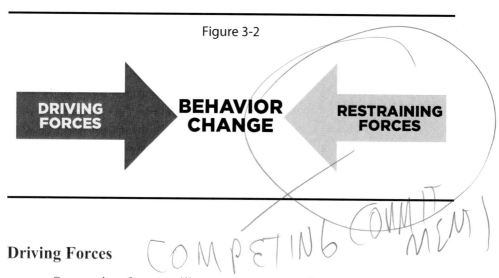

Figure 3-2

DRIVING FORCES → BEHAVIOR CHANGE ← RESTRAINING FORCES

COMPETING COMMITMENT

Driving Forces

Supporting forces will encourage your client to succeed in your identified area of behavioral change. They tend to help initiate change and keep momentum over time. Support could come from your client's manager and/or peers, but it could also be their own internal motivation to succeed in a new endeavor.

Restraining Forces

When considering the Force Field Analysis, Newton's third law of motion comes to mind: *"To every action, there is an equal and opposite reaction."* For each supporting force, there is likely to be an opposite force that serves to impede behavioral change. These preventing forces could come from your client's work environment or could be internal to their cognitive self-talk or attributional style. Force Field analysis focuses on ways of reducing the hindering forces and encouraging the positive ones. Force Field Analysis encourages agreement and reflection, through discussion of the underlying causes of a problem.

The decisional balance Force Field Analysis can help coaches weigh client resistances against motivations of achieving change. The table below can help guide coaches in a step-by-step procedure of facilitating the decisional balance Force Field Analysis.

Figure 3-3

Force Field Analysis

Envisia Learning Change Model	Force Field Analysis Steps	Facilitative Questions
ENLIGHTEN	**Step 1:** Defining the Problem	What is the nature of the current situation that is unacceptable and needs modification? It is useful to separate the specific problem from those things that are working well.
	Step 2: Defining the Change Objective	What is the desired situation that would be worth working toward? Be as specific as possible.
ENCOURAGE	**Step 3:** Identifying the Driving Forces	What are the factors or pressures that support change in the desired direction? What are the relative strengths of these forces? What are the inter-relationships among the driving forces?
	Step 4: Identifying the Restraining Forces	What are the factors or pressures that resist the proposed change and maintain the status quo? What are the inter-relationships among the restraining forces?
ENABLE	**Step 5:** Developing a Comprehensive Change Strategy	What can you do to strengthen and reinforce the "driving forces"? What can you do to remove or reduce any of the "restraining forces"?

Chapter 9:
Facilitating Motivation to Change Behavior

> "It is not the strongest of the species that survives, not the most intelligent, but the one most responsive to change.
>
> **CHARLES DARWIN**

As coaches, we all come across our clients' resistance and ambivalence toward progress. We often hear clear indicators of a lack of motivation to change. Do any of these statements sound familiar from conversations you have had with your coaching clients?

- *"Unless I am able to achieve my goal quickly and with little effort, it isn't worth pursuing."*

- *"I don't become motivated through threats and a fear of punishment!"*

- *"The professionals who preach change don't know what they are talking about."*

- *"My problem behavior is not a big deal; I am in control at all times. Why all the fuss?"*

- *"Change should be simple and easy to achieve; why am I having so much trouble?"*

- *"There must be something wrong with me."*

- *"The people around me constantly encourage me to change. It seems like I mean nothing to them unless I change."*

- *"The effort it takes to sustain change is too much; therefore, I will only work on attaining the change and leave sustaining the change for time to take care of."*

- *"If someone makes fun of or criticizes my efforts, I'll get demoralized and just give up."*

- *"For me to be successful, it is important for everyone to understand me and my need to change."*

- *"People should realize how hard it is for me to change; they should be more sympathetic."*

- *"My friend's health habits are worse than mine. He seems fine! No one is asking him to change."*

- *"Unless everyone supports me, I'll never succeed in changing."*

- *"Why are they making this so difficult? Are they using scare tactics to make me change?"*

- *"This 'change thing' is beginning to look like a plot by my manager who doesn't really understand me."*

- *"I've tried before and wasn't successful so why do you think I will succeed now?"*

Motivational Interviewing (MI) can help determine whether these types of comments represent a hindrance to change. There are two phases in Motivational Interviewing. The first phase involves *exploring ambivalence*, which includes building intrinsic motivation and self-efficacy for change. The second phase involves *strengthening the commitment to change* (Passmore & Tinwell, 2007).

200

Often, clients will demonstrate ambivalence when they feel reluctant to change. They may want to change, but they aren't deeply and intrinsically motivated. The coach's role is to help the client examine the "costs" and "benefits" of changing. This approach can lead the client to determine whether he or she feels it's worth it to continue with the behavioral change process.

Many coaches refer to "ballroom dancing" as a metaphor for Motivational Interviewing. Ballroom dancing can only occur when two people move together in a partnership. When done well, the movement unfolds through a series of subtle presses, or influences. As coaches, we do want to influence our clients to change, but we don't want to manipulate them into making changes that they are not ready for. Thus, the prescription for change must match the client's motivation level. A client that is very motivated may be willing to do more than a client that is moderately motivated (Passmore & Tinwell, 2007).

Factoid: Rehab is for Quitters

Psychologists Gregory Miller and Carsten Wrosch have found that when people quit unattainable goals, they may have better mental and physical health than those who persevere (Miller & Wrosch 2007). These findings build on previous research, which found that persistent individuals experienced higher levels of an inflammatory protein called C-reactive protein (an indicator of stress), as well as increased cortisol. They also reported lower psychological well-being.

Coaching Techniques for Effective Motivational Interviewing and Readiness Assessment

It is important for coaches to approach their clients in a non-judgmental manner, so those clients can appropriately identify their resistance. The following principles can help coaches increase a client's awareness about his or her resistance to change and, similarly, his or her motivation to change (Miller & Rollnick, 2002).

- *Express empathy,* by using reflective listening to convey an understanding of the client's point-of-view and underlying drives.
- *Develop the discrepancy* between the client's most deeply held values and current behavior.
- *Manage resistance,* by responding with empathy and understanding, rather than confrontation.
- *Support self-efficacy,* by building the client's confidence that change is possible.

Motivational Interviewing Case Study

Throughout the next section, we will review each of these techniques and encourage your application of them by utilizing the case study below to identify and overcome a client's ambivalence to change.

Chris is Senior Executive at a highly profitable manufacturing firm. He has a large team, and he seems to lack the interpersonal and leadership skills needed to fully engage and empower them based on his recent performance evaluation and 360-degree feedback results. Feedback from his manager and team indicate that he does not demonstrate a highly participative or involvement-oriented leadership style, does not solicit input from others, and does not involve his team in problem solving, decision making, or planning.

He is perceived to be highly defensive when constructive suggestions are given to him. In fact, when an external coach hired by the company met with Chris to review his 360-degree results with him, he demonstrated resistance toward changing any leadership practices and behaviors.

Motivational Interviewing Exercise #1:

Express Empathy Using OARS

Expressing empathy involves seeing the world through the client's eyes, thinking about things like the client thinks about them, feeling things like the client feels them, and sharing in the client's experiences. The expression of empathy is a critical element of Motivational Interviewing. When clients feel understood, they are better able to open up to their own motivations and resistance. The sharing of experiences allows coaches to assess when and where clients need support and what potential pitfalls clients can focus on. As a result, clients' defensiveness is disarmed, and they can actually accept their feelings of reluctance toward changing.

"OARS" is an acronym used to describe some of the *micro-skills* involved in expressing empathy with clients in a coaching intervention. "OARS" stands for *O*pen-ended questions, *A*ffirmations, *R*eflective listening, and *S*ummarizing. The most effective coaches tend to utilize the OARS technique as part of their coaching "toolbox" with their clients.

Directions: Practice applying each of the OARS micro-skills by writing a response you might have to Chris' statements below based on the case study presented earlier.

> <u>Chris:</u> *"I am completely surprised with my 360-degree feedback results. I have been one of the top performers in this department for many years so I can't really understand how nobody has shared any of these perceptions or issues with me before. I'm guessing that it's just a few critics that don't really reflect how the majority of my direct reports, peers and manager really view me."*

Open-ended Questions

Write an open-ended question in response to the statement that Chris made about his reaction to his 360-degree feedback results. Ensure you are asking questions in a way that allows Chris to open up.

Coach Response:

Affirmations

Write a response that ensures Chris feels valued and appreciated. Make sure you are providing positive reinforcement as you affirm Chris.

Coach Response:

Reflective Listening

Write a response that ensures Chris feels understood. Make sure you are seeking to clarify how Chris feels.

Coach Response:

Summarizing

Write a response that demonstrates that you have a clear understanding of Chris' situation. Summarize what you have understood in terms of the content of the conversation.

Coach Response:

Motivational Interviewing Exercise #2:

Identify Discrepancies

One important Motivational Interviewing skill is developing clients' awareness of the discrepancies between their current behaviors and ideal behaviors. By identifying and clarifying discrepancies, ambivalence and resistance are uncovered. Once clients see these discrepancies more clearly, they can begin to elicit change statements that enhance their motivation to want to initiate new behaviors.

Assessing discrepancies between clients' current states versus their future states can be illustrated through the use of *Motivational*

Rulers. This is a technique suggested by Miller and Rollnick (2002) that a coach can utilize to assess a client's stage of change. For example, motivation to change can be assessed by simply asking the client to rate the *perceived readiness to change* on a scale of 0 to 10, with 0 being "not at all interested in changing," and "10" meaning "they have already made the change." To assess *confidence to change,* a confidence "ruler" can be employed by the coach: "Why are you an X on the scale and not a zero?" "What would it take for you to go from X to a higher number?" Both of these "change rulers" help to elicit "change talk," which helps the client begin to see the advantages of initiating new behaviors and building confidence that can be successful over time.

Directions: In the space below, pose a question to Chris, utilizing either the readiness or confidence ruler to elicit "change talk", and explore in what way Chris feels a sense of control and optimism to succeed in his behavioral change efforts.

Identifying Discrepancies Exercise

Coach Response:

Motivational Interviewing Exercise #3:

Roll with Resistance

The role of the coach is not to confront or argue with a client's possible defensiveness or resistance to changing behavior but to "roll with it." Statements demonstrating resistance shouldn't be challenged! Instead, the coach can disarm this defensiveness by reflecting on the client's statements in a neutral way that validates the client's concerns. By using this approach, resistance decreases, as clients become less argumentative and less likely to play "devil's advocate" to the coach's suggestions. As a result, new perspectives are examined without imposing anything upon them.

Four techniques can be used to help clients move through resistance and increase their willingness to initiate or continue with successful change efforts. These include: 1) Reflection (seeking to understand your client's perspective through paraphrasing content and reflecting feelings expressed); 2) Shifting Focus (helping the client become solution focused through questions); 3) Agreement with a Twist (agreeing with your client and attempting to point out something they may have not fully considered or thought about); and 4) Reframing (suggesting a benefit or positive outcome of the behavioral change effort). Each of these when used strategically can be highly effective to help your client overcome potential barriers to implementing and sustaining new behaviors and practices.

Directions: Practice "rolling with resistance" by writing your responses to Chris' statements in the boxes below.

Chris: "If my staff demonstrated that they were competent, maybe I would be a bit more involvement oriented or participative and allow them to take the lead on decisions more frequently. Most are just too inexperienced or not motivated for me to trust they will come up with high quality decisions. I can't afford not to succeed at this stage of my career."

Figure 3-6

Reflection

Write a response that allows Chris to reflect on his resistant statements. For example, listen and summarize Chris' resistant statements in a way that conveys understanding and empathy of Chris' feelings.

Coach Response:

Shifting Focus

Write a response that helps Chris shift thoughts from obstacles and barriers to possible solutions.

Coach Response:

Agreement with a Twist

Write a response that demonstrates your agreement, with a slight twist, that moves the discussion forward.

Coach Response:

Reframing

Write a statement to reframe Chris' view by focusing on potential benefits or positive outcomes of behavior change.

Coach Response:

Motivational Interviewing Exercise #4:

Support Self-Efficacy for Change Talk

As clients are held responsible for choosing and carrying out actions necessary for change, coaches can help them focus on staying motivated by reinforcing and supporting their sense of self-efficacy and self-esteem. It's quite simple: If the client truly believes he or she can and will change, then he or she will. For example, the coach might remind the client about other successes he or she has made recently or explore his/her way of explaining previous successes.

Directions: Demonstrate this technique by writing sentences that would support Chris' self-efficacy in the boxes below.

Identify Signature Strengths

Write a statement that probes to uncover "signature strengths" (a skill that Chris is both competent and passionate about).

Coach Response:

Identify Areas for Improving Skills & Self-Efficacy

Write a statement that encourages Chris to identify his potential development areas.

Coach Response:

Exploring Client Motivation through their Attributional Style

Attributional style is the approach that clients use to explain their success and failures. If you listen carefully to your client, you will uncover three components:

1. **Internal versus External Perspective**. This involves how the client explains where the cause of an event arises. People experiencing events may see themselves as the cause (internal) versus as a result of circumstances that are outside their influence (external).

2. **Permanent versus Temporary Perspective**. This involves how the client explains the extent of the cause. Clients who see things as permanent typically see the situation as unchangeable

and will continue indefinitely as opposed to being short-term and over in some period of time.

3. **Pervasive or Specific Perspective**. This involves how the client explains the extent of the effects. Clients may see the situation as affecting all aspects of life (pervasive) or only this unique situation (specific).

Attributional style can be either described as optimistic or pessimistic. For example, clients who generally tend to blame themselves for negative events or failures in their life believe that such events are a direct result of their efforts, will continue indefinitely, and describe their lives in general. During the last 25 years, studies have shown that clients who profess pessimistic explanations for life events have poorer physical health, are more prone to depression, and have a less adequately functioning immune system (Peterson, 2000).

A pessimistic attributional style might interfere with successful goal setting and implementation. Coaches might consider using the exercises developed for this section with their clients to help assess their primary attributional style and help build a more optimistic explanation for the future to facilitate behavioral change success.

Figure 3-8

Sample OARS Exercise Answers

Open-ended Questions

Coach Response: *"What do you see as some of the positive advantages of being seen as more participative?"*

Coach Response: *"What's preventing you from getting started? Why?"*

Affirmations

Coach Response: *"You have demonstrated success in your work and performance. I believe your competence can help you achieve what you want to achieve."*

Coach Response: *"You have risen through the ranks at your firm. You have a consistent track record as a high performer also It appears that you must be able to work with different types of colleagues and team members if you want to."*

Reflective Listening

Coach Response: *"Chris, I get a sense that there is a lot on your plate right now, and that seems a bit overwhelming."*

Coach Response: *"You seem to be suggesting that acting closer to your team can actually hinder their performance on the job. Is that right?"*

Summarizing

Coach Response: *"Chris, what I'm getting from what you are saying is,…"*

Coach Response: *"You seem to be saying….."*

Sample Motivational Interviewing Exercise Answers

Identify Resistance

Coach Response: *On a scale of 1 to 10, how confident are you that if you made a decision to change, that you could change, with 1 representing not at all confident and 10 representing extremely confident? What led you to choose a 7, rather than a 3?*

Coach Response: *What would it take to move you from a 7 to an 8? Why are you a 7 on the scale and not a zero? What would it take for you to go from 7 to a higher number?*

Reflection

Coach Response: *"You seem to be saying that your direct reports, colleagues, and managers are overreacting."*

Coach Response: *"You seem to see the value of being more participative but feel as if it is a perspective not viewed equally by everyone on your team."*

Shifting Focus

Coach Response: *"Can you think about some of the positive consequences of making the changes we have discussed today either for you or your team?"*

Coach Response: *"You have described some good reasons for the situation. What do you see as some possible solutions that you can influence directly?"*

Agreement with a Twist

Coach Response: *"You've made a good point, and that's important. You are absolutely correct to point out that some of your some of your direct reports that your inherited aren't truly motivated or competent. What things can you influence and/or control though to increase their level of commitment and engagement on the job?"*

Coach Response: *"I see your point of view. We know that high potential talent expect leaders to constructively confront poor performance on a team. Any thoughts on how you can keep your high potential talent engaged and committed to the organization?"*

Reframing

Coach Response: *"I understand that you want to have a productive, hard-working team, let's explore some possibilities of LEADING them to ensure that they stay on top of their work."*

Coach Response: *"Despite those challenges, I sense that you are determined and that this change is important to you."*

Sample Motivational Interviewing Exercise Answers

Identify Signature Strengths

Coach Response: *"Chris, you are recognized as a top producer. What are some of the skills and qualities that you think have contributed towards your success?"*

Coach Response: *"Chris, name a time in your life when you had to overcome a huge obstacle. What did you do? How did you do it? What skills allowed you to become successful?"*

Identify Areas for Improving Skills & Efficacy

Coach Response: *"Chris, if you were a coach and I was your client, what would you advise me to do more, less or differently?"*

Coach Response: *"Chris, you have obviously demonstrated competence on many levels, according to your 360-degree feedback results. How can you utilize that competence to work on your perceived improvement areas?"*

Believe in the Client's Ability to Change

Coach Response: *"Chris, I'm impressed with your ability to stay focused on your behavior change goals given everything on your plate—truly impressive so keep up the great work!"*

Coach Response: *"I'd like to have a dozen clients like you that demonstrate the drive and commitment to move ahead despite some realistic challenges and barriers you have faced."*

Reinforce Change Talk

Coach Response: *"Can you name one person that you admire who has succeeded in changing his/her habits? What did they do? Is change possible?"*

Coach Response: *"Suppose you were the coach and I had some of these perceived areas for development. Based on that, what would you tell me?"*

Seven Tips on Assessing Client Motivation

1	Seek to understand the client's frame of reference.
2	Reinforce client's thoughts, so that statements encouraging change are amplified, and statements that reflect the status quo are dampened down.
3	Facilitate client statements that encourage change, such as expressions of problem recognition, concern, desire, the intention to change, and the ability to change.
4	Identify the client's stage of change and use stage appropriate techniques to increase "readiness" to change.
5	Express acceptance and affirmation.
6	Affirm the client's freedom of choice and self-direction.
7	Allow the client's resistance to exist. Don't argue with them!

Summary

People don't initiate new behaviors and sustain them over time *unless they are sufficiently motivated*. One of the important roles of coaching is to help clients increase their readiness to change behavior and translate goal intentions into actual implementation.

Motivational Interviewing (MI) is a proven and structured approach to help clients better understand their ambivalence about changing behaviors and increasing a desire to do things more, less, or differently to enhance their effectiveness. Using motivational interviewing techniques like the *Change Ruler* to facilitate "change talk" can help clients see the advantages of initiating and sustaining new behaviors. Another way to assess motivation is through identifying their attributional style in order to learn about client perceptions of prior behavioral change success and failures that might be beneficial or impede future change attempts. Coaches should become familiar with one or more of the theories and models of individual behavioral change and apply some of their techniques and exercises to help foster motivation and a sense of confidence to succeed in behavioral change efforts.

Recent research suggests that attempts to change people's intentions alone may not always result in successful maintenance of behavior over time (Lawton, Cooner & McEachan, 2009). Many clients often express a strong desire and intent to become more effective and to try new behaviors, but oftentimes, they rarely initiate or sustain a new change for very long.

Some recent evidence suggests that *perceived importance and concern* for the desired behavioral change end-point might be the *best predictor* differentiating non-intenders from those who are successful adopters of new behavior, whereas self-efficacy, perceived control, and being clear about the "cons" behind behavioral change are more important in discriminating successful maintainers from unsuccessful maintainers (Rhodes, Plotnikoff & Courneya, 2009).

Key Points

1. Nobody likes a change, except for wet babies. Keep in mind that unless a client understands and accepts feedback and is willing to use it to improve, his or her behavior will likely remain the same, despite anything a coach does.

2. Coaches need to help clients explore the advantages and disadvantages of changing behavior. Helping clients begin to talk about the advantages of change helps to convert *intentions* into actual *implementation* of goals.

3. Not all people who express an interest to change behavior will necessarily be *successful* in either implementing new behaviors or sustaining them over time. Behavioral change is complex, and coaches not only need to assess their client's internal motivation and readiness stage but the external support and environment that can help reinforce or punish new behaviors.

4. Pessimistic attributional styles (explanations of life events as being internal, permanent, and invasive) are likely to undermine a client's successful pursuit of behavioral change efforts and contribute to both psychological distress and helplessness.

⦿ ENCOURAGE EXERCISES

The following section includes various exercises related to the *Encourage* chapters.

Tips for Getting the Most from the Exercises in the Book

- **Take time to do the exercises.** These exercises are designed to help you and your client to move through the Enlighten, Encourage and Enable stages of successful behavior change.

- **Take time to reflect.** Spend some quality time on each exercise to answer the questions and reflect what they mean for you personally and professionally.

- **Pick and choose the most important exercises to use.** Each of the exercises has been specifically included to support the specific behavior change stage in our model. Some exercises will be more relevant than others for you and your client. However, each has a unique purpose but there is not a need to specifically do all of them or in any order.

- **Share with others.** Consider sharing your thoughts and feelings about one or more of the exercises with a partner, family member, friend or colleague. Seek their impressions and input about your reactions and commitments.

- **Commit to action.** Consider taking specific actions to translate these exercises into goals and new behaviors.

Each of the exercises included in the book and additional ones for each of the *Enlighten, Encourage* and *Enable* behavior change stages can be previewed and printed in a useable format for you and your clients to use for free by visiting our website at: www.envisialearning.com/clueless

ENCOURAGE EXERCISE #1

My Work and Life Balance

Think about your balance in life, and answer the following questions:

1. What do you want *more* of in your life?

2. What do you want *less* of in your life?

3. Do you need to *simplify or intensify* activities and responsibilities?

4. If you want to become *more balanced* in life, what do you need to do:

   More?

   Less?

   Differently?

5. What beliefs that you have about becoming more balanced could interfere with you actually making changes in your lifestyle or habits (e.g., I'd exercise more, but I just don't have the time)?

6. What do you need to give up in order to achieve the balance you want in life?

ENCOURAGE EXERCISE #2

Activities I Tend to Avoid

In the space below, list situations, people, and activities you put
energy into avoiding:

Home:

Work:

In Relationships:

In My Community:

What patterns, if any, do you notice about the things you avoid?

What changes, if any, would you like to make in any of these areas?

ENCOURAGE EXERCISE #3

Facilitating Change Talk

Step 1:

Think about the habit or behavior you are interested in changing. Write about *why* you are motivated to want to change this habit/ behavior below:

Step 2:

For each sentence you wrote, mark a letter corresponding to the *type of statement* you made:

D = desire statement
A = ability statement
R = reasons statement
N = need statement
C = commitment statement

Step 3:

How many statements did you make that were of the *Commitment* type? Research suggests that the more "commitment to change" statements you make (*change talk*), the more successful your change effort will be.

ENCOURAGE EXERCISE #4

Decisional Balance Worksheet

In this exercise, you will think about and record some of the important advantages and disadvantages of changing or continuing your current habits or behaviors. You will compare what you have to lose against what you have to gain. Think about a specific behavior or habit you are considering to change. When you are finished, review your answers, and weigh your reasons for change. Which way does your decisional balance tip?

Continuing Your Current Habit or Behavior

Changing Your Current Habit or Behavior

ENCOURAGE EXERCISE #5
Asking Others to Change
Give-Get-Merge-Go Technique

The "Give-Get-Go-Merge" communication technique can be effectively used to influence other people in an involvement oriented manner. Identify a family member, friend, or colleague at work and practice expressing each of the four steps below to practice this assertiveness technique.

Give your point-of-view, suggestion, recommendations or thoughts.

- Be concrete, specific, and objective.
- Be succinct!
- Own the statement by using "I," instead of "We."

Get their point-of-view, suggestion or thoughts.

- Directly ask others what they think about what you just said.
- Ask sincerely, or don't ask at all!
- Try a statement like, "What are your thoughts about that?"

Merge your points-of-view by actively clarifying what you have heard the other person saying.

- Use paraphrasing or reflection to test for understanding.
- Don't repeat back what you heard verbatim—nobody likes a parrot!
- Use a phrase such as, "So, you seem to be saying…"

$\underline{Go}$ ahead and summarize the areas of agreement and areas of disagreement.

- Briefly state the areas of agreement you both have expressed.
- Briefly state the areas of disagreement you both have expressed.
- If necessary, agree to disagree!
- Watch for indicators of defensiveness on your and the other person's part
- Put some closure to your discussion

ENCOURAGE EXERCISE #6

Asking Others to Change-DESC Technique

Effective communications can concretely and behaviorally describe behavior in a manner that enhances self-esteem and reduces the potential for defensive reactions. The DESC (describe, express, specify and consequences) technique behavior can be used in a variety of situations. Practice the "DESC" technique with another individual to increase your ability to influence change in others in a manner that minimizes defensiveness and helps build motivation to change.

D escribe the behavior, not the personality or attitudinal characteristics of interest.

- Be concrete, specific, and non-evaluative in your description of their behavior
- Focus on as recent of behavior as possible
- Model appropriate behaviors of interest to further clarify and reinforce

E xpress your own feelings about the behaviors.

- Use "I" statements to convey these feelings
- Use congruent non-verbal behavior

Specify the changes in behavior that you want in a precise and concrete manner.

Consequences of the desired behavior changes should be shared.

- Specify the consequences of changing in the desired direction first
- Specify the consequences of not changing in the desired direction

ENCOURAGE EXERCISE #7

How Others Can Support My
Behavioral Change Effort

Think of people at work, home, and school who have helped you the most in your life (e.g., mentors, coaches etc.).

1. Write down the names of these individuals below, and next to them, briefly write why they have had such an impact on you (i.e., what did you learn from them? What did they say or do?).

2. Write down someone at work, home, or school who has tried to help or coach you in the last year. Write down his or her name and summarize what he or she did or said to you and what you have learned from him or her.

3. What feelings do you have in writing down and summarizing how these key people have helped you to grow and develop personally and professionally?

4. What similarities or differences do you find in those people who have had an important impact on how you are today?

5. How can you enlist others to help you be successful in the behavioral change goals and efforts you are making today? Who can you ask to support and assist you?

ENCOURAGE EXERCISE #8

Mobilizing My Future Vision

The clearer you are about your desires, the better you will be able to focus your energy to achieve them. Answer the questions below to help mobilize your future vision into a reality.

1. Describe how things will be when your wishes become a reality (i.e., what does the *future state* look like for you in terms of a specific, behavioral goal)?

2. How will accomplishing your specific, behavioral goal *improve*:
   - Interpersonal Relationships/Interactions
   - Health/Well-Being
   - Career/Professional Success

3. What individual needs will you be satisfying by taking actions to achieve your future vision (i.e., successful completion of your specific behavioral goal)?

4. In the next week, what is your *prediction* about whether you will *implement* your specific behavioral goal?

ENCOURAGE EXERCISE #9

Assessing My Attributional Style

Try to imagine yourself in the following situations and answer the questions below for each one.

1. Try to imagine you have been recently laid off and are trying to find a new job.

a) Write down one main cause for the situation:

b) How likely is it that the cause you gave will continue to affect you (1= Never and 5=Always)?

c) Is the cause you gave something that just effects this situation or does it affect other areas of your life (1=Just this situation to 5=All areas of my life)

2. Try to imagine a friend or colleague is very upset with you.

a) Write down one main cause for the situation:

b) How likely is it that the cause you gave will continue to affect you (1= Never and 5=Always)?

c) Is the cause you gave something that just effects this situation or does it affect other areas of your life (1=Just this situation to 5=All areas of my life)

3. Try to imagine you have a serious injury.

a) Write down one main cause for the situation:

b) How likely is it that the cause you gave will continue to affect you (1= Never and 5=Always)?

c) Is the cause you gave something that just effects this situation or does it affect other areas of your life (1=Just this situation to 5=All areas of my life)

Scoring:
Calculate a total score by adding your responses to 1a+1b+2a+2b+3a +3c. Your score ranges will range from 6 to 30.

Interpretation:
- **6-12**: Your scores suggest a tendency to utilize more of an optimistic explanatory style.
- **13-18**: your scores suggest a tendency to sometimes utilize both an optimistic and pessimistic explanatory style.
- **19-30**: your scores suggest a tendency to sometimes utilize a pessimistic explanatory style.

ENCOURAGE EXERCISE #10

Building an Optimistic Attributional Style

Developing an optimistic explanatory style around life events takes some practice but can be enhanced through the following exercise which has four steps. Write down your responses to each of the questions for the steps below.

Step A

1. Write down one *bad event* that has happened in your life this week:

2. What type of event is it (e.g., health, social, personal, work, achievement, other)?

Step B

1. What is your *explanation* about why this event occurred?

2. How negative does it make your *feel* (1=Not at all negative to 5=Extremely negative)?

3. How strongly do you believe the cause for the event you wrote about in question #3 above?

4. Is this cause about you or other people/circumstances (1=Totally due to other people/circumstances to 5=Totally due to me)?

5. Will this cause be present in the future (1=Will unlikely to be present again to 5=Will likely to be always present)?

6. Does this cause effect just this event or others in your life (1=Affects just this event to 5=Affects all areas of my life)?

Step C

1. Write down one other positive yet realistic cause for why the event happened.

2. How negative does it make your feel (1=Not at all negative to 5=Extremely negative)?

3. How strongly do you believe the cause for the event you wrote about in question #3 above?

4. Is this cause about you or other people/circumstances (1=Totally due to other people/circumstances to 5=Totally due to me)?

5. Will this cause be present in the future (1=Will unlikely to be present again to 5=Will likely to be always present)?

6. Does this cause effect just this event or others in your life (1=Affects just this event to 5=Affects all areas of my life)?

Step D

- Now that you have gone through this exercise, how *strongly do you believe* the very first reason you gave was the reason the event happened?

- As you reflect on the situation you wrote about, do you *feel better*?

- As you reflect on the situation you wrote about, do you see some *new ways you can effectively cope with the situation in a positive manner?*

Encourage References

Dolan, M. J., Seay, T. A. & Vellela, T. C. (2006). The Revised Stage of Change Model and the Treatment Planning Process. Compelling Perspectives on Counseling. *Journal of Counseling and Psychotherapy, 3*, 79-94.

Dorn, F.J. (2008, April). Change Management: Theory and practice, strategies and techniques. Paper presented at the American Psychological National Conference, Boston, MA.

Fishbein, M. & Ajzen, I. (1975). Belief, attitude, intention, and behavior: An introduction to theory and research. Reading, MA: Addison-Wesley.

Kotter, J. P. (1996). *Leading Change*. Boston: Harvard Business School Press.

Lawton, R., Conner, M. & McEachan, R. (2009). Desire or reason: Predicting health behaviors from affective and cognitive attitudes. *Health Psychology, 28*, 56-65.

McEvoy, P. & Nathan, P. (2007). Perceived costs and benefits of behavioral change: Reconsidering the value of ambivalence for psychotherapy outcomes. *Journal of Clinical Psychology, 63*, 1217-1229.

Miller, W. R. & Rollnick, S. (2002). Motivational interviewing: Preparing people *for* change.

Miller, W. R. & Rollnick, S. (2009). Ten things that motivational interviewing is not. *Behavioural and Cognitive Psychotherapy, 2009*, 37, 129-140.

Miller, G. E. & Wrosch, C. (2007). You've gotta know when to fold'em: Goal disengagement and systemic inflammation in adolescence. *Psychological Science, 18*, 773-777.

Norcross, J., Mrykalo, S. & Blagys, M. (2002). Auld Lang Syne: Success predictors, change processes, and self-reported outcomes of New Year's resolvers and nonresolvers. *Journal of Clinical Psychology, 58*, 397-405.

Nowack, K. & Heller, B. (2001). Making executive coaching work: The importance of emotional intelligence. *Training Magazine*, trainingmag.com.

Passmore, J. (2007). Motivational interviewing – ambivalence, intrinsic motivation, and self-efficacy. Addressing deficit performance through coaching – using motivational interviewing for performance improvement at work. *International Coaching Psychology Review, 2*, 265-275.

Peterson, C. Optimistic explanatory style and health. In: J.F. Gilham (Ed.). The science of optimism and hope: Research essays in honor of Martin E.P. Seligman (pp. 145-162). Philadelphia: Templeton Foundation.

Prochaska, J. O., Diclemente, C. C. & Norcross, J. C. (1997). *In search of how people change: Applications to addictive behaviors.* In A. G. Marlatt and G. R. VandenBos (Eds), Addictive behaviors: Readings on etiology, prevention, and treatment (pp. 671-696). Washington, DC, US: American Psychological Association.

Rhodes, R. E., Plotnikoff, R. C. & Courneya, K. S. (2008). Predicting the physical activity intention-behavior of adopters and maintainers using three social cognition models. *Annals of Behavioral Medicine, 36,* 244-252.

PART IV:

Enable

> "When it is obvious that the goals cannot be reached, don't adjust the goals; adjust the action steps. **CONFUCIUS**

Introduction:

How Do I Go About Changing?

> "You miss 100 percent of the shots you don't take.
>
> **WAYNE GRETZKY**

If three squirrels are sitting on a tree and two decide to jump off to another branch, how many are left? The answer is three. You might ask why but the answer is simple because there is a big difference between *deciding* and actually *doing*. A strong intention to act does not guarantee behavioral change. This is the difference between *goal intentions* and *implementation intentions*. People often fail because they may confront problems during the process of attaining their goals; that is, they either fail to get started or they get derailed along the way.

Factoid: Intentions Are Overrated

A review of health behavior practices (e.g., condom use, exercise, cancer screening) found that people acted on their strong intentions only 53 percent of the time (Gollwitzer & Sheeran, 2006).

Not all enlightened and truly motivated clients are successful at changing their styles or specific behaviors that may contribute to future "derailment." This *Enable* section describes the process of setting and accomplishing goals. It begins by providing ways to design goals that will increase the likelihood of attaining them. It then details the process for and components of turning new behavioral practices into long-term habits. This section will then move on to describing ways relapse occurs and provides preventative intervention strategies. It ultimately identifies various methods and approaches for talent development and sustaining change, and it introduces the Envisia Learning, Inc. *Performance Coaching Model* to target internal and external coaching of talent at all levels of the organization.

Chapter 10:

Goal Setting

> "The tragedy in life doesn't lie in not reaching your goal. The tragedy lies in having no goal to reach.

BENJAMIN MAYS

Formulating goals is a *key* to successful implementation. People are much more likely to develop when they decide which competencies or skills to focus on. Goals should include clear actions that break down learning into manageable steps. For example, when a client achieves success on specific developmental goals, it paves the way for setting new and more challenging goals. It is important to stretch individuals by structuring goals into small, attainable, and manageable steps. Generally, in order to stretch clients, it is particularly important to maximize choice.

Coaches have two primary roles to help their clients with the goal setting process: 1) Helping client set development goals; and 2) Providing ongoing feedback regarding progress. Beck and his colleagues argue that in order for coaches to help their clients develop awareness, skills and abilities, they should take a "multiple goal perspective" (Beck, Gregrory & Carr, 2009). They emphasize three important recommendations to help clients pursue both developmental goals in tandem with regular work goals:

1. *Set development goals with high expectancies.* It is important that the goals set by clients are achievable and to set goals early

on that are easily accomplished (research suggests that goals that can be achieved easily help build self-efficacy).

2. *Provide feedback on development progress.* Beck et al. (2009) point out that goals that receive the most feedback are typically perceived to be most important and this translates into more time and effort on behalf of the client. Such feedback should be given with careful attention to the learning style and personality of the client.

3. *Identify incentives for development.* Coaches should help clients identify incentives that are associated with their development goals to enhance motivation and minimize relapse (e.g., emphasizing future outcomes and rewards).

Indeed, the coach typically plays a large role in the goal setting process. He or she may want to refrain from *providing* the goals to his or her client. Rather, the client should be able to generate his or her own goals, with the help of the coach to refine them. Some research has indicated that the client's involvement in setting his or her own goals, either autonomously or collaboratively, increases the commitment to the goals, when compared to goals that are instead assigned to them (Locke & Latham, 2002).

Goal Setting Factors

In order to effectively establish goals, it is a good idea to consider all the factors involved. There are a number of variables that influence the level of goal pursuit individuals engage in (Koo & Fishbach, 2010). Some of these variables include the difficulty of attaining the goal or the designated timeframe for that attainment (Shilts, Horowitz, & Townsend, 2004). Other factors that determine the success or failure of attaining goals include personality factors and the personal habits of the client. Let's look at five important factors that affect goal setting and successful accomplishment.

1. *Goal Difficulty*

Research suggests that challenging goals lead to greater effort, focus, and persistence than moderately difficult or easy goals. It has also been suggested that people who perceived their goal as difficult to attain reported higher positive emotion, an increase in job satisfaction, and perceptions of occupational success (Latham & Locke, 2008).

2. *Proximity*

Goals are often distinguished by how far forward they project into the future. Schunk (2001) suggests that proximal short-term goals are achieved more quickly and result in higher motivation and better self-regulation than more distant and long-term goals. Further, these researchers suggest that if long-term goals must be established, subdividing them can produce greater benefits.

3. *Time Frame*

The time frame for completion needs to be reasonable in order for goals to be attained (Latham & Locke, 2006). Research suggests that individuals are more likely to maintain goals in the face of obstacles and challenges when more time remained for goal pursuit than when less time remained. (Schmidt & Deshon, 2007).

4. *Multiple Goals*

Individuals can accomplish more than one goal at a time, assuming that these goals do not conflict with each other in some way (Locke & Latham, 1990). It becomes difficult to achieve multiple goals when each goal alone is attainable, but together the goals cause conflict (Schunk, 2002).

5. *Specificity*

Research shows that *specific* goals raise performance because they clarify the amount of effort required for success. They also boost self-efficacy and confidence by providing a clear standard against which to determine progress (Schunk, 2002).

Personality Correlates with Goal Setting and Implementation Intentions

Naturally, individuals with different personality types will commit to their goals differently. Coaches should be aware of how their clients' personality traits will play a role in goal achievement. The reason it is important to understand this is because it can help coaches and clients establish goals that are realistic and suitable for a client's personality type. The following traits have been associated with successful *goal attainment* in various research studies:

1. *Core Self Evaluations (CSE)*

Judge, Locke, & Durham (1997) defined core self-evaluations as basic conclusions or bottom-line evaluations individuals hold that constitute a higher order construct of one's self-concept. Core self-evaluations are composed of four personality traits: self-esteem, generalized self-efficacy, emotional stability (low neuroticism), and locus of control (Erez & Judge, 2001). In other words, the more an individual typifies the core self-evaluation traits, the more likely he or she is to attain the goals he or she sets out to achieve. For example, people with low self-efficacy are unlikely to choose or commit to an ambitious goal, whereas people with high self-efficacy not only commit to ambitious goals, but set even more ambitious ones once they've reached their initial goals (Latham & Locke, 2008).

2. *Psychological Capital*

Recent empirical evidence that *psychological capital* can be used to explain how employees are motivated to acquire, maintain and foster the necessary resources to attain successful performance outcomes (Peterson, Luthans, Avolio, Walumbwa & Zhang, 2011). Specifically, an individual's motivation and choices towards goal initiation and completion can be explained by four psychological resources that include self-efficacy, hope, optimism and resilience which in turn affect both motivation and performance.

Psychological capital has been defined as having more measurement stability than emotional states, but not as stable as personality consisting of four psychological resources that increase the probability of success based on motivated effort, persistence and goal attainment/performance (Peterson et al., 2011).

The first component of this higher-order core construct is *self-efficacy* which is defined as the confidence and belief about one's abilities to motivate both internal and external resources to execute tasks and contribute to high performance. Second, is *hope* which is defined as a positive motivational state that facilitates goal directed energy and success. Third, is *optimism,* which is defined as an explanatory style that helps interpret negative and positive events in a way to optimize goal success as well as a positive orientation towards the future. Fourth is *resilience* which is defined as the ability to bounce back from failure or challenges. Psychological capital has been demonstrated to be a significant predictor of job performance and work success and may be changed based on

243

developmental interventions, repeated feedback from leaders, peers or even the job itself (Peterson et al., 2011).

3. *Perfectionism*

Some people set goals that are truly *impossible* for them to attain. They may, nevertheless, persist in pursuing such goals because their self-worth (self-esteem) is contingent upon goal attainment (Latham & Locke, 2008). People who are perfectionists might set unreasonable goals or be unwilling to back off and quit, despite clear signs that the goal is unattainable.

4. *Conscientiousness/Drive*

Achievement striving, dependable, and conscientious individuals are more likely to set and achieve their goals (Barrick, Mount, & Strauss, 1993). Since conscientiousness is related to traits such as organization, persistence, and purposefulness, these traits are similar to the need for determination, deliberation, caution, and reliability, which are necessary for goal achievement. Research shows that personality variables, such as conscientiousness, are related to goal level, self-efficacy, and performance (Mitchell, Thompson, & Falvy, 2000). Conscientious individuals are highly meticulous, detail-oriented, and driven, so they are more likely to put forth the appropriate effort to enact and sustain change.

5. *Grit*

"Grit" is a trait that is based on an individual's passion for a particular long-term goal or a particular end state of a goal. Individuals who are "gritty" often have a powerful motivation to achieve their objectives (Duckworth, Peterson, Mathews, & Kelly, 2007). Measurement of "grit" includes items that tap into both perseverance of effort as well as strength of interests or passion. This type of client would tend to set long-term goals and not be deterred by setbacks, initial failures, or ongoing challenges. As such, individuals high in Grit are able to maintain their determination and motivation over long periods of time despite experiences with failure and adversity.

6. *Mood*

Research indicates that "one's mood at the moment can influence goal choice" (Mitchell et al., 2000). Thus, people with a more positive mood may report higher confidence levels and, as a result, set more challenging goals. Additional research suggests that when individuals are in a bad mood, they tend to fixate their energy on their negative affect over cognitive and behavioral efforts towards attaining their goals (Gollwitzer & Sheeran, 2006).

Learning Goals vs. Performance Goals

An individual's goal orientation describes the goals that they choose and the methods used to pursue those goals (DeShon & Gillespie, 2005). There are differences between *learning goals*, which involve acquiring/learning new skills or strategies, and *performance goals*, which focus on performing well. Instead of focusing on the end result, a learning goal focuses attention on the discovery of effective strategies to attain and sustain desired results (Seijts & Latham, 2006).

When trying to accomplish a learning goal, the individual will learn to master all the necessary skills that are associated with acquiring that goal. In the process, he or she may ask for feedback and reflect on progress in order to master whatever it takes to learn the new skill. On the other hand, trying to attain a specific performance goal can place additional demands on people, so much so that they may be unable to devote the necessary cognitive resources to mastering them. Performance goals can be appropriate when the necessary skills to perform a task are already mastered and the primary focus is to exert more effort to reach a higher level of performance.

Seigt & Latham (2006) found that individuals with learning goals demonstrated the following advantages over those with performance goals:

1. They took the time necessary to acquire the knowledge to perform the task effectively and to analyze the task-relevant information that was available to them.

2. They showed an increase in self-efficacy as a result of the discovery of appropriate strategies for task mastery. Other research supports the notion that learning goals are especially effective in enhancing self-efficacy and self-regulation (Schunk, 2001).

3. They had a higher commitment to their goals than did those with a performance goal.

It is a good idea to set up goals that will allow your clients to focus on mastering the skills necessary to perform a new behavior as well as goals that target specific outcomes. For instance, a client may have a performance goal of creating a more productive team or losing a specific amount of weight. By establishing a learning goal, the client would focus on acquiring the skills to build a high performance team and to maintain a healthy weight.

Implementation Intentions

Once goals have been designed, it is important to identify when, where, and how a client will complete them successfully. This process is referred to as an *implementation intention*, which helps clients create an appropriate and prescriptive plan of action. For instance, if a client has an intention to start exercising, implementation plans specify:

- *When* this person will exercise (every day after work)
- *What*, exactly, she will do (running), and
- *Where* she will do it (at the gym)

Research has found that implementation intentions promote effective management of various problems that individuals might face in attaining goals, thus increasing rates of goal attainment (Gollwitzer & Sheeran, 2006).

Implementation intentions are described as "if-then" plans that provide clients with time and place cues about opportunities or critical moments to act, then links those cues to responses. The "if-then" goes as follows: *"If situation X is encountered, then I will perform behavior Y."* A goal intention, however, specifies a desired event, like, *"I intend to meditate frequently."* On the other hand, an implementation intention follows the form of *"After I get out of bed in the morning, I will sit down and meditate for 10 minutes."* After a while, getting out of bed (the situational cue) would be associated with meditating.

Ultimately, setting implementation intentions can help clients form stronger habits. This is achieved because behaviors are repeated at specified times. The client does not have to rely solely on willpower to achieve the behavior; instead, he or she can rely on cues that automatically initiate responses. Coaches collaboratively work with clients to establish these plans by creating an implementation intention for each one of their goals.

Asking Clients about Future Predictions of Behavior to *Increase* Implementation Intentions

There is considerable evidence that repetitive behaviors (both unhealthy and healthy) are very difficult to change, even when people intend to do so (Webb & Sheeran, 2006). Therefore, methods to strengthen or disrupt behavior repetition would appear to be beneficial to sustaining desirable change over time. Current research suggests that asking questions regarding *future behavior* can lead to significant changes in that behavior (Chandon, Smith, Morowitz, Spangenberg, & Sprott, 2011).

When asked to make predictions about future behavior, people think about what they normally do (past behavior) and what they think they should do (personal norms). In one experiment, Chandon and colleagues (2011) asked college students to predict whether they would read books or watch the news in the next week. Compared to a control group, students asked to predict their behavior were more likely to repeat what they had done the week before. Asking about future exercising led students who had only exercised for 10 minutes in the week before to exercise for an estimated 94 additional minutes in the next week (an increase of 138 percent). Apparently, when people have set targets about how much they should engage in a behavior for themselves, asking them to predict whether they will engage in that behavior in the next week makes them think about what they should do and increases the likelihood of implementing their intention. However, asking questions led to an estimated 23 fewer minutes of exercising (a decrease of 11 percent) among those who had exercised for 150 minutes in the week before.

When *personal norms are weak* or not accessible at the time of the prediction request, asking people about their future behavior strengthens behavior repetition. People become more likely to repeat what they normally do. However, when personal norms are strong or made accessible at the time of the prediction request, behavior prediction appears to actually weaken behavior repetition. People become less likely to repeat what they normally do.

SMART Development Goals

Goals that are clear, with well-defined metrics to determine success, are often referred to as "SMART" goals. The acronym SMART can help with goal-setting processes. SMART goals are those that are *Specific, Measurable, Action oriented, Realistic, and Time bound*. The benefits of using SMART goals are that these goals are more planned out, focused, concise, and specific and are, therefore, significantly easier to visualize. In order to achieve goals, all five criteria should be in place.

As an example, suppose an overweight individual wants to create weight-loss goals. It probably won't help this person reach the goal if he or she simply to be thinner and lose weight. SMART goals help translate the goal intentions into clear and measurable goal implementations.

Figure 4-1

"SMART" Goals

Specific	**Clear and Concrete** (I want to lose 10 pounds)
Measurable	**Easily Observable** (I will weigh myself each week to check progress)
Action Oriented	**Behaviorally Based** (I will exercise each day for one hour from 6-7pm)
Realistic	**Actions that can be Accomplished** (I will wake up an hour earlier each morning to exercise)
Time Bound	**Have Start and End Dates** (By the 10th of next month, I will have lost 10 pounds)

A Dozen Goal-Setting Tips

1	Share your goals with others, and seek their support and help to achieve them.
2	Declare what you will achieve, and own it!
3	Create goals that are motivating, with a desired payoff.
4	Create goals that will help you be more effective at your current position and in the future.
5	Leverage your current strengths to help you be successful in your goal attainment.
6	Have short, medium, and long-term timeframes; focusing on the long-term allows clients to cope with the inevitable minor setbacks.
7	Visualize the end result.
8	Focus on becoming better, rather than simply winning: "Winning isn't everything; it's the only thing" is a well-known quote in sports, but those who focus on the journey of becoming better seem to be even more motivated to learn, experiment, and grow professionally and personally.
9	Ask what can I do more, less, or differently?
10	Match specific competencies to your identified goals, so that you can see a clear link between what you want to accomplish and what will help you develop that skill.
11	Create implementation intentions for your goals (i.e., SMART goals).
12	Focus on the remaining tasks and actions of a particular goal. This can influence the success of moving up the goal ladder, as opposed to only celebrating actions that have been completed. It will help you have a higher aspiration to achieve more.

Chapter 11:
Facilitating Goal Implementation

> "Motivation is what gets you started. Habit is what keeps you going.
>
> **JIM ROHN**

Once goals have been set, achieving them requires persistence, the proper techniques, social support, and preventative measures that help avoid relapse. This chapter will review what can go *wrong* in implementing goals and in strategies for sustaining them.

Ingredients for Learning a New Behavior

There is, in fact, a big difference between those who possess expertise vs. those who are expert in what they do. In *The Cambridge Handbook of Expertise and Expert Performance*, a recent book co-edited by Anders Ericson (2006), the authors conclude that great performance comes mainly from two things:

- Regularly *obtaining* concrete and constructive *feedback*
- *Deliberate practice*

Ericsson and others use the phrase "deliberate practice" to mean focused, structured, serious, and detailed attempts to get better. Deliberate practice has to be challenging and difficult. As it turns out, expert performance requires about 10 years, or 10,000 to 20,000 hours of deliberate practice. Little evidence exists for expert performance before *10 years of deliberate practice in any field* (Anders-Erikson, 1996).

Recent research by Phillippa Lally and colleagues from the U.K. suggests that new behaviors can become automatic after, on average *18 to 254* days, but it depends on the complexity of the behavior you are trying to put into place and your personality (Lally, 2009). Lally and her colleagues studied volunteers who chose to change an eating, drinking, or exercise behavior and tracked them for success. These volunteers completed a self-report diary, which they entered on a Web site log. They were asked to try the new behavior each day for 84 days. For the habits, 27 chose an eating behavior, 31 a drinking behavior, 34 an exercise behavior, and four did something else, like practicing meditation.

Analysis of these behaviors indicated that it took 66 days, on average, for a new behavior to become automatic and a new "habit" to seem natural. The range was anywhere from 18 to 254 days. The mean number of days varied by the complexity of the habit:

1. Drinking averaged about 59 days
2. Eating averaged about 65 days
3. Exercise averaged about 91 days

Although there are many limitations in this study, it does suggest that it can take a *large number of repetitions* by a person for a new behavior to become a habit.

Therefore, creating new habits requires tremendous self-control to be maintained for a significant period of time before these habits become automatic, and performed without any real self-control. For example, think about how much time you spend consciously operating your car when you are driving. For most people, it takes about *three months of constant practice* before a more complicated, new behavior gets set in our neural pathways as something we are comfortable with and something that is seemingly automatic. Adopting a new physical workout routine or learning to become a more participative leader might take a great deal of practice before becoming a habit.

The Neuroscience of "Practice" and Learning a New Behavior

In addition to an individual's self-control, discipline, and the time spent in forming a habit, research has indicated that mentally focusing on practicing a new behavior can contribute greatly to learning a new behavior. Harvard University neuroscientist, Alvaro Pascual-Leone conducted an experiment on how humans practice by comparing mentally practicing a task with physically practicing a task. He experimented with a group of individuals that spent five days learning to play piano for two hours each day. They were instructed to play piano as fluidly as they could by trying to keep up with the metronome's 60 beats per minute. At the end of each day's practice session, they sat beneath a coil of wire that sent a brief magnetic pulse into the motor cortex of their brain.

This transcranial-magnetic-stimulation (TMS) test revealed how much of the motor cortex controlled the finger movements needed for the piano exercise. When the scientists compared the TMS data on the two groups, they found that those who actually played the piano and those who only imagined doing so resulted in the following: The region of motor cortex that controls the piano-playing movement of fingers also expanded in the brains of volunteers who imagined playing the music, just as it had in those who had actually played it (Pascual-Leon, Amedi, Fregni, Lotfi, & Merabet, 2005).

Figure 4-2

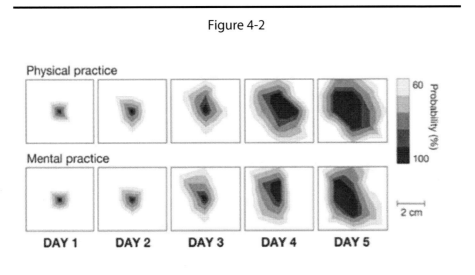

Figure 4-2 illustrates the following:

1. Comparison of a mental practice group on the piano versus a physical practice group (both two hours per day for five days) showed nearly similar changes in cortical pathways

2. Mental practice, plus two hours of physical practice, resulted in equal performance at the end of the five-day study period

Additionally, Tartaglia, Bamert, Mast, & Herzog (2009) conducted research on "mental imagery" and found that perceptual learning can occur by mentally visualizing an act of a behavior as much as it can occur via the physical action of the actual behavior. In other words, they suggest that *thinking about something repeatedly* could be as good as doing it. In a series of experiments, the researchers asked some participants to practice identifying which line in a series of three parallel lines a central line was closest to and to identify it by pushing the correct button. In follow-up post-training exercises, these participants improved their baseline performance significantly. The other group of participants, who instead were asked to *imagine* the bisecting line's proximity, improved their performance significantly. Therefore, training through imagery was actually sufficient for perceptual learning.

These findings provide important implications for learning new habits and behaviors. Perhaps in addition to spending time physically practicing a new behavior, clients can also devote time to *being mindful* and imagining their success at learning a new task.

The Four Stages of Learning a New Behavior

When implementing goals, it is important to understand the process by which individuals learn a new behavior. Abraham Maslow posits that there are four stages to achieving competence and eventually mastering a new behavior. According to his model, *learning is the process that moves from incompetence to competence.*

Think of something in your own life that you learned how to do really well: driving a car, riding a bike, skiing, etc. Once you have learned how to do this, it becomes automatic; you rarely think about the activity anymore. Between not knowing that something needs to be learned and mastering a skill, every individual undergoes four stages of learning:

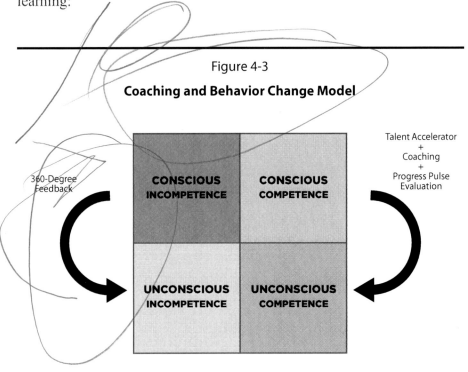

Figure 4-3

Coaching and Behavior Change Model

1. **Unconscious Incompetence**: *"I don't know what I don't know."*

   The individual neither understands nor knows how to do something, nor recognizes this deficit. During this stage, the client is unaware that his or her behavior needs to change. The coach finds ways to assess the client in order to provide feedback.

2. **Conscious Incompetence**: *"Now, I know what I didn't know."*

   Though the individual does not understand or know how to do something, he or she recognizes the deficit, without yet addressing it. During this stage, the client receives feedback and understands the need to take on a new set of behaviors. The client may receive feedback on his or her performance, and gets ready to begin learning a new behavior.

3. **Conscious Competence**: *"I know what I know."*

    The individual understands or knows how to do something. However, demonstrating that skill or knowledge requires a great deal of consciousness and concentration. At some point, the client begins to realize a certain level of mastery with his or her behavior. The client may not be an expert, but knows that he or she has some expertise. For instance, say the client is trying to learn how to become an active listener. He or she may realize that it's easy to listen when not being criticized. This insight facilitates practice to actively listen to people even if they are providing criticism.

4. **Unconscious Competence**: *"I'm not aware of what I know."*

    The individual has had so much practice with a skill that it has become "second nature" and can be performed easily (often without concentrating too deeply). He or she may be able to teach it to others, depending upon how and when it was learned. For example, after driving a car for a few years to a certain destination, a driver may not even be aware of how he or she arrived there because the same route has been taken so many times that it has become automatic.

Factoid: Stuck in the Middle

When people work toward goals, they monitor their progress in two ways; what they have achieved so far and how much they have left to do. It appears that individuals switch between the methods depending on how close they were to reaching their goal. Research with University students asked to pursue a specific goal (e.g., correcting errors in an essay) were less motivated halfway through the tasks, which likely reflects the point where they switch their focus from how much they got done to how much they had left to do.

Additional research suggested that a shift in attention from the starting point to the end point occurred halfway through the task, so this might be one of the most important times for coaches to follow up with their clients (Bonezzi, Brendl, & De Angelis, 2011).

Chapter 12:
Measuring Goal Progress

> ❝ Life is change. Growth is optional. Choose wisely. ❞
>
> ## KAREN KAISER CLARK

Defining a Way to Measure Success

Evaluating an individual's progress at achieving goals is critical to the success of goal attainment. There are various ways coaches and clients can track, monitor, and evaluate progress. The measurement process will vary, depending on the type of clients and their needs. For example, a manager in an organization may participate in annual performance reviews, whereas a client seeking health and wellness may utilize tools that monitor his or her stress levels.

1. **Annual Performance Reviews**

   Clients working in organizations that provide annual reviews can utilize this form of feedback despite some obvious limitations of appraisal systems today (Culbuert & Rout, 2010). Ongoing feedback about performance by one's manager may be better to provide a metric around goal achievement and success.

2. **Performance Conversations**

   Clients working in organizations can ask their co-workers or colleagues for feedback. It is a good idea to ask the opinions of those that have direct contact with the clients. Clients can also seek the feedback of family and peers. Oftentimes, close individuals will be able to determine change and progress. It is a good idea to seek feedback from those individuals they trust.

3. **Team Feedback**

If an individual is part of a group or work team or even leads a team, it is a great opportunity to ask questions for better feedback. Because each team member has a slightly different perspective, gathering feedback from all colleagues on a team might accurately clarify strengths and potential development areas. In addition, the process of asking for feedback can lead to better rapport and trust in relationships.

4. **Mini-Surveys of Progress**

The purpose of mini-surveys is to continue monitoring progress and new areas for development. Mini-surveys are a simple and efficient way to measure behavioral change. They are short and focus only on the behavioral goal. They are designed to help coaches track performance in small increments. The Envisia Learning, Inc. *ProgressPulse* is an example of a tool to measure and assess goal progress and effectiveness. Participants are able to ask other raters to provide specific feedback on whether others have noticed increased effectiveness based on their development plan efforts resulting in a brief evaluation report as shown below:

Figure 4-4

Introduction

This Mini-360 report provides you with feedback on the competency you selected to work on as part of your professional development plan. This report compares your own self-perception to those of others who have provided you feedback on this specific competency.

Your report summarizes feedback from the following type and number of raters (Note: you must have at least two raters in each category to be included in this summary report except for "Manager" who responded to ensure anonymity and confidentiality):

TYPE AND NUMBER OF RATERS		EFFECTIVENESS SCALE	
Manager	1	Much Less Effective	-2
Peer	2	Slightly Less Effective	-1
Direct Report	2	Unchanged	0
Team Member	2	Slightly More Effective	+1
		Much More Effective	+2
		Not Applicable	NA

Adaptability/Stress Tolerance

Maintains balance and performance under pressure and stress. Copes with ambiguity and change in a constructive manner.

	-2	-1	0	1	2	NA
Manager			1			
Peer			1	1		
Direct Report				2		
Team Member				2		
Total			2	5		

COMMENTS

Can be really impatient and raise his voice at times
-Manager

Can still show impatience--cut off a conversation that was a bit controversial last week
-Peer

Seems a bit more calm in the face of constructive criticism from others

5. Experiential Techniques

Reading books, listening to podcasts and attending seminars may be useful, but current research suggests that successful behavioral change can be facilitated much more rapidly and deeply by using more active group and experiential approaches, such as work sample simulations, case studies, and on-the-job activities (e.g., special projects, stretch assignments, etc.). For example, in our coaching practice, when we assess clients through video assessment role-plays, we find a tremendous amount of specific detail about our clients' progress. Using experiential techniques can help our clients assess their current level of proficiency and skills and point out additional areas for them to consider working to enhance their effectiveness.

6. Reminders ("Professional Nagging")

Reminders have been widely used as tools to help facilitate behavioral change and have been extensively studied in both health psychology and behavioral medicine literature (Fung, Woods, Asch, Glassman, & Doebbeling, 2004). Reminders to clients and patients in the form of e-mails, text messages, phone calls, and other tools appear to be particularly effective in improving an adherence to new behaviors and preventing relapse.

Coaches should utilize the full range of reminder tools and techniques with their clients to help them focus on practicing and sustaining new behaviors. Some vendors also offer automated reminder systems (e.g., *Talent Accelerator* by Envisia Learning, Inc., provides e-mail reminders about their goal progress to clients who have created their online development plans). The most effective coaches seem to be positive "professional nags" for their clients, encouraging them to stay on course with the implementation of their goals.

There are also numerous free or inexpensive Web-based or Smart Phone apps and calendar systems that provide text and e-mail reminders that can be creatively used. Coaches can make recommendations on which system might be best, based on their client's interest and behavioral goals.

Tracking and Monitoring Progress

What do you think is the *top motivator* of performance for individuals at all levels? If you thought it was recognition, rewards, incentives, interpersonal support, specific feedback, or clarity of goals, you would be wrong. Teresa Amabile and Stephen Kramer (2010) completed a multi-year study tracking the day-to-day activities, emotions, and motivational drives of over 600 managers in diverse settings to determine what really motivates workers.

The number one drive for motivation was making progress or headway on goals and work activities. In Amabile and Kramer's research, days when individuals reported making headway in their jobs, or days when they received support that helped them overcome obstacles, their emotions were the most positive and their level of satisfaction was highest. On days when they felt they were "spinning their wheels" or experiencing barriers to meaningful accomplishment, their emotions, moods, and motivations were significantly lower.

Being *able to see progress* is a *key* to sustaining motivation to continue with the goals, tasks, and activities that have been initiated. Systems for tracking, monitoring, and evaluating progress on goals can serve as useful mechanisms to reduce lapses and relapses with new behaviors. For example, Envisia's online goal setting and reminder system *Talent Accelerator* is designed to provide a visual tracking and monitoring system to help clients see the progress they are making. Based on the research of Amabile and Kramer, such tracking systems should help clients stay on track to complete goals and specific action plans.

Figure 4-5

Example of Tracking and Monitoring Goals Using Talent Accelerator™

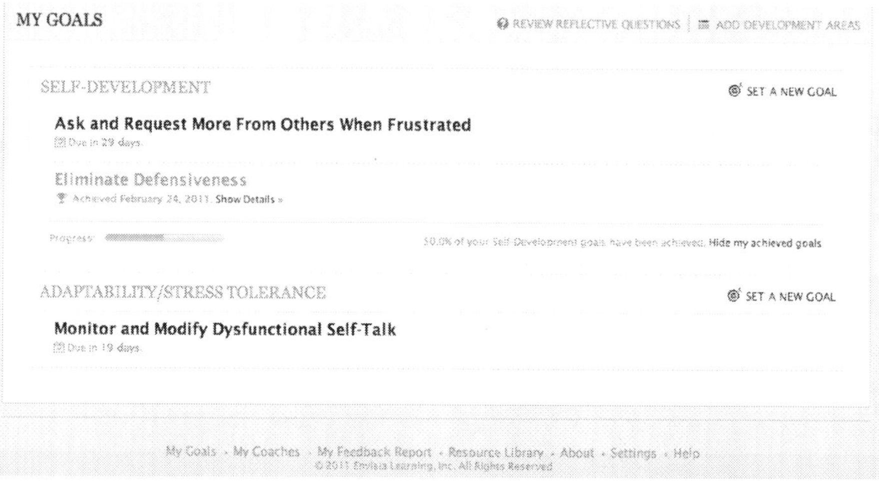
MY GOALS
REVIEW REFLECTIVE QUESTIONS
ADD DEVELOPMENT AREAS
SELF-DEVELOPMENT
SET A NEW GOAL
Ask and Request More From Others When Frustrated
Due in 29 days.
Eliminate Defensiveness
Achieved February 24, 2011. Show Details »
Progress:
50.0% of your Self-Development goals have been achieved. Hide my achieved goals
ADAPTABILITY/STRESS TOLERANCE
SET A NEW GOAL
Monitor and Modify Dysfunctional Self-Talk
Due in 19 days.
My Goals · My Coaches · My Feedback Report · Resource Library · About · Settings · Help
© 2011 Envisia Learning, Inc. All Rights Reserved

Figure 4-6

Example of Tracking and Monitoring Goals Using Talent Accelerator™

envisia
LEARNING

talentaccelerator

SET A NEW GOAL FOR SELF-DEVELOPMENT   Step 1 of 2

Your goal is the outcome of what you want to accomplish in a particular development area you have selected based on your assessment feedback. We have a few suggestions below that you can start with or you can scroll to the bottom of the page to create your own.

Once you select or create your development goal, we will walk you through some very brief steps to help translate this goal from intention into successfully implementation using our resource library that contains over 5,000 books, articles/blogs, audio, video and other resources.

Choose a suggested goal:

AVOID OVERUSING YOUR STRENGTHS   ⊛ USE THIS GOAL

All of our strengths, when over used, can be experienced as our liabilities or weaknesses by others. If you are assertive and outspoken and willing to share your thoughts and feelings others might perceive this behavior as pushy, overly directive or controlling. These people may see your behavior as rather rigid and lacking behavioral flexibility. Ask a trusted co-worker to give you feedback about when they experience you as overly opinionated or rigid in your behavior or thinking. Recognizing when you are being inflexible is the first step to changing your behavioral repertoire and becoming more adaptable.

AVOID PEOPLE THAT MAKE YOU FEEL BAD   ⊛ USE THIS GOAL

Build supportive relationships and spend less time investing in unhealthy ones. You will always have more self-control around others that energize you!

BE YOUR OWN HERO   ⊛ USE THIS GOAL

Perform the short exercise of writing down all the attributes that you admire in others. Be it benevolence, honesty, humor, integrity, whatever the case write it down. Go ahead, make it a long list. The more you note the attributes in others you'll begin to see the type of person that you truly want to be. Begin emulating these attributes into your own life one-by-one until you get through the entire list. Be prepared to enjoy the immense benefits of being your own hero and how it can influence your ability to maximize your self-control.

265

Figure 4-7

Example of Tracking and Monitoring Goals Using Talent Accelerator™

YOUR GOAL FOR SELF-DEVELOPMENT

I'VE ACHIEVED THIS GOAL

YOUR GOAL IS:
Ask and Request More From Others When Frustrated

Due March 26, 2011 / Edit Goal

Action Items and Resources

ADD ACTION ITEM AND RESOURCES

Check the box to the left of each action item as you complete it and make progress towards your goal.

7 Habits of Highly Effective People: Powerful Lessons in Personal Change
By: Stephen Covey, Ph.D. | from www.amazon.com

Millions of copies sold: "With a balance of theory and practical examples, this guide to personal and professional life describes seven principles of life management. Targeted toward anyone who is interested in personal change, it guides you through private victory, public victory and renewal."

CrazyBusy: Overstretched, Overbooked, and About to Snap! Strategies for Handling Your Fast-Paced Life
By: Edward M. Hallowell M.D. | from www.amazon.com

Look at what's happened to the usual how-are-you exchange. It used to go like this: "How are you?" "Fine." Now it often goes like this: "How are you?" "Busy." Or "Too busy." Or simply "Crazy."

Without intending for it to happen or knowing how, when, or why it got started, many people now find that they live in a rush they never wanted. If you feel busier than you've ever been and wonder how this happened and how you can keep up the pace much longer, you are hardly alone.

Chapter 13:

Relapse Prevention

> "Rather than viewing a brief relapse back to inactivity as a failure, treat it as a challenge, and try to get back on track as soon as possible.
>
> **JIMMY CONNORS**

For most people, willpower and determination alone aren't enough for sustaining new behaviors that are healthy or changing old ones that are potentially damaging. Coaches should educate their clients that *relapse* is a normal part of most behavioral change processes. They can educate their clients about what leads to these "lapses" and how to effectively cope with periods of personal stress that will enable them to continue to grow and learn over time without totally relapsing back to old entrenched behaviors and habits.

Principles of relapse prevention include identifying high-risk situations for relapse (like a change in season) and developing appropriate solutions (like finding a place to walk inside during the winter). Helping people distinguish between a *lapse* (e.g., a few days of not participating in a planned activity) and a *relapse* (e.g., an extended period of not participating) is thought to improve adherence.

How Does Relapse Occur?

Marlatt & Gordon (1985) created the Relapse Prevention model that provides a set of cognitive-behavioral strategies to prevent or limit relapse. A central aspect of the model is the detailed classification of factors or situations that can precipitate relapse or contribute to such episodes. While much of this research is geared toward addictive behaviors, the concepts surrounding relapse prevention can be applied to all types of behavioral change interventions. Research suggests that a number of specific factors contributing to relapse include the following:

1. **Negative emotional states:** Anger, anxiety, depression, frustration, and boredom are emotional states that are associated with the highest rates of relapse (Marlatt & Gordon, 1985).

2. **Situations that involve another person or group of people:** Interpersonal situations like conflict can trigger relapse.

3. **Social pressure:** Being around individuals who model clients' old habits can trigger relapse (e.g., attending a party where many people are smoking and drinking when seeking to quit).

4. **Positive emotional states:** A client who smokes or drinks may be more likely to revert to old habits during a celebration.

Factoid: Five Hours of Temptation

According to psychologist, Saul Shiffman, the number one predictor of behavior lapses is emotional: the level of negative affect during the four to five hours leading up to the lapse (e.g., anger, anxiety, depression, or a bad mood that ramps up over a period of hours).

Clients' reactions or responses to different situations can trigger relapse. However, a client that can execute effective coping strategies is less likely to relapse, compared to a person who is lacking those skills. Coaches must teach clients to anticipate the possibility of relapse and to recognize and cope with situations that can trigger each individual differently. They can help their client's awareness of cognitive, behavioral, and emotional reactions in order to prevent a lapse from escalating into a relapse (Marlatt, 1999).

Relapse Prevention Strategies for Coaches

1. ***Identifying and Coping with High Risk Situations:*** In order to anticipate and plan for situations that trigger clients to revert back to old habits, the client must first identify the different situations in which he or she may experience difficulty coping. These situations can be identified through the coaching process and through various assessment processes.

2. ***Enhancing Self-Efficacy:*** Marlatt (1999) recommend preventing relapse by the use of strategies designed to increase a client's sense of mastery and sense of being able to handle difficult situations without lapsing. They recommend an emphasis on collaboration between the client and therapist or coach.

3. ***Eliminating Myths:*** It is important for coaches to counteract the misperceptions about a client's current behavior. For instance, thinking that smoking is "not that bad" and helps release stress is a myth that an individual may hold in order to keep him or her from altering his or her behavior. Or a manager who believes that micromanagement is what helped his or her employees become productive may hold an inaccurate belief that needs to be shifted into reality. The coach's role is to help clients understand these misperceptions and provide them with accurate information about the consequences of their behaviors.

4. ***Lapse Management:*** According to research, "despite precautions and preparations, many clients committed to

abstinence will experience a lapse after initiating abstinence" (Larimer, Palmer, & Marlatt, 1999, p. 151). This notion holds true for any behavior that is an addiction or even a regular habit. Lapse-management strategies focus on halting the lapse and combating the abstinence violation effect to preventing an uncontrolled relapse episode. The coach and client can discuss a "lapse management plan" that includes all the different steps the client can take to get back on track in progress and development.

5. **Cognitive Restructuring:** This concept is also known as "Reframing" (as discussed in the *Encourage* section). It is used to assist clients in modifying their attributions for and perceptions of the relapse process. Specifically, coaches can train clients to reframe their perceptions of lapses and not to view them as failures, but as signals to alter or increase the plan to cope more effectively.

One way of doing this would be to eliminate "black-and-white thinking". According to Larimer, et al., (1999), black-and-white thinking can turn a minor lapse into a major one. After a small slip, many people simply give up because they believe one failure means they don't have the ability to change. This "abstinence-violation effect" is the belief that anything less than perfection is a total failure. It leads the quitter to conclude that they just don't have the willpower to succeed (McGowen, 2010).

It is important for coaches to educate clients about the process of relapse prevention. Behavioral change is a process, and relapse is an inevitable part of the journey. Despite the occurrence of relapse, clients should also be aware that they *can* actually improve. In fact, it is suggested that if handled the right way, a relapse can actually be an opportunity for lasting behavioral change. It provides opportunity to develop and improve techniques for anticipating and overcoming bad habits (McGowen, 2010).

Chapter 14:

Building a Support Group

> "Oh, you hate your job? Why didn't you say so? There's a support group for that. It's called everybody, and they meet at the bar.
>
> **DREW CAREY**

Individuals seeking to change behaviors and sustain those changes may need the support of professionals, peers, friends, or family members to help sustain momentum. Professional help, family support, and planning are required just as much as a desire and commitment to change. Coaches can refer clients to groups or associations that focus on an individual's growth. These groups can provide those individuals with support and a network of others that can relate to them.

Many researchers have found evidence that suggests social support is a promising technique for promoting healthy behavioral change. They suggest that social support is more effective when two individuals have similar characteristics or issues (Center of Excellence for Training and Research Translation, 2008). For example, a recent study on the effect of support groups on individuals seeking to quit smoking suggests that positive and negative support are both important factors in the early phase of quitting, but it is the continued minimization of negative support that predicts the maintenance of nonsmoking (Lawhon, Humfleet, Hall, Reus, & Munoz, 2009).

Types of Social Support to Facilitate Successful Behavioral Change

The following are common sources of networking and social support that can help foster behavioral change, both at work and away from the job:

- **Family, Friends, and Peers**: Peers, family members, friends, and networking groups all contribute to sticking through change plans. On the other hand, if family members, friends, and peers do not support change efforts, individuals may be more prone to relapse. For example, if a smoking addict is surrounded by friends that smoke, he or she is exposed to a "high-risk" situation that can hinder efforts to quit smoking.

- **Coaches and Counselors:** Without the help of a coach or counselor, clients may have a harder time overcoming change. Coaches should ensure that clients have the proper support to overcome challenges and sustain change.

- **Organizational Support:** Clients within organizations can utilize the support of their colleagues, mentors, peers, human resource personnel, and managers. While the support of these individuals depends on the organizational culture and its receptivity to change efforts, it is still useful to seek someone in an organization that can act as a "role model" to change efforts.

- **Specialized Support Groups:** There are various support groups that have been demonstrated to be effective for individuals seeking change. Individuals of similar circumstances meet either monthly, weekly, or during weekend-long events to discuss and share experiences with change efforts. Such groups include self-discovery programs, leadership programs, business retreats, spiritual courses, addiction and recovery centers, etc. These groups can be particularly helpful in that people can learn from the experiences of one another and gain a sense of belonging.

- **On-line Goal Setting and Tracking Systems:** Beyond social networking sites, there are online tools that can essentially act as online coaches. For instance, Envisia Learning's *Talent Accelerator* provides recommendations for change, tracks improvements, and provides various accountability systems to ensure behavioral goal progress (www.envisialearning.com).

The Benefits of a Social Support Network

Numerous studies have demonstrated that having a network of supportive relationships contributes to psychological well-being. Having a social support network can be beneficial in the following ways:

- **Sense of Belonging.** Often times, individuals feel they are alone in the change process. However, being surrounded by others that are going through similar circumstances, can help them feel part of an entity where their challenges and growth opportunities is perceived as common.

- **Increased Sense of Self-Worth.** Being around individuals to connect and exchange support with can be gratifying and increase a sense of self-value.

- **Feelings of Security.** A social network provides clients with access to information, advice, guidance, and other types of assistance, should clients need them. Clients can feel understood and safe when they have individuals that can be of help or have similar circumstances. In addition, individuals have an easier time opening up about their challenges when they are surrounded by others that can empathize with them.

- **Sustaining Development.** When clients are surrounded by individuals that can support their progress, they may be less likely to lapse back into old habits.

Avoiding "Toxic" Individuals

Oftentimes, clients have a difficult time sustaining progress because of the individuals around them. It is very important for clients undergoing change efforts not to surround themselves with individuals that trigger emotional stress and lead them toward high-risk relapse situations. A coach should assess clients' environment and set boundaries around those individuals that are likely to be influential in a toxic way.

Engineering Social Networking Online

With the growth of online social networking in people's lives, it would seem convenient for individuals to utilize online networking sites for support. Existing online peer groups or the creation of virtual support groups is common (Center of Excellence for Training and Research Translation, 2008). Popular social sites like Twitter, Facebook, LinkedIn, Google+, etc., can also be tools to build a social coalition with individuals that face similar situations. For instance, a leader that is seeking to work better with his or her employees may look to particular blogs and posts on one of the online sites that provides a network of individuals that share blogs, articles, thoughts, advice, and questions, through postings and chat rooms.

Chapter 15:

Approaches to Developing Talent

> "Success comes from knowing that you did your best to become the best that you are capable of becoming.
>
> **JOHN WOODEN**

Developing talent at all levels of an organization is critical to facilitate retention and engagement and to remain globally competitive. However, "The Coaching Conundrum 2009: Building a coaching culture that drives organizational success," a recent survey by Blessing White, Inc., revealed that about 84 percent of all managers are expected to coach talent, but only 52 percent actually do (only 39 percent in Europe), and only 24 percent are rewarded or recognized for coaching and developing talent.

Managers and internal coaches should consider a variety of ways to develop talent, including focusing on activities, assignments, and work-related projects to enhance knowledge, skills, and experience. These might include:

- Start-up Assignments
- Fix-it Assignments
- Stretch Assignments
- Professional Development, Mentoring, or Coaching
- Non-Work Activities

Figure 4-8 summarizes some suggestions for activities, tasks, and assignments designed to support talent development at all levels of the organization. These behavior-based activities are likely to be more powerful than just attending internal workshops or taking self-directed online webinars or programs. Of course, most organizations will put more energy into their *high-potential and high-performing* talent than those who are poor performers or who have serious personality and skill deficits making them high risk for potential "derailment."

Figure 4-8

Activities, Tasks, and Assignments to Support Talent Development

Activity, Task or Assignment	Examples
Start-Up Assignments These activities, tasks, and assignments emphasize leadership, delegation, problem solving and decision making skills, learning new content quickly, working under time pressures, and working collaboratively with groups of people.	1. Chair a task force on a business problem. 2. Go off-site to troubleshoot problems or improve processes. 3. Install a new system, program, or procedure. 4. Initiate a large-scale change project within the organization. 5. Plan an off-site meeting, conference, or convention. 6. Serve on a new project or product review committee. 7. Work on a short-term international start-up initiative.
Fix-It Assignments These activities, tasks, and assignments emphasize team building, individual responsibility, dealing effectively with different people including executives, peers and direct reports. These assignments may require being responsible for dealing with a specific crisis where conflict is likely.	1. Manage a group of inexperienced people. 2. Manage a dysfunctional team. 3. Resolve conflict among subordinates. 4. Manage a group of low-competence and low-performing talent. 5. Assign a challenging project that failed previously. 6. Close down a department, unit, or failing business.
Stretch Assignments These activities, tasks, and assignments emphasize intellectual challenge, problem analysis and influencing skills. In many cases, individuals taking on these assignments may lack experience or skills in some areas.	1. Conduct a competitive analysis. 2. Create a strategic plan for a department. 3. Conduct a market analysis with recommendations for gaining market share. 4. Coordinate a process improvement initiative. 5. Chair or participate in a cross-functional team.
Professional Development or Mentoring These activities, tasks, and assignments emphasize learning, training, mentoring, and coaching.	1. Teach someone how to do something they are not an expert in. 2. Seek an external executive coach. 3. Seek and utilize an internal or external mentor. 4. Work with a senior leader who is particularly successful.
Non-Work Activities These activities, tasks, and assignments take place away from work and emphasize individual leadership, contribution to a cause, and working with new people.	1. Join a community board. 2. Become active in a volunteer organization. 3. Work with a charitable organization. 4. Become active in a professional association in a leadership role.

Envisia Learning Inc. Performance Coaching Model

The use of a *performance coaching model* can provide managers and coaches with a framework to enhance the skills and productivity of talent at all levels of the organization. This performance-based coaching model helps to clarify contracting, the definition of specific goals, typical assessments to be used, and approaches to maximize both individual goals and organizational outcomes.

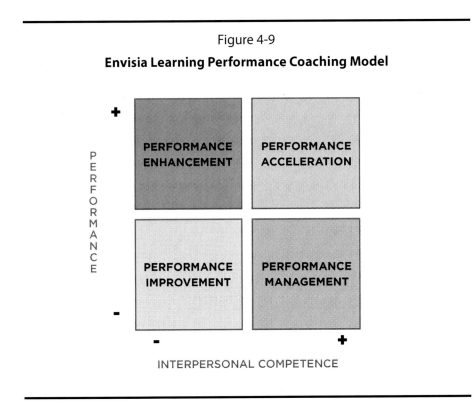

Figure 4-9

Envisia Learning Performance Coaching Model

The Envisia Leaning, Inc., *Performance Coaching Model* is based on two important factors: 1) Overall job performance and 2)

Interpersonal competence. Figure 4-9 provides a typology of four coaching approaches, each targeting specific goals and methods aimed at facilitating both "what gets done" (performance) and "how things get done" (social competence) for all employees within an organization. A manager or coach can use this model to quickly identify the best coaching approach to facilitate the development of talent at all levels.

Performance Enhancement Coaching
(High Performance/Low Interpersonal Competence)

- Employees at all levels who demonstrate generally high job performance but are characterized as less likable or interpersonally competent can best be helped by utilizing a *Performance Enhancement* model of coaching.

- These employees are at risk for potential "derailment" at some point in their career and might be described as "competent" but "difficult" to deal with. As a result, others may find collaborating and interacting with these individuals challenging and attempt to avoid them when possible.

- In this model, the focus of improvement is developing social, interpersonal, and communication skills that might potentially derail the client. Generally, coaches will utilize both personality/ style and multi-rater feedback assessments (such as a focus on emotional intelligence) to help illuminate the interpersonal "blind spots" of the client.

- Most coaching assignments will require a lengthier intervention to ensure that these employees fully understand how they are experienced and perceived by others and the potentially negative impact of their leadership, communication skills, and interpersonal style. Such clients are expected to be somewhat defensive and challenging as they sometimes lack the "self-awareness" or self-insight characterized by relatively low emotional intelligence. A great source of resources for additional information about emotional intelligence is the Consortium for Research on Emotional Intelligence in Organizations at www.eiconsortium.org

Performance Enhancement Developmental Strategies:

- Provide direct and candid feedback, asking for what you want the person to do more, less, or differently particularly in the interpersonal area

- Consider utilizing coaching to avoid derailment

- Utilize a 360-degree feedback process and development plan, focusing on enhancing interpersonal competence

- Measure and monitor team, department, and staff engagement

- Introduce and utilize a "balanced scorecard" to emphasize both task and interpersonal factors associated with performance

Performance Improvement Coaching
(Low Performance/Low Interpersonal Competence)

- Employees at all levels who demonstrate generally low job performance and also could be characterized as less likable or interpersonally difficult, can best be helped by utilizing a *Performance Improvement* model of coaching. These employees are sometimes offered coaching as a last resort before outplacement by many organizations. The use of outside coaching services should be questioned, as these low performers typically show little return on investment for such interventions.

- Coaches approached by companies asking for help with such employees should carefully contract with the client system to clarify potential issues around assessment, confidentiality, and the role of human resources in the coaching intervention. Often, organizations believe that offering coaching services to these chronically poor performers will help minimize any possible wrongful termination lawsuit that could develop.

- This is another reason coaches should carefully structure the intervention if they decide to proceed with this type of client. It is easy for coaches to feel pressured by these employees' managers or even by human resources, for a candid evaluation about the suitability or "fit" of the client. Make sure that as a coach you don't become a natural part of the progressive discipline process by simultaneously playing an evaluation and coaching role within the client system and with the client, respectively. Too many non-experienced (and experienced) coaches have been tempted by these types of requests for help by an organization, only to realize too late that the hidden agenda was not to truly help the client but to gather additional information confirming that the client was a poor fit.

- In this particular coaching model, the focus is on the immediate and significant performance improvement of the employee. These employees are often in the low-performing 10 percent that many companies look to eliminate by offering specific outplacement and severance packages. Such poorly performing and low-potential employees can cripple morale, interfere with team functioning, and take tremendous management time away from high performers. Coaches who work with such employees typically have concrete and specific developmental action plans to support the efforts of management to "turn these employees around" and enhance current performance.

Performance Improvement Developmental Strategies:

- Diagnose if the performance deficit is due to lack of knowledge, skills, or motivation

- Seek human resources consultation about documentation and your progressive discipline process

- Set concrete performance goals and expectations

- Follow up to ensure performance improvement targets are met

- Reinforce and reward desired behaviors

Performance Acceleration Coaching
(High Performance/High Interpersonal Competence)

- Employees at all levels demonstrating a high level of performance and demonstrating interpersonal competence can further be developed by utilizing a *Performance Acceleration* model of coaching. These high-potential clients are the "lovable stars" that organizations want to retain over time.

- In this model, the focus is on leveraging the strengths of these employees and enhancing their "star" potential. Generally, coaches will utilize diverse approaches for assessment, including targeted interviews with critical stakeholders, personality/style tools, and skill-based multi-rater feedback instruments.

- These employees are expected to be fairly responsive, open, and eager to learn, making the coaching engagement typically easier. As such, they will be looking for greater specificity in feedback and targeted resources to facilitate their development. Such employees will tend to keep coaches challenged, because they are motivated, as well as interested in learning as much as possible to leverage what they do well and become even better.

Performance Acceleration Developmental Strategies:

- Carry an assignment from beginning to end
- Become involved in a merger, acquisition, strategic alliance, or partnership opportunity
- Implement an organization-wide change initiative
- Negotiate agreements with external organizations
- Operate in a high-pressure or high-visibility situation
- Head a visible committee or organization-wide task force
- Look for relevant volunteer opportunities outside of the organization.
- Engineer "stretch assignments" and developmental activities
- Consider using an executive coach to enhance "signature strengths"
- Encourage work-life balance
- Champion future career potential with other senior managers
- Structure a mentoring relationship

Performance Management Coaching
(Low Performance/High Interpersonal Competence)

- Employees at all levels who demonstrate one or more deficiencies in specific competency areas (e.g., planning, oral presentation, writing, delegation, time management) but are seen as basically collaborative and likable can best be developed by utilizing a *Performance Management* model of coaching. These employees are highly responsive to coaching specifically geared toward facilitating key competencies and skill areas that might be preventing high performance.

- In this model, the focus of improvement is in developing specific techniques, skills, and abilities. Coaches might utilize more interactive approaches to model behavior, video tape clients in action, and use employee simulations to help facilitate learning. Most coaching assignments will be task-focused and shorter in duration, based on a demonstration of skill acquisition by the client to key stakeholders within the organization. Such clients will typically have high emotional intelligence and respond to specific instruction and more pragmatic techniques and tools.

Performance Management Developmental Strategies:

- Use skill-based training programs (internal or external)
- Utilize strategic developmental experiences to enhance specific competencies related to performance
- Model desired behavior, provide instruction, support skills practice, and reinforce desired behaviors
- Consider short-term, skill-based coaching

Evaluating Performance Coaching Interventions

It is important to think about metrics and approaches to evaluating coaching at the beginning of the intervention. Each of the four performance coaching models should be evaluated based upon the specific, agreed upon goals of the intervention. Figure 4-10 shows a comparison of the four performance coaching approaches and ways to evaluate them. Some of the following should be considered as part of an overall "performance coaching evaluation scorecard:"

- Analyze a change in scores before and after 360-degree feedback assessment (12 to 24 months following the first administration).

- Analyze the progress made on the employee's professional development plan (e.g, ProgressPulse).

- Analyze "post-then" change scores from the client on self-perceived changes in knowledge, skills, and behavior. This is the comparison of self-ratings before the intervention began, which is known as the "then" perspective, to those after the coaching intervention is done, which is known as the "post" perspective.

- Analyze post-coaching progress viewed by key stakeholders within the client system (e.g., the client's manager, internal and external customers, colleagues, etc.).

Figure 4-10

Envisia Learning Performance Coaching Comparisons

Type of Coaching	Focus	Duration	Coaching Effectiveness	Typical Metrics
Performance Improvement	Enhance Current Performance	1-3 Months	Very Low	Performance Improvement Measures Performance Reviews Grievances / Complaints
Performance Acceleration	Enhance Interpersonal Competence	3-12 Months	Very High	Staff / Customer Satisfaction Promotion / Succession Employee Engagement / Climate Surveys
Performance Enhancement	Enhance Strengths	3-12 Months	Low	Emotional Intelligence Assessment Employee Engagement / Climate Surveys Retention / Turnover competency Based 360-Degree Feedback
Performance Management	Enhance Task Management Performance	1-3 Months	High	Role Plays / Simulations Competency Based 360-Degree Feedback Video Tape Review Direct Observation

Summary

As reviewed throughout the *Enable* section, it is imperative for coaches to approach every stage of a client's learning with carefulness and detail. When designing goals, coaches and clients should collaborate to identify goals that are appropriate. Using the goal-setting tips, such as setting SMART goals and implementation intentions can be effective. In addition, providing knowledge and expectations about the process of learning new behaviors can help clients through their journey. In particular, coaches should view slips and setbacks as a part of the learning process, so that high-learning goals will repeatedly be set. If failures are judged severely, less difficult or vague and abstract goals are likely to become the norm (Latham & Locke, 2006).

Various measurement tools can be useful resources to track client progress. When client goals are not achieved, it is time to assess the reasons why. For example, coaches need to gauge their clients' "set points" around their abilities. Perhaps a goal that was perceived as attainable during its creation was soon realized as "unattainable" when practiced. Under these circumstances, the goals may need to be altered to fit the client's set points of ability.

Managers and coaches can employ the Envisia Learning Performance Coaching model as a way to target specific developmental goals based on a client's current job performance and interpersonal competence. This model offers specific approaches for enhancing specific skills and tools for talent at all levels of the organization.

Key Points

1. Intentions to change behavior aren't necessarily a good predictor of whether an individual will *actually* change behavior. Goal intentions do not always result in goal implementations.

2. Coaches can guide clients to translate goal *intentions* into *implementation* by using SMART goals.

3. It's easy to "lapse" and even easier to relapse to return to our old habits. Coaches can utilize *relapse prevention* tips and strategies to help clients prepare for and cope with lapses.

4. Creating the right supportive environment at work and away from work helps to maintain deliberate practice and helps facilitate neural circuits to make the behavior automatic (*unconscious competence*).

5. Coaches can help clients develop using a variety of developmental tasks, exercises, and assignments, such as activities outside of work (e.g., volunteering), and using the Envisia Learning *Performance Coaching Model.*

6. Coaches should use frequent reminders, encourage clients to track and monitor goal progress and evaluate effectiveness to help reinforce maintenance of behavioral change efforts.

ENABLE EXERCISES

The following section includes various exercises related to the *Enable* chapters.

Tips for Getting the Most from the Exercises in the Book

- **Take time to do the exercises.** These exercises are designed to help you and your client to move through the Enlighten, Encourage and Enable stages of successful behavior change.

- **Take time to reflect.** Spend some quality time on each exercise to answer the questions and reflect what they mean for you personally and professionally.

- **Pick and choose the most important exercises to use.** Each of the exercises has been specifically included to support the specific behavior change stage in our model. Some exercises will be more relevant than others for you and your client. However, each has a unique purpose but there is not a need to specifically do all of them or in any order.

- **Share with others.** Consider sharing your thoughts and feelings about one or more of the exercises with a partner, family member, friend or colleague. Seek their impressions and input about your reactions and commitments.

- **Commit to action.** Consider taking specific actions to translate these exercises into goals and new behaviors.

Each of the exercises included in the book and additional ones for each of the *Enlighten, Encourage* and *Enable* behavior change stages can be previewed and printed in a useable format for you and your clients to use for free by visiting our website at: www.envisialearning.com/clueless

ENABLE EXERCISE #1

My Professional Board of Directors

Research shows that organizations and people perform better in environments where they are supported and encouraged. The stronger our relationships are, the greater our strengths become and the more value we add to our organization.

Imagine the oval below represents the table of your very own Board of Directors. Put yourself at the head of the table, and write the names of people you would like to be sitting around the table guiding, supporting, and helping you with your career.

1. Do the people on your Board of Directors know they are members?

2. Would the people that you work with put you on their Board?

3. Who isn't on your Board that perhaps should be?

4. What makes these relationships successful?

ENABLE EXERCISE #2

My Interpersonal Network

If you envision yourself as the hub of your social network and extend outward, you can describe how you utilize each, what needs of yours are being met, and how satisfied you are. Strong social networks are associated with personal and professional success, physical health, and psychological well-being. How's your interpersonal network?

Spouse/Partner/Significant Other:

- What type of support do I give and receive from this network?
- How would I describe my level of *satisfaction*?
- What can I do to strengthen this network?

Family/Friends:

- What type of support do I give and receive from this network?
- How would I describe my level of *satisfaction*?
- What can I do to strengthen this network?

Manager/Colleagues/Organization:

- What type of support do I give and receive from this network?
- How would I describe my level of *satisfaction*?
- What can I do to strengthen this network?

Community:

- What type of support do I give and receive from this network?
- How would I describe my level of *satisfaction*?
- What can I do to strengthen this network?

ENABLE EXERCISE #3

My Relapse Prevention Plan

Situations of High Risk (e.g., social settings, stressful situations, etc.):

Warning Signs and Combating Them:

- Early warning sign:
- Productive or Positive Thoughts and Behaviors:

Dealing With Potential Lapses:

- Lapse Behavior:
- What led to the Lapse?
- What could I do differently in the future?
- What do I need to do to get back on track?

ENABLE EXERCISE #4

Coping With Stress to
Avoid Relapse—Meditation Exercise

- Choose a quiet environment that is not too brightly lit. Allow yourself five minutes at first, and gradually work up to 20 minutes.

- Sit upright with your spine erect. Your feet should be flat on the ground, with your hands resting in your lap. Close your eyes, and keep your body still.

- Start with some deep breathing: Inhale and exhale deeply, letting all your breath out. Pause, then inhale, letting the breath flow naturally, using your abdomen muscles.

- Now allow your breathing to become natural and slow. As you exhale, count, "one." Continue counting each time you exhale. If thoughts enter your mind and you forget to count, simply notice the thoughts, and dismiss them. Do the same with sounds and bodily sensations. Simply notice and dismiss them.

- If you wish to time yourself, use a non-ticking timer. When you are done, rock gently back and forth before slowly getting up. Practice at least once daily.

ENABLE EXERCISE #5

My Behavioral Change Self-Contract

Behavior Change Goal

- I agree to (specific behavior):
- Under the following circumstances (specify where, when, how much):

Environmental Planning

- In order to help me do this I am going to arrange my physical and social environment by:
- And control my internal environment by:

Consequences

- Provided by me if contract is kept:
- Provided by me if contract is broken:
- Provided by others if the contract is kept:
- Provided by others if the contract is broken:

ENABLE EXERCISE #6
Creating a SMART
Development Implementation Plan

Choose one goal identified in the previous exercise and create a SMART development goal using the following outline:

Specific Goal	
Measurement	When I achieve this goal, I will know I am successful because: Other people will notice the following difference(s):
Actions	What actions will I take? What will I do differently?
Reality Checklist	How is this goal achievable? Why is this goal important? What resource(s) do I need?
Timeline	When will I start? When do I expect to meet my goal?

ENABLE EXERCISE #7

Savoring Our Successes

Savoring is defined as the emotions of joy, awe, excitement, and gratitude derived from an experience. Studies have shown that whether a person is able to savor experiences predicts his or her degree of happiness and reinforces the positive benefits of that experience.

See yourself and think about the successful completion of a new behavior or habit that you are working on. Answer the following questions:

1. What positive thoughts did you have about successfully completing the new habit or behavior?

2. What positive emotions or feelings did you have about successfully completing the new habit or behavior?

3. How can you extend the length of time that you have had these positive thoughts, feelings, and emotions about your successful new habit or behavior?

ENABLE EXERCISE #8

My Allergic Responses to Others
Who Impede My Goal Progress

We can learn the most from those we have the strongest allergic reactions to.

Analyze the personality and behaviors of those you have an allergic response to (i.e, those who you experience as difficult, challenging or annoying), as you begin to build your personal support system at work and home to become a successful adopter of new behaviors and habits.

1. What are you allergic to in others (i.e., what is it about others that "pushes your buttons")?

2. How does it make you feel?

3. How do you typically react?

4. What might this say about your own personality and style?

ENABLE EXERCISE #9

Sample Coaching Evaluation

The following performance coaching questions could easily be asked of the client's manager (or other key stakeholders in the organization).

Please indicate the progress made by circling a number below. If you are unable to answer, please skip the question.					
■ Compared with six months ago, has this individual's credibility, respect, and effectiveness increased (circle 4 or 5), stayed the same (circle 3), or decreased (circle 1 or 2)?	1	2	3	4	5
■ Compared to six months ago, has this individual's self-awareness regarding the impact of his/her decisions and actions on others increased, stayed about the same, or decreased?	1	2	3	4	5
■ Compared with six months ago, have favorable perceptions of this individual as a leader within this organization improved, stayed about the same, or diminished?	1	2	3	4	5
■ Compared with six months ago, has the morale of this individual's direct staff in the organization improved, stayed about the same, or diminished?	1	2	3	4	5
■ Compared with six months ago, has the leader's overall performance on the job improved, stayed about the same, or diminished?	1	2	3	4	5
■ Please add any additional comments relevant to this individual's development as a leader below:					

ENABLE EXERCISE #10

My Daily Progress Checklist

Near the end of each work day, use this checklist to evaluate your progress or setbacks. What can you do to best facilitate progress at work given that even *small steps forward* are highly correlated with mood and work/job satisfaction?

My PROGRESS	My SETBACKS
Describe 1 or 2 events today indicated progress or even a breakthrough.	Describe 1 or 2 events today indicated a small or large setback or even a possible crisis.
Describe *catalysts* that helped contribute to progress (actions that directly support work such as support from others):	Describe *inhibitors* that contribute to setbacks (actions that fail to support or actually hinder work):
Describe *nourishers* that helped contribute to progress (events such as praise, recognition or words of encouragement):	Describe *toxins* that contribute to setbacks (discouraging or undermining interactions or events):
What can I do tomorrow to enhance the *catalysts* and *nourishers* to enhance my progress?	
What can I do tomorrow to reduce the *inhibitors* and *toxins* to enhance my progress?	

Enable References

Amabile, T. & Kramer, S. (2011). The power of small wins. *Harvard Business Review,* *89,* 70-80.

Barrick, M. R., Mount, M. K. & Strauss, J. P. (1993). Conscientiousness and performance of sales representatives: Test of the mediating effects of goal setting. *Journal of Applied Psychology, 5,* 715–722.

Beck, J. W., Gregory, J. B. & Carr, A. (2009). Balancing development with day-to-day task demands: A multiple-goal setting approach to executive coaching. *Industrial and Organizational Psychology, 2,* 293-296.

Bonezzi, A., Brendl, C., & De Angelis, M. (2011). Stuck in the Middle: The *Psychophysics of Goal Pursuit, Psychological Science,* 7, 2011, doi: 10.1177/0956797611404899.

Chandon, P., Smith, R., Morowitz, V., Spangenberg, E. & Sprott, D. (2011). When does the past repeat itself? The interplay of behavior prediction and personal norms. *Journal of Consumer Behavior, 38,* 420-430.

Cooper, C.L. & Barling, J. (Eds.), (2008), *Sage Handbook of Organizational Behavior.* 1, 234-261). Thousand Oaks, CA: Sage.

Culbert, S. & Rout, L. (2010). Get rid of the performance review. New York: Business Plus.

DeShon R. P. & Gillespie, J. Z. (2005). A motivated action theory account of goal orientation. *Journal of Applied Psychology, 90,* 1096 – 1127.

Duckworth, A. L., Peterson, C., Matthews, M. D. & Kelly, D. R. (2007). Grit: Perseverance and passion for long-term goals. *Personality Processes and Individual Differences, 92,* 1087.

Dweck, C. S. & Leggett, E. L. (1988). A social-cognitive approach to motivation and personality. *Psychological Review, 95,* 256-273.

Erez, A. & Judge, T. A. (2001). Relationship of core self-evaluations to goal setting, motivation, and performance. *Journal of Applied Psychology,* 86, 1270-1279.

The influence of experience and deliberate practice on the development of superior expert performance. In Ericsson, K. A., Charness, N., Feltovich, P. & Hoffman, R.R. (Eds.), *Cambridge Handbook of Expertise and Expert Performance,* 683-703. Cambridge, UK: Cambridge University Press.

Ericsson, K. A. (1996). The acquisition of expert performance: An introduction to some of the issues. In K. A. Ericsson (Ed.). The road to excellence: The acquisition of expert performance in the arts and sciences, sports, and games, 1-50.

Fung, C., Woods, J., Asch, S., Glassman, P. & Doebbeling, B. (2004). Variation in implementation use of computerized clinical reminders in an integrated healthcare system. *The American Journal of Managed Care, 10*, 878-885.

Gollwitzer, P. M. & P. Sheeran, (2006). Implementation intentions and goal achievement: A meta-analysis of effects and processes. *Advances in Experimental Social Psychology, 38*, 69-119.

Hölzel, B., Carmody, J., Vangel, M., Congleton, C., Yerramsetti, S., Gard, T. & Lazar, S.W. (2011). Mindfulness practice leads to increases in regional brain gray matter density. Psychiatry Research. Neuroimaging, *191*, 36-43.

Judge, T., Locke, E. & Durham, C. (1997). The dispositional causes of job satisfaction. A core evaluations approach. *Journal of Applied Psychology, 83*, 17-34.

Judge, T. & Ilies, R. (2002). Relationship of Personality to Performance Motivation: A Meta-Analytic Review. *Journal of Applied Psychology, 87*, 797–807.

Koo, M. & Fishbach, A. (2010). Climbing the goal ladder: How upcoming action increase level of aspiration. *Journal of Personality and Social Psychology, 99*, 1-13.

Lally, P. (2010). How are habits formed: Modeling habit formation in the real world. *European Journal of Social Psychology, 40*, 998–1009.

Locke, E. A. & Latham, G. P. (1990). *A theory of goal setting and task performance.* Englewood Cliffs, NJ: Prentice Hall.

Locke, E. A. & Latham, G. P. (2002). Building a practically useful theory of goal setting and task motivation. A 35 year odyssey. *The American Psychologist*, 57, 705-717.

Lombardo, M. M. & Eichinger, R. W. (1989). Eighty Eight Assignments for Development in Place. Center for Creative Leadership.

McGowen, K. (2010). The New Quitter: Falling Off the Wagon-Whether by Bakery Binge or Drug Bender-Doesn't Mean Total Defeat. *Psychology Today*, 78-84.

Larimer, M. E., Palmer, R. S. & Marlatt, G. A. (1999). An Overview of Marlatt's Cognitive Behavioral Model. *Alcohol Research & Health, 23*, 151-160.

Mitchell, T. R., Thompson, K. R. & George-Falvy, J. (2000). Goal setting: Theory and practice. In C. L. Cooper & E. A. Locke (Eds.), *Industrial and organizational psychology: Linking theory with practice* (pp. 216– 249). New York: Wiley-Blackwell.

Nauert, R. (2011) Brain Structure Changes After Meditation. Retrieved January 24, 2011, from http://psychcentral.com/news/2011/01/24/brain-structure-changes-after-meditation/22859.html.

Pascual-Leone, A., Amedi, A., Fregni, F. & Lotfi, B. (2005). The Plastic Human Brain Cortex. *Annual Review of Neuroscience, 28*, 377-401.

Peterson, S., Luthans, F., Avolio, B., Walumbwa, F. & Zhang, Z. (2011) Psychological capital and employee performance: A latent growth modeling approach. Personnel Psychology, *64*, 427-450.

Pope, D. & Simonsohn, U. (2011). Round Numbers as Goals. Evidence from Baseball, SAT Takers, and the Lab. *Psychological Science, 22*, 71-79.

Schmidt, A. M. & Deshon R. P. (2010). The moderating effects of performance ambiguity on the relationship between self-efficacy and performance. *The Journal of applied psychology, 95*, 572-81.

Schmidt, A. M. & DeShon, R. P. (2007). What to do? The effects of goal-performance discrepancies, superordinate goals, and time on dynamic goal prioritization. *Journal of Applied Psychology, 92*, 928-941

Schunk, D. H. (2001). Self-regulation through goal setting. ERIC/CLASS Digest, 1-6, Retrieved January 24, 2011, from http://www.eric.ed.gov/PDFS/ED462671.pdf.

Schunk, D. H. (1995). Self-efficacy and education and instruction. In J. E. Maddux (Ed.), Self-efficacy, adaptation, and adjustment: Theory, research, and application (pp. 281-303). New York: Plenum Press.

Seijt, G. (2006). Learning goals or performance goals: Is it the journey or the destination? *Ivey Business Journal, 70*, 2-6.

Shilts, M. K., Horowitz, M. & Townsend, M. S. (2004). Goal setting as a strategy for dietary and physical activity behavior change: A review of the literature. *American Journal of Health Promotion, 19*, 81-93.

Tartaglia, E. M., Bamert, L., Mast, F. W. & Herzog, M. H. (2009). Human Perceptual Learning by Mental Imagery. *Current Biology, 19*, 2081-2085.

Webb, Thomas L. & Sheeran, P. (2006). Does changing behavioral intentions engender behavior change? A meta-analysis of the experimental evidence. *Psychological Bulletin, 132*, 249-268.

About the Authors

Sandra Mashihi, Ph.D.

Dr. Sandra Mashihi is an Organizational Psychologist and Senior Consultant at Envisia Learning. She specializes in executive coaching, personal brand development, interpersonal relationships, cultural diversity, and sales training. Prior to her work at Envisia Learning, she was the Organizational Development Consultant for a national financial firm in Los Angeles, where she was responsible for employee retention, sales training, and leadership development initiatives. Sandra has a track record of coaching executives and managers on leadership development, interpersonal relationships, and team building. She has extensive knowledge and expertise with behavioral assessments, 360-degree feedback tools, and personality-based inventories.

Sandra received her B.S. in Psychology from UCLA and received her M.S. and Doctorate in Organizational Psychology from the California School of Professional Psychology. She has further developed her coaching skills at the Coaches Training Institute. She is also a member of Society of Industrial Organizational Psychology (SIOP) and the American Society of Training & Development (ASTD). Her professional career has been within the financial, non-profit, and healthcare industries.

Kenneth Nowack, Ph.D.

Dr. Kenneth M. Nowack is a licensed psychologist (PSY 13758) and President & Chief Research Officer of Envisia Learning. He is charged with providing strategic vision and leadership, conceptual product design and development, research, public relations, and advanced client relations.

Ken has over 20 years of experience in the development and validation of human resource systems, assessment tools, organizational climate surveys, questionnaires, simulations, and tests. He has developed 360 degree feedback systems and assessment centers, as well as employee selection, succession planning, performance appraisal, and management development training programs for a number of clients in the public, private, and not-for-profit sectors. Ken has conducted research and published extensively in the areas of 360-degree feedback systems, health psychology, survey research, training evaluation, assessment, and personnel testing. He has also authored numerous assessment instruments and learning systems.

Ken also serves as President and Chief Research Officer of LifeHub, Inc. (www.getlifehub.com) and is a member of the Consortium for Research on Emotional Intelligence in Organizations. He received his B.S. and M.S. degrees in Educational Psychology at the University of California, Davis, and his Ph.D. in Counseling Psychology from UCLA, where he is a guest lecturer at the Anderson School of Management.